MOUNTAIN IN

A Search for

THE CLOUDS

the Wild Salmon

Bruce Brown

SIMON AND SCHUSTER
NEW YORK

Published by Simon and Schuster
A Division of Gulf & Western Corporation
Simon & Schuster Building
Rockefeller Center
1230 Avenue of the Americas
New York, New York 10020

SIMON AND SCHUSTER and colophon are trademarks of Simon & Schuster
Designed by Eve Kirch
Manufactured in the United States of America

10 9 8 7 6 5 4 3 2 1

Library of Congress Cataloging in Publication Data

Brown, Bruce.
Mountain in the clouds.
1. Pacific salmon. 2. Fishery management—Washington
(State) 3. Fishery resources—Hatchery vs. wild stocks.
4. Indians of North America—Washington (State)—
Fishing. 5. Pacific salmon fisheries—Washington
(State)—Political aspects. 6. Wildlife conservation—
Washington (State) I. Title.
QL638.S2B76 333.95'6 82-3245
ISBN 0-671-43583-3 AACR2

I am grateful for the assistance I received from many people during the course of writing this book. The following gave me advice, encouragement, and often a place to sleep: Malcolm Brown, Marian Brown, Jeff Cederholm, Joel Connelly, Bob Cumbow, Harold Eby, Pat Feeley, Tony Floor, Joanne Foster, Steve Green, Jim Harp, Karen Harp, Bruce Johansen, Larry Lestelle, Carolyn Marr, Lane Morgan, Murray Morgan, Rosa Morgan, Curt Madison, Jerry Parker and all the people at the Little River farm, Jim Porter, Dan Seligman, Charles Simenstad, Harold Sisson, Nile Thompson, Robert L. Wood, Yvonne Yarber, Brian Youngberg.

I am also indebted to the people at S&S, especially Michael Korda, who demanded the best work I was capable of producing, and Leon King, who gave so unstintingly of his time.

Bruce Brown

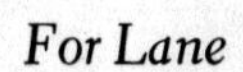
For Lane

CONTENTS

Unnamed and Unknown

ONE

We followed the fluttering shadow of our helicopter over the bluff and into the valley of the Queets. It was a hot, Indian summer afternoon, and the ridges all around were cloaked in drifting smoke from the slash fires along the coast. Ahead, the valley rose over a mile from the river to the glacier-studded face of Mount Olympus and the tumult of peaks beyond.

We swung to the north, hugging the descending foothills. Dark waves of cedar and spruce ran past under the clear bubble of our craft for the first few miles, but soon the ancient rain forest was broken by logging and road construction. These broad, geometric areas of bare earth and debris grew larger and more numerous until we rolled high over a shimmering grove of cottonwoods and dropped into the canyon of trees bordering the river itself.

Braiding back and forth between green pools and clear, racing riffles, the Queets led into the mountains. I leaned out the open door of the helicopter and scanned the river. Off to our right, an immaculately forested hillock jutted up from the valley floor where Tshletshy Creek's long glacial canyon meets that of the Queets. Beyond, where the valley seemed to vanish between the rock walls of Kitma Peak and Mount Pelton, the upper valley began, and the best modern maps became fuzzy.

The Queets River, which rushes from the highest mountains of the Olympic Peninsula to the Pacific Ocean in less than fifty miles, was first traversed in 1890, the year that the American frontier was officially pronounced closed. At that time the Queets valley was alive with tremendous trees and large quantities of game such as elk, ducks, and seals. Here, as elsewhere along the North Pacific coast, however, the most conspicuous natural marvel was the salmon.

Early chroniclers were amazed by the numbers of these fish found in the rivers of the West. The Lewis and Clark expedition noted "great quants. of salmon" when it passed along the Columbia River in the fall of 1805. In 1854, zoologist George Suckley wrote that the salmon were "one of the striking wonders of the region . . . These fish . . . astonish by number, and confuse with variety." As late as 1899, Richard Rathbun of the Smithsonian Institution said simply, "the quantities of salmon which frequent these waters is beyond calculation, and seems to be so great as to challenge human ingenuity to affect it in any way."

A century later, I was speeding to test the current condition of both the salmon and "human ingenuity." The destination was a gravel bar on the upper Queets midway between Hee Haw Creek and an unnamed stream. There I would be dropped off to join a Quinault tribal salmon survey crew that was going to search for wild salmon in the upper Queets. Salmon surveys like this are now conducted annually by federal, state, and tribal governments on major salmon rivers throughout the West. Our plan was to travel light and fast, in the manner inadvertently pioneered by Private Harry Fisher, the first man to explore the river from the headwaters to its mouth.

It is one of history's gentler ironies that Fisher feared at first that he might starve to death on the Queets. Alone, lost and hungry after becoming separated from the U.S. Army survey party that made the first ascent of Mount Olympus, Fisher soon found he could throw away his meager store of flour and bacon. "Eagles and ravens were quite numerous today, and dog salmon running lively," he wrote in his journal for September 24, 1890. "At noontime I waded out into water deep and swift and speared a large salmon, and in the scuffle I lost my balance upon the slippery stones and was washed down with the current, losing spear and salmon, but retained my staff. I had one other barb, and used it to better effect."

Fisher came to savor salmon meat and the sport in catching the fish, but he soon found that their presence posed certain unexpected problems. "Although warm and comfortable," he wrote of the night of September 25, "I might as well have selected a camp in Barnum's Menagerie so far as sleep was concerned. Located near a shoal in the stream, great salmon threshed the water all night long, in their effort to ascend the stream. Wild animals which I could not see snapped the bushes in all directions, traveling up and down in search of fish."

The salmon that fed Fisher and so many other creatures on the Queets that fall were members of a race of Chinook or king salmon, *Oncorhynchus tshawytscha.* Known to weigh as much as 125 pounds and measure more than five feet in length, Chinook are the largest and—by many accounts—the finest of the Pacific salmon. In their prime they resemble a burnished blade whose upper edge has been darkened with a delicate tracing of black spots. At other times, they may display a sootiness that gives them two more of their many local names: black salmon and blackmouth. Their tails are exceptionally broad and straight, their backs strong and sleek, their heads bulletlike with clear, unblinking eyes.

Like the other four species of Pacific salmon—coho (or silver), sockeye (or red), pink (or humpy), chum (or dog)—Chinook are exceptional swimmers. The Kwakiutl Indians, who venerated the salmon, addressed their prayers and offerings: "O Supernatural Ones, O Swimmers." Salmon can accelerate faster than a car over short distances, or glide without apparent effort on unseen currents and drifts. Motion is central to their lives. They feed by it, communicate by it, and, one has to suspect, enjoy it too. It is only late in life when their bodies have been deformed by the spawning process that they lose their mastery of water.

Spawning males often develop a humpback and hooked snout with a wicked set of canine teeth, while the females' tails may fray to stumps of bare bone as they dig their nests in the riverbed. Life begins for the salmon within the gravel bowl of that nest. At the climax of protracted and passionate mating rituals, male(s) and female simultaneously release sperm and eggs into the bottom of the nest, where they are buried by further nest excavation. Two months later the eggs hatch tiny alevins that live in the gravel until the yolk sacs attached to their stomachs diminish. Of the 5,000 eggs that might be laid by a Chinook female, the majority will not live this long.

Those that do, however, are recognizable as fish for the first time. As fingerlings, they can live in the river of their birth for as long as a year before going through the silvery transformation known as smoltification. This allows them to survive in salt water and immediately precedes their migration to the sea. Following the prevailing North Pacific currents in thousand-mile-long gyres, the young salmon grow rapidly on zooplankton, squid and small fishes. Many Chinook live four years in the ocean, traveling 10,000 miles or more during the course of several circuits around the great oceanic grazing grounds. Then at the height of their strength and beauty, they return homeward, seeking out their natal streams to spawn the next generation. Once they reenter fresh water, Pacific salmon will not eat, and within a few weeks of spawning they all die.

I continued to study the river as we passed through the bend into the upper valley, but saw no sign of either the fish or the more obvious nests (known as redds) they dig where the water is swift. Finally, a little after 3 P.M., we tilted toward a gravel bar where I could see two figures standing by the edge of the river. My pilot, a silver-haired man with a leg brace showing below the cuff of his pants, eased us back around and set the machine down in a cyclone of fine gravel and jet fumes. Once the copter was on the ground, I shook hands with the pilot, grabbed my gear and bent double like an ape, dashed toward the two men I had spotted from the air. By the time I reached them, the helicopter had disappeared down the valley and the only sound was the roar of the river.

Larry Lestelle, a fisheries biologist for the Quinault Indian Nation, and Dino Blackburn, a member of the Quinault Tribe, were finishing a candy bar when I joined them. We had already reviewed the basics of salmon nest identification before leaving the village of Queets that morning, and so after a few moments of gear adjustment and slightly embarrassed banter, we took the plunge. Lestelle led the way across a swirling, thigh-deep eddy to the faster but shallower water on the riffle beyond. Both he and Blackburn were wearing the preferred attire of Quinault salmon surveyors: T-shirts, gym shorts, long underwear bottoms, brightly striped athletic socks and tennis shoes. The idea, Lestelle explained cheerfully as the icy water lapped the backs of his knees, was to combine wet warmth with quick drying. I felt somewhat frumpy in my blue jeans, but discovered that after numbness killed the pain, the sultry September afternoon made the snowmelt river seem like an ideal place for a stroll.

The bright current that carried an occasional leaf between our legs was fed by melting glaciers high on the flanks of Mount Olympus. Although it is the tallest peak in the range, Olympus comes as close to being invisible as is possible for a 7,965-foot mountain. The surrounding peaks of Mount Queets, Mount Carrie and Mount Appleton stand in such close rank that Olympus itself can only be seen from a handful of unmarked vistas around the periphery of the peninsula. And even here, it is generally swathed in the clouds that deposit 200 inches—or 16 feet—of rain a year on its flanks. Viewed on a map, Olympus is the hub of a wheel of rivers running out from the center of the peninsula in all directions. To the west, these rivers feed the Pacific Ocean; to the south, Grays Harbor; to the north, the Strait of Juan de Fuca; and to the east, Hood Canal, an arm of Puget Sound.

Blackburn, Lestelle and I skirted Kilkelley Rapids, the worst on the Queets, by way of an animal trail that gamboled over boulders, logs and bushes. Above us towered a forest of old-growth conifers that looked as though a Christmas tree flocking machine had run amok in its upper reaches. Everything was covered with green growing matter, and yet the understory of salmonberry had a trim, almost tidy look. Shafts of sunlight plunged at intervals to the mossy forest floor where we found chanterelle mushrooms and a cluster of cloudberries in a nook by the side of the trail. This deep red fruit was a favorite of the Haida Indians of the Queen Charlotte Islands until deer introduced by whites destroyed it as a food source, but it has apparently always been rare on the Olympic Peninsula.

Lestelle called a brief halt on the other side of the rapids, partially to let me catch up, and partially to let him relace his brand new high-topped tennis shoes. A tall man with a boyish, clean-shaven face, he had a great deal of trouble with his ankles and knees the last time he walked the Queets, and the new shoes were part of his precautions to avoid a repeat performance. "Relax, Larry, the weak-kneed shall inherit the earth," I said as he sat on a big, round rock adjusting his elastic knee supports. He laughed good-naturedly, but in fact both religion and fish are a very serious matter to him.

Lestelle first saw the Queets River on a fishing trip with his father when he was in sixth grade. "We drove out and parked at the Matheny Creek bridge and fished a clear, shallow riffle that you could see didn't have any fish in it," he told me once, adding "I thought it was the most beautiful river I'd ever seen." A little experience showed him that Dolly Varden trout could sometimes be found in backwater pools, and by the time he was a teenager he had decided to become a fisheries biologist. He steadfastly pursued his goal through high school and upon graduation from the University of Washington was hired as the Quinault Tribe's Queets River biologist. After three years on the front line of the Northwest salmon wars, Lestelle was still known to slow down at every bridge to look at the river below.

"Well, who's going to see the first salmon?" he asked as he got to his feet. Neither Blackburn nor I made any promises, but it did seem that we should start seeing them soon if they were in the river. Although Chinook have the physical strength to climb Kilkelley Rapids, there are no records of them spawning above Hee Hee Creek, Hee Haw's lower companion. We were now a mile from Hee Hee, and the river was beginning to split into spurs and side channels as the gradient of the valley diminished. To cover these multiplying stream-sized channels, Lestelle divided the party. Blackburn, a stocky man with long, tightly curled hair and a Pancho Villa moustache, would cover the right, while Lestelle and I would cover the left.

Since Chinook are most fond of big water spawning, we were looking for places where the main river broke across a broad gravel bed, or twisted tight under the cover of an overhanging bank or tree. Although the river had appeared clear from the helicopter, the rock flour ground in the Queets's glacial headwaters made it opaque as jade to waders. For this reason, Lestelle instructed us to stay in the water as much as possible. He wanted us to flush the fish with our feet. There was also a chance that we would locate one of their redds by stepping in it. Remembering that Chinook nests can be more than a foot deep, I began to wonder if our survey would be a record of the number of times we were wet to the crotch.

As it turned out, we didn't find any salmon at all on the first stretch of river, the big gravelly bend that followed, or the next stretch approaching the cliffs on the south side of the valley. It wasn't until a little after 4:30 that a glimpse of something surprisingly large, almost out of scale with the water that contained it, first caught my eye. Crossing the gravel bar, I found a female spring Chinook that must have weighed twenty-five pounds lying in the mouth of a small side channel. When Lestelle came over to join me, the fish started and shot across the main river with such force that she beached herself on the opposite shore. Lestelle said her thin appearance indicated she was spawned out, but he grabbed her by the tail and threw her back into the water anyway.

Starting at the surprisingly clear mouth of the side channel, we traced it back through a wasteland of gravel and uprooted trees. There were six more leopard-spotted Chinook lounging in the lower portion of the stream. Most were holding quietly in water so shallow that their backs and tails were almost entirely exposed. They seemed entranced as we approached, but once one had seen us they all became fidgety, and dashed away upstream to hide. We followed until, turning a corner, we found the stream emerging whole from a bed of dry gravel. By the time we got back to the main river, Blackburn had gone on without us, crossing an immense tangle of fallen old growth spruce that vaulted fifty feet off the ground, and then winding his way through a group of small, tree-covered islands below.

Leaning on a newfound staff and cleaning my glare-resistant Polaroid glasses, I asked Larry why these Queets Chinook were known as spring or summer Chinook. "It has to do with the time they return to the river as adults," he said. "We call them springs or summers based on the general season of their migration, but it's a somewhat arbitrary distinction. The fish begin entering the river in little spurts from March on . . . Some of these fish have been in the river waiting to spawn for seven months now." Because of the extra fat needed to sustain them over their long fast, early running salmon, such as the Queets spring Chinook, are considered choicer eating than their later running relatives. They also tend to be more vigorous and secretive.

On the next riffle I made the mistake of trying to cross the river in an area of standing waves. White water welled up over my waist as the river tore the stones out from under my feet. "Keep moving," Lestelle shouted from the other side. "You can't stand still!" With a dozen yards of thrashing water between me and him, I decided to back out and retrace my steps. Soon after I regained the shore, three red-breasted mergansers swooped in and landed immediately upriver from me. They preened themselves nonchalantly as the current bounced them through the standing waves toward a dead spruce that was loudly ploughing water across more than half the river. Still unaware of my presence, the three ducks dived simultaneously in front of the sweeper and then bobbed up on the other side where the river relaxed into a smooth glide.

There they thrust their rakish heads under the water again and again. At first I thought they were drinking, but then it occurred to me that they were probably scouting for prey, preferably young salmon. During late summer they would be looking for the flash of white on the anal fins of coho salmon, or the more shadowy steelhead. At other times, these powerful swimmers pursue all five species of Pacific salmon native to North America, as well as the two anadromous relatives of the Atlantic salmon, steelhead and cutthroat trout. (A sixth species of Pacific salmon, the diminutive cherry salmon, is found only in the rivers of Asia.) I rested on the log until the birds had drifted out of sight and then backtracked to cross the river thirty yards upstream.

Lestelle estimated that we were less than a mile from Alta Creek, our planned camp for the night. We were discussing Blackburn's whereabouts when Lestelle spotted a dark torpedo in the water close to a bank of overhanging alders. He approached cautiously, but once again the fish started, this time driving downriver until it died right in front of me and floated on its side, head down. Despite the white fungus that covered her tail, this was a handsome fish, measuring thirty-four inches and weighing an estimated twenty-eight pounds in her emaciated post-spawning state. I steered her onto a nearby gravel bar with my staff, marveling how easily even a stiff, lifeless Chinook could glide through the water.

Looking back from a big log at the next bend, I saw Lestelle, a tiny figure in blue gym shorts, bending over the dead fish while the darkening wilderness rose to the long shafts of light that still flushed the upper peaks. Judging by the fossil remains found in the sea cliffs near here, salmon and their ancestors have been running in these rivers for at least five million years. The earliest known salmonid is *Smilodonichthys rastrosus*, a ten-foot-long creature of the Pliocene. The giant skulls of these fish, which are characterized by extremely large canine teeth and numerous gill rakers (or plankton sieves), have been found in Washington, Oregon and California. Ted Cavender of Ohio State University and Robert Miller of the University of Michigan have speculated that *Smilodonichthys* may have been a direct ancestor of the Pacific salmon, among whom it bears the closest resemblance to sockeye and chum.

Within the last two million years, repeated glaciation has by turns depleted, multiplied, isolated and mixed the salmon to a considerable degree. When the glaciers were at their greatest advance, both Atlantic salmon and steelhead abandoned their northern haunts for rivers like the Rhône on the Mediterranean and the Colorado on the Gulf of Mexico. Pacific salmon are believed to have survived the most recent glaciation in two refuges, one each on the North American and Asian continents. With the glaciers' retreat 10,000 years ago, the salmon fanned out and recolonized millions of miles of rivers draining into the North Pacific.

Spawning at times in the shadow of the withering glaciers, the salmon led the return of life to the ice-scarred valleys. They were not the only means by which nature reclaimed the wasteland of gravel, boulders and clay, but they were among the most important, for they provided the only way of capturing large amounts of nutrients at sea and returning them to the land. (Many biologists believe this is why all Pacific salmon die after spawning, unlike the Atlantic salmon of the more nutrient-stable East Coast.) Running in such numbers that many rivers like the Olympic Peninsula's Hamma Hamma (or "Stinky Stinky") were known for the marvel of their rotting, the salmon helped recreate the soil which supports the rococo excesses of the modern Olympic Peninsula rain forest. At the same time, as Harry Fisher learned, they attracted animal life.

At sea, when salmon are preparing to begin their spawning run, seals, sea otters and porpoises congregate to feed on them, and in their wake come the voracious killer whales. Faster than the fastest porpoise, killer whale packs overtake their prey from behind and eat them alive. Off British Columbia's Nass River nineteenth-century whaler Charles Scammon observed orcas with salmon "in their bristling jaws, shaking and crushing their victims, and swallowing them apparently with great gusto." Once the salmon are in the river, bears, cougars and coyotes take their toll, and then the carcasses of the fish that survived to spawn become the dinner of bald eagles and other scavengers. The salmon's eggs are eagerly sought by the trout that shadow the big fish in their last days, and so in time are the young salmon by diving ducks, cormorants and squawfish.

During much of his residence on the North Pacific coast, man too has been among the principal salmon predators. Virtually every riparian culture along 10,000 miles of coastline was dependent, often to a large extent, on the salmon as a staple of their diet. The people of the Kamchatka Peninsula and neighboring Siberia used salmon to make a pounded, breadlike dish, a variety of cakes and blinis, and used the oil to fry their choicest delicacy: a mashed combination of sarana lily bulbs, marrow of the purple fireweed, sweet grass, cloudberries and crowberries. Indian tribes of the North American coast like the Kwakiutl, Nootka and Chinook ate smoked salmon and made a type of "cheese" out of the eggs, which were also used as a dip for salmonberry shoots and fern rhizomes that had been boiled and peeled like bananas. When fresh, the fish were simply boiled, roasted or fried in a little grease, preferably bear.

In the early days of European and American settlement in the North Pacific, the white man was as dependent on salmon as the Indian, eagle or otter. Small frontier communities such as the socialist Puget Sound Cooperative Colony on the north side of the Olympic Peninsula followed the migrating salmon to obtain their store of winter food, and many citizens of the area's towns and cities did the same. In 1891, when a young man named Joshua Green came to the metropolis of Seattle, salmon was an important local subsistence crop. Green, who later founded one of the largest banks in Washington State, remembered on his hundredth birthday in 1969: "We had *plenty* of salmon then. In those days, I fished just like the Indians did. I had a little skiff, and I put a line around my neck in a loop, and I'd row, and the rowing would move the spoon I was trolling, and that's a grand way. . . . I caught two barrels of salmon the first season I was here—besides working."

It was nearly dark by the time we found our Indian companion crouching near several Chinook at the mouth of Alta Creek. We conferred briefly and then headed up the bank, squishing softly as we walked. After kindling a fire on a grassy flat grown thick with ghostly white-barked alders, we changed into dry clothes and set our wet ones to drying around the blaze. I had been told to bring no food, and so watched with interest as my companions pulled the elements of our dinner out of their packs. Dehydrated soup, beef franks and plain white hot dog buns appeared one after another and were devoured in as much time as it took to scorch them to the taste of the chef. I passed around some dried fruit I had smuggled in for dessert, and then the three of us drew close to the fire, laughing as we strained to read the tiny print that revealed the multisyllabic ingredients in the soup (lactalbulin, monosodium glutamate, hydrolized vegetable protein, potassium carbonate, disodium inosnate, disodium guanylate).

We all agreed that salmon would have been preferable, but we would be happy enough just to see the fish at this point. Queets spring Chinook have declined to one-third their number a century ago, with the population dropping from 2,300 to 1,300 in the last decade alone. Early signs had suggested that this year's spring Chinook run in the Queets would be considerably larger than it has been in recent years, but we were not finding the fish to confirm that hopeful forecast. Tallying the day's count in his yellow waterproof notebook, Lestelle figured that the three of us had seen twelve redds and twenty-three fish in five miles of river, none of which, curiously, were adult males. "There should have been fish in that first bend below Hee Hee Creek, and then on the right-hand riffle above that nice deep pool," he said, shaking his head.

The tone in Lestelle's voice told how important it was to him that we find salmon spawning on the Queets. Already the English-speaking world had exterminated two substantial wild salmon resources within the last two hundred years. First the English pillaged the wild Atlantic salmon in rivers like the Thames, and then the Atlantic salmon of the Eastern United States met the same fate at the hands of the Americans. In both instances, the cause of the problem was well known. "There is no question," as one nineteenth-century observer put it, "but salmon were most plentiful before civilization had begun its work, and when dams, traps and other obstructions and hydraulic mines were unknown, when the sources of the river were unsettled and undefiled by the sewerage of the cities, the forests at the headwaters still untouched by man, the country yet in a natural state."

The same process of "civilization" has been at work on the Pacific salmon since the California gold rush of 1849. During the intervening years, Pacific salmon have declined to less than half their former number along the entire West Coast of North America. Many significant runs have been wiped out entirely, and virtually every surviving run has been reduced in number and range. On the Columbia River, which 100 years ago boasted the largest runs of Chinook, coho and steelhead on the face of the globe, these same fish have declined to the point of receiving serious consideration for the federal government's threatened or endangered species list. And since artificially propagated hatchery salmon now make up more than half the remaining fish in Washington State, the choicer wild salmon probably total less than a quarter their number before the coming of the white man.

It is not surprising to learn, therefore, that there are no subsistence salmon fishermen in San Francisco or Seattle, and no wild salmon in the streams that drain their famous hills. The Olympic Peninsula on the other hand would seem to offer a different prospect. This 6,000-square-mile area of mountain and forest, located directly opposite Seattle across Puget Sound, is one of the wildest places remaining in the contiguous United States, and the upper Queets is as wild as any place on the peninsula. Ninety years after it was first explored there is still some confusion about the names of prominent features, and the description "unnamed and unknown" appears with frequency on fisheries survey maps.

If the wild salmon can no longer survive here, one might ask, where can they?

TWO

THE LAST STARS STILL SHONE in the west when we rolled out of our sleeping bags the next morning. Our clothes had not dried entirely, and there was some yodeling as we pulled them on. After a cup of hot chocolate and a few mouthfuls of last night's leftovers, we scattered the fire and headed for the river. The water was stupendously cold, but our spirits were buoyed by the sight of the sun creeping down Kitma Peak into the blue valley.

Fording the Queets just above Alta Creek, Blackburn and I found that one of his fish from the night before had been dragged up on shore and partially eaten while we slept. Hundreds of tiny blue butterflies fluttered above the bright water as we traveled the length of the first serpentine side channel, but there were no Chinook, dead or alive. Returning to the main river below Pelton Creek, we clattered out to the end of a rocky point and lay down on our backs in the sun to wait for Lestelle.

Twenty minutes later, he reported more disappointing news from his side of the river. Although it was only a little after 9 A.M., the valley was already quite warm and utterly without clouds. The mountains still encircled us, but seemed less imposing, as if they had all taken one step backward. We found a few redds in the next two miles, but nothing compared to our first sighting above Hee Hee the preceding day. Finally, Lestelle decided to divide the party again as we approached a pair of large side channels near Paradise Creek that had contained many Chinook in the past.

The upper side channel, which Blackburn and I covered, was entirely empty of fish and largely dry, apparently because of a major shift in the riverbed the year before. Beyond, however, we came to the mouth of Paradise Creek, a cool green tunnel framed by a swirling pool and the face of a sunbaked cliff. I was on one side of the channel and Blackburn was on the other, with the pool in between. We consulted at the top of our lungs for a few moments, and then I proceeded up the stream alone. The first redd was waiting for me there in the sunlight by the cliff. Hanging a yellow marker on a nearby bush, I stepped into the lush shade of heavy old growth spruce and an almost luminescent stand of maple and alder. I had a hunch there were salmon here, and probably other creatures as well, for this was a pure portion of the Olympic Peninsula rain forest.

At first glance, the most impressive thing about the forest is the sheer size of its trees. Except for a few redwood and sequoia farther south on the Pacific rim, they are the tallest trees on the face of the earth. The world's largest western red cedar, 19 feet thick at the butt and 180 feet tall where its crown has been snapped by a gale, grows near the town of Forks, a few miles north of the Queets River. The largest western hemlock is in the Quinault Valley to the south; and both the champion Sitka spruce and the record-holding Douglas fir grow in the Queets Valley. The latter tree, known simply as the "Queets fir," is more than 14 feet through and 221 feet tall at the point where its crown has been broken.

The overwhelming impact of the rain forest cannot be conveyed by cold statistics, however, for the big trees are only the skeleton upon which the great body of the forest is hung. Research at Oregon State University has shown that the variety of mosses, lichens and ferns increases as the trees grow taller. In fact, because the trees do not grow perfectly vertically, they are each home to two different worlds of plants: flat, leaflike lichens predominate on the upper, or drier side, whereas liverworts are more common on the wetter undersides. Typically, the trees of the rain forest carry 20 percent additional weight in extravagant living draperies, and some, like the Queets fir, are festooned with huckleberries and wild flowers for more than 100 feet up their trunks.

Although observed less frequently, animals inhabit the forest from the floor to the canopy, and above. Many are dependent on the trees for their survival, just as the trees themselves rely on animals and other plants to complete certain crucial life functions. Small rodents like the Townsend chipmunk, for instance, eat the potatolike truffles found in the earth around the trunks of the big trees. These truffles contain the spores of mycorrhizal fungi that grow among the outer root cells of the trees and enable them to absorb nutrients from the soil. Mycorrhizal fungi are essential to the survival of all trees in the western forests, and their only means of dispersal is by rodents, who spread fungi and forest with their droppings.

The salmon, too, receive benefits from the forest they helped create. In the winter, when the rains roll off the Pacific, the forest soaks up and retains immense amounts of water, thereby blunting the natural tendency of the peninsula's rivers to flood and destroy the salmon's redds. Later in the year, when there is a danger that lethally warm water will kill the young salmon before they are ready to go to sea, the forest releases its cool store of moisture and shades the rivers and streams from the direct sunlight for at least part of the day. Spawning spring Chinook are particularly aware of the trees along the rivers where they mate; whenever possible, they dig their nests in dark, shady water.

I found the second redd on Paradise Creek in the manner

Lestelle had advocated the day before—by stumbling into it. Jolted by the shock and unaccustomed to the deep midday shade, I paused to take my bearings. The stream was about twenty feet wide, and no more than a foot deep in the pools between the big round rocks. As my eyes adjusted to the light, I was impressed to find that I was standing among a half dozen spring Chinook and their redds. On one nest behind the projecting roots of an alder, I saw the biggest Chinook yet, a forty-five-inch, thirty-five-pound dame with iridescent white halos around the spots on her long, curved back. Like all the fish in Paradise Creek that day, she was extremely docile, and let me watch her from as close as a dozen feet. Six more redds, and as many salmon, followed until I reached a bottle-glass-green pool with three ancient cedars piled over one end.

Lestelle had instructed us to be on the lookout for sockeye salmon in Paradise Creek because of previous sightings. Just as I was recalling what he had said, I was stopped dead in my tracks by the sight of a flame-red fish with a vivid green head hovering motionless in a shaft of light that slanted through the forest into the middle of the pool. He was a little more than half the size of a Chinook and was plainly watching me with his golden eye. I stood completely still and tried to estimate the rarity of what I was seeing. Sockeye, *Oncorhynchus nerka*, almost always require the presence of a large lake somewhere within reach of the rivers they frequent for successful propagation. There are no lakes on the Queets or its tributaries, and if this sockeye was part of a true river-rearing population, his tribe could not number more than a handful.

Halfway back I met Lestelle, who was hanging long, numbered yellow flags in place of the increasingly skimpy markers that I was forced to leave as the number of redds outstripped my limited supply of flagging. He verified the fifteen Chinook redds I had counted in the lower half mile of the stream (along with one shallow, perfectly round sockeye redd), and puzzled with me over the curious mass spawning area just above the forks. Nowhere near this many spring Chinook had ever been observed spawning in Paradise Creek before, and Lestelle speculated the fish moved into the creek when floods devastated the upper side channel, just as the surviving wild salmon of the Toutle and Cowlitz rivers sought new spawning grounds when the eruption of Mount St. Helens killed those rivers.

Rejoining Blackburn on a gravel bar in the blazing early afternoon sun, we grabbed a quick lunch of cheese, Ritz crackers and jerky. After eating, I walked over to the river to fill my canteen while Blackburn and Lestelle discussed our plans. Paradise Creek had been the richest find of the trip, but it was already 2 P.M., and we had fourteen miles of river and a tricky ford ahead of us in the six hours of daylight that remained. I poured a generous draught of water over my head and said I didn't think we could make it. "If we can't make it," Lestelle said smiling, "we'll just camp wherever we are when we run out of light."

A hot wind was rising in the west, stirring the falling leaves of the maples and cottonwoods, and carrying with it the smell of smoke. Hurrying past two unnamed streams, we entered an area where the Queets braided into two, three and four shallow channels. It was here that we found the first carcass of a big male lying half out of the water with his eyes eaten out. He had a thick muscular body and hooked snout; his tail was white with rot. A little farther on, we came upon a disoriented jack—or small precocious male—flitting aimlessly in a warm exposed section of water from which he apparently could not escape.

As the sun sank in our faces, the river took on a blinding dazzle, and the air seemed to grow still hotter despite the loud gusts of wind. I saw an immature bald eagle flap silently out of a snag a quarter mile away, and Blackburn spotted several more redds beside an eroding flat of alders and oxalis. We increased our pace with each passing hour, and by 6 P.M. we had set off at a jog on the park trail from Bob Creek to the roadhead at the Queets Campground. Ten miles remained, but we could already see that we were coming to the edge of the wilderness by the towering columns of smoke in the sky to the west.

Brown and sinuous, these beacons marked the slash fires set by logging companies at the completion of clearcuts. Somewhere up on Matheny Creek and over in the Clearwater Valley, the last vestiges of another old-growth forest were going up in smoke. The big trees would have already been cut down and hauled away, and now nearly every other growing thing over hundreds of acres would have been scraped into piles by bulldozing and ignited. Clearcutting and controlled burns are part of a "high yield" forestry program designed to obliterate the old-growth forest and replace it with a simpler system where commercially valuable trees like Douglas fir predominate.

The fires are deliberately lit to prevent worse wildfires. Herbicides such as 2,4,5–T and 2,4–D are then sprayed to kill quick growing "weed trees" that will shade out Douglas fir. Because burning, suppression of nitrogen-fixing alder and increased rain runoff all rob the soil of nutrients, chemical fertilizers must be applied to assure growth. A good stand of Douglas fir that has been given this care will grow exceptionally fast, reaching a height of fifteen feet at ten years, forty-five feet at twenty-five years, and 100 feet or more at fifty years. It will be much more expensive to grow than a natural grove, but it can be harvested earlier, allowing a quicker payout. Where second-growth trees were commonly harvested at eighty-five years of age, third growth is now normally taken at fifty-five years, and much is cut as young as thirty-five years, the infancy of trees that can live to be more than 1,000 years old.

Cutting at fifty-five rather than eighty-five maximizes annual growth, or yield in pounds of wood, but it does not produce wood of the same quality. The spans are shorter, the strength less, and in the case of western red cedar, the famous water and rot-resistant quality diminished. A shake roof made of old-growth cedar is a marvel that may last fifty years, even on the sodden west side of the Olympic Peninsula. A roof of second-growth cedar shakes or shingles probably will not last half as long. Reflecting this superiority, the price paid per board foot for old growth is substantially higher than that for the younger "wonder trees."

Ecologically, the impact of clearcuts is as extreme as might be expected. Virtually every creature with the capacity to transport itself leaves after logging. A month or so later the first crows and deer may return, passing through on their way somewhere else. By reducing the depth of habitats from the 200-foot-tall old-growth forest to the two-inch-tall blade of grass or Douglas fir seedling, logging literally flattens many creatures' chances for life. "What you commonly see in areas that have been clearcut is fewer species and less individual creatures than before," said Fred Maybee of the Washington Department of Game. Some important insect-eating birds and nitrogen-fixing lichens are dependent on old growth for their habitat, and will perish without it. The fisher, the brown creeper and the spotted owl, which is currently under consideration for the federal government's threatened or endangered species list, are among the animals becoming rare for this reason.

Salmon, too, are affected by logging, for the removal of the trees can change the drainage pattern of a valley, and alter the very nature of the river that flows within it. According to Robert Curry of the University of California at Santa Cruz, logging typically produces "a wider, shallower stream flowing at a somewhat steeper gradient" which erodes its banks, chokes on its own sediment and eventually splits into a maze of individual channels that alternately scour out or go dry. "We seem to believe that the biological portions of a watershed can be changed . . . without a concomitant change in the physical system," Curry said, "but energy ties both together."

This appears to be what happened on the Quinault River, which neighbors the Queets on the south and is the main seat of the Quinault Tribe. Clearing for farms began around Lake Quinault before the turn of the century, and during the First World War the U.S. Army logged a considerable amount of the magnificent Sitka spruce above the lake for war plane manufacture. Not all trees in any given area were taken, but the operation apparently caused the upper Quinault to unravel like a piece of yarn. Early settlers pictured the upper river as a "stream of narrow portion, banked by miles of heavily timbered soil." After logging, the Quinault became a river of many braided channels constantly shifting across a broad waste of gravel and debris.

Millions of wild salmon were thereby killed before they even hatched. Freshets washed some out of their nests while others strangled in the air when the channel went dry. Siltation killed still more salmon by cementing the interstices between the gravel and transforming their redds into sealed tombs. Based on modern experience, it is likely that the early logging on the Quinault also caused respiratory disease among fry and eliminated large numbers of the creatures they eat in fresh water.

The Quinault salmon that suffered this travail were arguably the single most famous run on the Pacific coast of North America. When the whites arrived on the Columbia, they found that the choicest fish came not from that mighty salmon producer, but rather from a small river about eighty miles up the coast. In April 1813, a geographer for the Northwest Company named David Thompson wrote of his stay at the mouth of the Columbia that "Comcomly [a chief of the Chinook Tribe] brought a few beaver in trade, and some Queenhithe dried salmon, which were excellent—the best fish I have seen on the Columbia." The Chinook Tribe, which owned the premier fishing grounds on the Columbia, esteemed the Quinault sockeye so highly that they used it as an all-purpose term of excellence. Whites after Thompson picked this up and mistakenly applied the name to the most prized of the Columbia's runs, the salmon now known as the Chinook. For half a century Chinook salmon were known as "Quinnat," and even today the name persists in Europe and New Zealand.

It is difficult to determine exactly how large the Quinault sockeye run originally was. We know that early explorers shot the blueback for sport with their revolvers as the fish leaped from the waters of Lake Quinault, and the Quinault Indians traded them in dried form from the Columbia to Cape Flattery. The largest early catch reported was 367,260 sockeye in 1915, with an estimated run size that year of at least 600,000 fish. The run was probably larger once though, for that same year a report to the U.S. Commissioner of Fisheries noted that "the salmon [run] in the Quinaielt Lake and River has materially decreased in recent years." With increased logging along the fishes' primary spawning grounds above the lake, the catch of sockeye in the Quinault fell to 15,665 in 1920, the "smallest ever known to that time."

The Commissioner of Fisheries' remedy for the problem on the Quinault was to construct a salmon hatchery on Lake Quinault, which also took place during the First World War. Although acutely aware from the Bureau of Fisheries' own reports of the damage logging was doing, he chose to avoid any direct confrontation with the loggers or the timber interests that stood behind them. Only when the hatchery itself was imperiled did the U.S. Bureau of Fisheries raise a timorous voice of protest. The rest of the time it was more than willing to use unchecked logging abuses as a justification for expanded hatchery work. "While there is at present no positive proof of the efficiency of propagation as carried on by the [Quinault] hatchery," a bureau report from the 1930s noted, "it would seem, owing to the present hazardous conditions under which natural propagation must take place, that the hatchery should be of considerable value in maintaining the runs of sockeye salmon."

With its long, low hatchery building full of wooden troughs, running water sluiced from a nearby creek, and pack horse supply system, the Lake Quinault federal fish hatchery was typical of the period. Its purpose was to incubate the eggs of sockeye salmon that would otherwise have spawned in their native streams. The hatchery collected the eggs and sperm from the fish, mixed them and laid the fertilized eggs in the troughs. Upon hatching they were released into the lake. It was supposed that more juvenile sockeye in Lake Quinault automatically meant more adults returning later, but this did not prove to be the case.

During the first two decades of its existence, the Lake Quinault hatchery was more bane than boon to the blueback.

Assuming that runs of sockeye in different rivers were interchangeable, the hatchery imported sockeye eggs from Afognak Island in the Gulf of Alaska. As these Alaskan fish interbred with the bluebacks they dulled the native fishes' hereditary adaption to the river, making the wild sockeye less efficient reproducers. The Afognak transplants were also heavily infected with a viral fish disease known as IHN. Fisheries biologists like Larry Gilbertson speculate that IHN may not have been such a serious problem on the Quinault before the hatchery. Thousands more Quinault sockeye were killed during the 1920s by the Bureau of Fisheries counting weir at the outlet of Lake Quinault. One year, 1921, the Bureau of Indian Affairs figured that almost half of that year's spawning escapement had been killed when the fish were caught in the weir and drowned.

Logging, meanwhile, became steadily more widespread and destructive. The Quinault Indian Reservation, which occupies 190,000 acres on the west side of the Olympic Peninsula, is generally considered to have been the most savagely logged area in the state of Washington. Beginning in 1922, reservation timber was sold by the U.S. Bureau of Indian Affairs in large blocks, which were progressively clearcut following the railroad logging practices of the day. Tens of thousands of acres were stripped of valuable timber in a continuous line as the rails pushed deeper into the wilderness. No effort was made to clear the heavy load of cedar slash that covered the land, or to reforest it, and in the 1930s a series of huge fires swept and reswept the area until the mycorrhizal fungi were killed and the soil would support nothing but the brush deserts that cover it to this day.

The last of the great Quinault sockeye runs occurred during the 1940s. Old Indian fishermen at the Quinault village of Tahola still remember how thick the quick little fish were in those years, their weight in the nets, and the money they made. In 1941, Quinault Indian fishermen caught 509,140 blueback, the most on modern record. With a faraway war raging in Europe and Asia, it seemed for a few years that the world had passed the Quinault by. The sockeye ran strong in 1940, 1941, 1942, 1947 and 1949, but after that there were no more catches of 200,000 fish, and after 1956 there were no more catches of even 100,000 fish. When Lake Quinault hatchery was closed in 1947 it was revealed that the wild sockeye that once may have numbered 1,000,000 were now barely able to sustain one-tenth that.

The years right after the Second World War also saw another increase in logging activity. Using trucks instead of railroad flatcars to get the trees out of the woods, logging outfits were able to exploit steeper, previously inaccessible hillsides. Because of the terrain and road building techniques, mud slides became increasingly frequent along the rivers and streams of the Quinault Reservation. It was a time when "it wasn't too rare to actually find spawning salmon pinned on the redd by felled trees," as one biologist recalled. Trees were commonly dragged —or yarded—across salmon spawning and rearing areas, and many blocks to salmon migration were created. Some controlled burning was practiced, but it was still more common for logging debris to be left where it lay.

Floods often picked up the debris and stacked it into deep jams that can cause flooding and act as a barrier to migrating salmon. Even small streams on the Quinault developed extensive tangles in the wake of logging. This has been observed throughout the Olympic Peninsula, and the rest of the Northwest as well. One recent example occurred early on the morning of December 2, 1977. At that hour logging debris riding a flood of heavy winter rain jammed behind the State Highway 410 bridge over the Greenwater River in the foothills of the Cascade Mountains. The surging rivers rose in a few moments to the level of the roadway, and then suddenly cut a new channel around the bridge and through the middle of the town of Greenwater, a good part of which washed away.

Modern truck logging came to the Queets in the early 1940s, but it was not until the 1960s that the big push began. Then the Washington Department of Natural Resources, which manages most of the watershed not included in the Olympic National Park, began to let large timber contracts. The land to be logged was part of the trust that supports public schools in Washington, and the proceeds could only be used to build new school buildings for the state's elementary, junior and high schools. The Department of Natural Resource's plan was to log all its old growth on the Queets as soon as possible. On the Clearwater River, which is the Queets's largest tributary, this meant that more than 50 percent of the watershed would be clearcut before 1990.

To understand why Washington Commissioner of Public Lands Bert Cole would decide to liquidate the old growth at a time when the crest of the World War II baby boom had already passed and school enrollments were not expected to increase, one must examine the timber supply situation in the Northwest. Despite expensive advertising campaigns designed to create exactly the opposite impression, the large Western timber companies have grossly overcut their land. Tree farms and reforestation programs ensure that there will be some timber in the future to be sure, but not as much or as quickly as needed at current levels of consumption. The U.S. Forest Service's Oregon-based Pacific Northwest Forest and Range Experimental Station concluded in 1971 that overcutting was so widespread that the region would lose 2,000 jobs annually between then and the year 2000 as a result of the declining supply of timber in the woods.

And so with the last old growth on the Quinault Reservation already in sight, logging interests on the west side of the peninsula were looking for some more public timber to log. Bert Cole, a former lumberman who was heavily supported by timber firms during his six successful campaigns, obliged by opening up the Queets on very sweet terms. For 10 percent down DNR would sell you the right to cut a parcel of timber within three to five years. The remaining 90 percent was not due until the timber was actually cut. As the value of the disappearing old growth climbed steadily through the 1960s and 1970s, it was possible to acquire timber in the Queets for a fraction of the sales price, which was itself a fraction of the timber's value at the time it was paid for. Salvage logger Ray Koon of Joyce, Washington, has estimated that "the profit [from such operations] could well have been $10 on an $.80 investment . . . most of it at public expense."

Dirt logging roads snaked in across the swales of the lower Queets, and the timber rolled out. By 1971 nearly two billion board feet of the world's finest Douglas fir, western red cedar and Sitka spruce had been logged along the mainstem Queets and Clearwater. That same spring, two massive landslides caused by new logging roads sent 20,000 cubic yards of dirt, rock, mud and trees plunging into the headwaters of Stequaleho Creek on the upper Clearwater. Native coho populations in this stream declined significantly in the years right after the slides, and fisheries biologists like Larry Lestelle believe that the slides affected salmon throughout the Clearwater and lower Queets. Subsequent research by Jack Tagart at the University of Washington showed that juvenile coho were both larger and more numerous in the streams on the Clearwater that had not been logged.

Spraying of herbicides to control "weed trees" also became something of a problem in the Clearwater as logging advanced. In 1979, DNR charged ITT-Rayonier with four counts of illegal spraying on the Clearwater and Dickey rivers where it appeared that 2,4-D had drifted off timberland into the trees along the riverbank and the water itself. Although the charges were later thrown out on ITT's appeal that the evidence might have been contaminated, there were a number of reports from the Olympic Peninsula during the late 1970s of poor herbicide use, including the spraying of streams, homes and in at least one incident, a person directly. To salmon, herbicides can be directly lethal in minute doses, and can be indirectly responsible for their death by changing their behavior so that they, say, do not migrate at the proper time.

Sometimes the effects of logging are not so subtle. Take the case of the steelhead near Dingaling Creek. In 1973, Lestelle and biologist Jeff Cederholm, who are good friends, learned that a couple of dozen beautiful adult summer-run steelhead had washed ashore on the upper Clearwater. Investigating, they found the fish in a canyon beside a new logging operation and concluded that the fish had been killed by blasting. "Probably somebody threw a stick or two of dynamite into a pool," said Lestelle. "They took what they wanted and left the rest." There was no way of knowing whether loggers had actually killed the fish, but without the construction of the logging road to the side of the stream and the presence of people in the area, it was a good bet that those fish would not have died.

Historically, the Department of Natural Resources, which manages five million acres of state trust land, has resisted efforts to make logging less damaging to salmon and other wildlife. When the state legislature passed Washington's Environmental Policy Act in 1971, Bert Cole and the department unilaterally decided that the new law did not apply to logging on the land they managed. Sued by environmental groups to force compliance, Cole lobbied the legislature for bills to exempt Natural Resources from state law. When this failed, the department decided to prepare one general environmental impact statement for most logging over the next 120 years. The draft of this document was attacked as incomplete, misleading and inaccurate by virtually every federal, state and county agency with responsibility for the environment, and then was adopted without change by the Board of Natural Resources.

The Washington Department of Game recently detailed an impressive list of destructive Department of Natural Resources practices statewide, including "an operation on Fish Creek where the Department of Natural Resources burned a 100-ton slash pile in the stream." In 1978 the Seattle *Times* reported on another logging operation on Natural Resources land: "Two large piles of slash and debris mark the site. A culvert spanning a small creek, which is in violation of the permit, has not been removed. And there is evidence of heavy vehicle traffic along the creek bank—another violation." The *Times* story by Lou Corsaletti quoted a Natural Resources spokesman who said, "small logging operations are often left in a similar state."

Not that DNR was the only guilty party in this respect. Logging on private land was generally worse, and worst of all was logging on Indian reservations, which are managed by the federal government. A report issued by the U.S. Fish and Wildlife Service in 1979 showed that 50 percent of recent logging operations on the Quinault Reservation had a direct and deleterious effect on salmon, killing them by "suffocation, poisoning, starvation, thermal shock and disease." Toxic cedar slash was left piled in streams, culverts were installed so that the fish would have to be able to fly to pass through them, logs were dragged through spawning gravel, and streamside vegetation was leveled, according to the report. In half these cases, the damage occurred after both the Bureau of Indian Affairs and the logging company had received official warnings from Fish and Wildlife regarding the danger to salmon.

Compared with the rest of the state, in fact, logging on DNR land in the Queets and Clearwater was almost a model of propriety and consideration. In the years following the Stequaleho Creek slides, flumes were installed on all culverts to reduce erosion, unstable road building methods were abandoned, and nearly half the logging roads in the area were paved. Buffer strips of uncut trees were left along some sections of river to provide shade and cover for salmon, and most of the slash was burned to prevent wildfires of the sort that devastated the Quinault Reservation. The man responsible for these changes was E.C. "Gock" Gockerell, DNR area manager for the Olympic Peninsula. An avid sport fisherman who recently caught a near-record steelhead in the nearby Bogachiel River, Gockerell read the Clearwater research produced by Tagart, Cederholm and their associates, and tried to modify his methods accordingly. Brian Boyle's defeat of Bert Cole in 1980 brought some significant changes to DNR, but it did not completely obviate the basic impact of the logging. Even with all the road paving, for instance, DNR plans still called for twice as many miles of unpaved logging roads in the Clearwater as Cederholm believes the salmon can safely tolerate.

You can see the process best from the summit of Kloochman Rock, a 3,300-foot escarpment on the ridge separating the Queets and Clearwater valleys. As late as the 1960s Kloochman offered "the best view of old growth forest on the peninsula," according to author and mountaineer Robert L. Wood. Today the weathered platform atop Kloochman surveys a dramatically different scene. There is the Queets winding down from Olympus in a steep valley, but it is heavily forested only to the point where it emerges onto the dozen-mile-wide bench that separates the mountains from the Pacific. Here and farther west whole mountainsides have been crisscrossed with dirt logging roads and stripped of much vegetation and animal life. To the north in the valley of the Clearwater, the logging has been even more widespread, covering half the visible land and resembling the scabby, shaved skin around a series of sutured wounds.

THREE

WE ALL KNEW we had come to the end of the line. We had been jogging with full packs for the last mile, but it was no use. It was so dark that we could no longer see our feet on the trail, let alone any obstacles that might be blocking our path.

As we swung out into the twilight on the cliff above the river, Blackburn and I stopped and waited in silence for Lestelle. Moments later he emerged from the inky forest. "I guess we'd better spend the night here," he said with a sigh.

Blackburn and I threw off our packs and sank down onto them while Lestelle rummaged in his for the walkie-talkie. We figured we were about four miles from the Queets Campground where a Quinault tribal pickup awaited us. It was a little after nine o'clock, and a long line of clouds was rising in the west.

Lestelle walked out to the end of a little promontory and spoke into the box. "Adam one, this is Adam four, Adam one, this is Adam four . . . Doesn't seem to be anyone answering in Queets," he said finally. "I guess I'll try Tahola."

Raising the walkie-talkie again, he turned toward the south and addressed the little bats flitting over the river. "Calling Tahola, calling Tahola . . . Come in, Tahola." We listened to the crackling static for several seconds before there was a mildly curious reply on the line.

"This is Tahola. Who are you?"

Lestelle smiled and explained that we were a tribal salmon survey team radioing from inside the Olympic National Park on the Queets. He said we would not be making it out that evening as planned, and asked the man on the other end of the line, who turned out to be a tribal policeman, to call his wife and Blackburn's girl friend.

"Happy to," came the reply, "and sleep tight."

Turning our attention to a camp, we found that might be a problem. On one side of the path was a sixty-foot drop to the river, and on the other was thick tangled forest. The path itself was flat and clear, of course, but none of us was too eager to sleep there. Before nightfall we had seen the fresh tracks of bear and a large herd of Olympic elk running for some distance along the trail. Further investigations with a flashlight failed to turn up any other options, however, and so finally we bedded down side by side with our upper bodies on the margin and our legs on the smooth, packed earth.

Blackburn immediately drifted off without complaint about the cold that had him eating a couple of packages of cough drops a day, but Lestelle and I fell into conversation. Weary as we were from fourteen hours of hard tramping on no dinner, our words took on the dreamy, attenuated rhythm of late-night intimacy. We discovered we had attended neighboring high schools in north Seattle and were soon recalling scenes from that American suburb: the little theater beyond the public golf course that used to show Japanese horror movie matinees, the concrete immensity of Northgate (which claims to have been the first shopping center built in the nation), the cars peeling out of parking strips after school in the fall. "Why is it that the river always sounds louder at night?" I wondered.

What seemed like moments later, I was awakened by Lestelle sitting bolt upright and beating his arms against his body. Off in the darkness, an animal diverted from the trail crashed past in the bushes behind us. "What was that?" I asked, thinking—no doubt as my companions were also thinking—bigger than a coyote, bigger even than a deer. Doesn't have the bounding stride of an elk though. Too violent and direct, except for maybe a . . . bear. "I don't know," Lestelle said, still shining the flashlight in the direction that the animal had just passed. "Well, whatever it is, it ought to get some sleep," Blackburn said, rolling over loudly.

When I awoke a little less than two hours later, Blackburn was already up building a small fire on the bluff overlooking the Queets. Since there was not much food left, we warmed our hands briefly, and then started down the trail through patches of low drifting fog. Another tribal salmon survey crew had already covered this section of the Queets the day before. We would not know what they found until we got back to the truck at the Queets Campground, but Lestelle said the general pattern for salmon was to begin spawning in the headwaters and then work their way downriver as the spawning season progressed. It was still a little early for this section of the river, but later when the Chinook hit their peak with the fall run, this would be the center of the action. "The early homesteaders say the river used to be black with them," said Lestelle.

Just then the teakettle whistle of a bull elk pierced the fog. Blackburn raised his hand to his mouth and answered. Trumpeting is a part of the elk's mating ritual, a booming declaration of virility. Considering that the Olympic elk, or wapiti, can stand five feet at the shoulder and nine feet at the tip of their intricate, branching antlers, I hoped the animal didn't decide to settle with Blackburn. Once found throughout the United States, these tawny animals are common today in only two areas, the Rockies and the Olympics. They were hunted for their hides and teeth (which were prized as watch fobs by members of the Benevolent and Protective Order of Elks), and probably would have perished on the peninsula if not for President Theodore Roosevelt. Appalled by the slaughter, Roosevelt closed 620,000 acres of the Olympic Peninsula to elk hunting in 1909 when he proclaimed the area a national park.

Light in the pack, as well as the stomach, we made good time to Coal Creek, which we crossed by hopping boulders. The sky was clearing overhead and the forest smelled softly of sweet hedge nettle and vanilla leaf. Around 9:30 we came to a fifty-acre meadow of grass and wild flowers. A wave of flying grasshoppers buzzed noisily in front of us as we made our way toward a large, weathered old barn standing against the tall trees at the far side of the clearing. Off to the side was a solitary fruit tree leaning over a pile of blackberries where a house probably once stood. A small Park Service sign announced that we had arrived at Andrews Field, the remains of one of the many homesteads that lined the Queets forty years ago.

Homesteading got underway here in 1890, the year that Fisher made his solo trip down the Queets. In fact, the first person Fisher encountered was a homesteader out hoeing his garden near Tacoma Creek. Public land could be claimed under a number of laws during the nineteenth century, the most common of which was the Homestead Act of 1862, which entitled every head of a household to 160 acres after five years' residence, payment of a nominal $10 fee, and "proving up" the claim. Originally intended to encourage the expansion of the free farmers who fed the Union Army during the Civil War, the Homestead Act succeeded so handsomely that forty years later there was virtually no unclaimed arable land left within the boundaries of the forty-eight states.

Despite the emphasis on farming, however, one did not have to sit in the woods pulling stumps for five years to claim public land. If one had capital, it was possible to cut the residency requirement by paying an additional fee to the government. Claims totaling more than 1,000 acres could be filed by the same person using a combination of enabling acts; and by hiring squads of "floaters" or "entrymen" to stake claims it was possible to amass large holdings without ever leaving Seattle or San Francisco. This is, in fact, how many of the early timber empires were acquired. In a contemporary account of land fraud on the Olympic Peninsula, Thomas Murphy wrote in the Port Townsend *Leader* in 1890:

> I heard considerable complaint while in the valley of men taking up claims for syndicates, being provided by the latter with supplies, and receiving a few hundred dollars for their claims after proving up. This dodge was attempted some time since on a section, which, it was understood, was to be shortly surveyed. Information was filed at the surveyor general's office of the crookedness of the matter, and as a consequence the survey has been postponed for an indefinite period, on account of which there is much wailing and gnashing of teeth.

The pattern on the Queets was typical of the peninsula, and of much of the West for that matter. The true homesteaders clustered along the river bottom on the best agricultural land, while much of the land along the benches and ridges was acquired by "syndicates." Often isolated by a day or more's hike from the nearest road, the homesteaders prospered on a mixed subsistence economy. With their hay fields, root crops and livestock, they tried to raise as much as possible of what they needed to live every year. Their only cash money came from guiding, logging on the Quinault Indian Reservation to the south, or working in the salmon cannery that operated near the mouth of the Queets during the 1920s. Homesteaders also relied on wild salmon, venison and fowl. Robert Brown, a Queets area homesteader now in his eighties, still recalls "the silvers [cohos] flashing in the moonlight—the river just full of them." He caught forty salmon one afternoon at the confluence of the Queets and Tacoma Creek.

A paved road was completed along the west side of the peninsula for the first time during the Great Depression, and in 1937 President Franklin Roosevelt toured the area by car. Agitation for the creation of the Olympic National Park was then at its height, and Roosevelt wanted to see for himself what was involved. All day the big limousine rolled past sections of magnificent old-growth forest, logged-off land and the occasional farm where homesteaders piled potatoes and cabbages under signs that read, "See What This Land Will Grow, Mr. President." The next year Roosevelt happily signed the bill creating a 680,000-acre Olympic National Park. Consulting with Secretary of Interior Harold Ickes, Roosevelt further determined to enlarge the park so that one of the rain forest rivers was preserved from the mountains to the sea. The river they chose was the Queets.

Early in 1938 the Works Progress Administration began contacting property owners along the Queets. The government was offering to pay $10 an acre for land it had recently let go for as little as $.16 an acre. Finding few takers, the WPA filed dozens of condemnation suits under the right of eminent domain. One homesteader ran the government's representatives off his place with a gun, but by the late 1940s the government had won every case. The result was the Queets corridor, a one-mile-wide strip of wilderness running for twenty miles along the lower river between Tshletshy Creek and the boundary of the Quinault Indian Reservation. The corridor contains some of the most impressive old growth remaining (the Queets fir, for instance, is located there), but its narrowness meant that the river was not really protected. Although the homesteaders were evicted, timber firms such as Polson Brothers (which subsequently became a part of ITT) were allowed to keep their holdings. Subsequent logging here and on state land in the Clearwater has degraded the Queets and the life it can support.

Deep rancor still exists among surviving homesteaders over this last twist. "They said it [the corridor] was for wildlife preservation," recalled Robert Brown, who was awarded $20 an acre by a jury in 1941 for his family's home near Kalaloch Creek. "That land has been butchered by logging! They've told me they wish I wouldn't use that word 'butchered,' you know, but it's true." There was a catch in his voice. "We got five tons of hay to the acre. . . . It was very productive land." The situation on the lower Queets has, in fact, almost exactly reversed itself since the creation of the corridor. Where human activities used to be restricted to the narrow area around the river, they now cover the bulk of the valley. The wilderness, meanwhile, has been restricted to what was formerly the area of human habitation.

We found the old barn on the far side of the clearing was still in good shape. High roofed and bleached pearly on its weathered sides, it appeared to be the sometime home of pack horses, winter campers, a rich assortment of rodentia, skunks and an owl. Beyond Andrews Field, in a glen of massive moss and lichen-encrusted maples, we heard the calling of more elk. The trail began to widen, and then the roar on our left told us we were coming back to the river. "Wet one more time, and we're home," Lestelle said, as we picked our way down to the water's edge. Our destination, the Queets Campground, lay on the other side of the river about a quarter mile below where we now stood. In between, the Sams River joined the Queets from the other side, considerably swelling its flow.

Lestelle and Blackburn hoped we could ford the Queets above the confluence with the Sams, but this proved difficult. The river was much too fast and deep until just above the mouth of the Sams, where it cast itself across a broad riffle. A turbulent pool and another broader, deeper riffle followed. Blackburn scouted around the point, but came back shaking his head. "I think my legs are a little too short no matter where we try it," he said wryly. It was clear that Lestelle's long legs (knees and ankles included) were about to have their finest hour. "Well, what do you think?" I asked. "Looks to me like our best bet is right across the tail of the riffle there," Lestelle said, indicating the thirty-yard-wide section immediately upriver from the cascading entrance of the Sams.

Wading in, I noticed bits of gravel dancing like marionettes in the current behind a big stone. The river was swift and dazzling in the morning sun, clearer than I had ever seen it before, but no less green. The numbness sucking at my knees gave me a moment of giddiness, but I knew that the only bad stretch was at the very end, where one had to cross the deepest water fast enough to keep from being swept into the confluence. About halfway across, the water rose to my waist and I experienced a sudden feeling of weightlessness. I was bouncing forward toward the far shore, but for every foot's progress in that direction I was being swept three feet downriver in the direction I didn't want to go. I tried to keep myself pressed against the bottom, but the more I pressed, the higher the water rose around me, and the more I was carried downriver. Lestelle and Blackburn turned to watch my antics from the safety of the shore, laughing. I couldn't see the humor at just that moment, but by the time I stumbled out of the water I was laughing hardest of all.

The truck, an old blue Dodge with Quinault Nation license plates, was waiting for us at the end of the road. It growled to life under Lestelle's hand while I searched for cookies in the glove box. The road was a one-lane washboard running through a low tunnel of vegetation. At 30 m.p.h., we bounced with the rhythm of my home blender's "purée" setting. There was lots of loose gravel in the bends, and pullouts to let oncoming cars pass every quarter mile or so. It turned out the other crew hadn't left us anything edible, but from their notes we confirmed Lestelle's earlier hunch that the run had not really gotten going yet in the lower river. The three of us had flagged sixty-one redds on the upper ten miles of river, compared to thirty-four redds on the lower ten miles. Paradise Creek was strong—the strongest on the river in fact—but overall the spawning population seemed to have slipped another notch. Based on ours and other surveys, Lestelle eventually estimated the run of 1979 Queets spring Chinook at 1,100 fish, down 200 from the previous year.

"Why can't these salmon overcome logging the way they overcame the glaciers?" I asked Lestelle. "I'm not saying logging hasn't done some gross things, but on the upper river where the spawning grounds are deep within the park, you'd think they'd be able to handle it."

Downshifting for a blind curve, Lestelle answered, "We're burning the candle at both ends. We've got problems with logging here in the valley, and then we've got overfishing at sea. . . . River systems like the Queets still have the potential to be tremendously productive [for wild salmon], but how can the runs rebuild when not enough fish return from the ocean to spawn? The big threat to these early Chinook probably isn't what's happening here," he said, nodding at the river through the trees. "It's what's happening in the ocean."

Unlike sockeye, Chinook will readily strike a baited line at sea. This phenomenon, which is due to their preference for feeding on fish rather than plankton, has made them one of the principal targets of the growing commercial and sport troll fleets. Trollers fish the high seas in relatively small boats outfitted with many, multihooked lines. By motoring with their lines deployed off long poles, they attempt to mimic the herring, anchovies and pilchard that make up the bulk of an adult Chinook's diet. Performed correctly, trolling comes close to an art, especially when the quarry is Chinook. As Joe Upton wrote in *Alaska Blues:* "Kings [Chinook] bite on different gear in different areas at different times. The color of the sky, the time of day, the flow of the tide: all these are important. . . . King salmon trolling means knowing the bottom and being able to keep the gear close to it, but without snagging and ripping the gear. Kings . . . often prefer rockpiles that only the cleverest troller can fish."

In the early days, when sail-powered trollers worked the banks off Cape Ommaney near Port Alexander, Alaska, the troll fleets seldom ventured more than 100 miles from their home ports. After World War II, however, poor catches in many established fishery areas, larger boats and sophisticated fish-finding gear encouraged the trollers to go farther into previously unfished waters. As their numbers swelled into the thousands, they spread out and covered the entire coast between Cape Foulweather, near Newport, Oregon, and Cape Fairweather, 150 miles north of Sitka, Alaska. By the 1960s the trollers were the dominant factor in the coastal fishery, often accounting for over half the total catch of Chinook and coho in Washington. Between 1940 and 1970, Washington trollers increased their catch of Chinook and coho nearly 100,000 to 958,408 fish.

The key to the trollers' success was simple: first shot at the fish. The history of commercial fishing on the Pacific is essentially a tale of one group after another finding a way to fish in front of the others. Thus the cannery owners built traps in front of the Indians' weirs, the gill-netters went out in front of the traps, the purse seiners moved beyond the gill-netters, and finally the trollers got to the head of the line by pursuing the fish into the ocean itself. High fuel costs were incurred because of the distances traveled, but this was more than offset by the fact that salmon caught in the sea are at their brightest and freshest and therefore command the highest price. There was also more leeway financially since, unlike fishermen working within the three-mile limit then claimed by the United States, trollers fished without limit: seven days a week, spring through fall.

The impact of trolling appears to have been heaviest on the wild salmon of the Washington and Oregon coast. Studies by the Washington Department of Fisheries have shown that 95 percent of some coastal spring Chinook runs are taken by trollers before the fish can return to their native rivers. This rate of harvest is higher than either wild or hatchery salmon runs can biologically sustain. In recent years, the less efficient hatcheries have often been unable to return their seed, and all coastal hatcheries have experienced declining returns, according to Washington Director of Fisheries Gordon Sandison, who attributed the trend to "an increasing harvest rate." On the Queets, the number of wild Chinook spawners dropped from 3,000 to 1,000, and then kept right on going until fewer than 700 Queets spring Chinook spawned in 1976.

The one group of salmon fishermen on the Washington coast

that did not participate in the prosperous plunder was the Indians. Fishing with nets at inherited stations along rivers such as the Queets, Hoh and Humptulips, the Indian fishermen of Washington found both their catch and their range declining. Indian fishermen on the Queets, for instance, took an average of 2,000 spring Chinook in the early 1950s. By 1964, the Indian catch was down to 1,210; in 1969 it reached 780; and in 1974, a year when Washington trollers caught more than half a million Chinook, the Queets fishermen netted only 481 Chinook. Less than half that number was caught in 1976, and Queets coho returns were, if anything, worse. In 1978, the Queets lost their entire fall season because the trollers overfished the Queets coho so heavily that the run could not stand an Indian catch of even one fish.

That winter the thirty or so Queets Indian fishermen sat on the bank and took stock of their situation. As far back as anyone could remember, their people had lived on the Queets and made their livelihood fishing for salmon. Chinook, coho and steelhead were the staple of their traditional culture, and since the coming of the white man they had been both staple and a major source of cash income. Harry Fisher, who was fed and feted by the Queets Indians at the end of his solo descent from Olympus, caught a glimpse of their salmon wealth in September 1890. "Although the water was four feet deep in front of the [Indian's long] house," he wrote, "the large salmon created a V-shaped ripple, and some of the children gave alarm, and all rushed pell mell, eager for the sport. They possessed a fine gill net, but nets and traps were useless during the run of salmon, as [the salmon] could be taken with the spear in endless quantities."

And yet for all the plenty, Fisher noted that the Indians did not waste fish, or take more than they needed. "Many large salmon shot through the water as we sped by," he recalled of a canoe ride with a Queets fisherman, "but he only viewed them with pride, as a farmer would his cattle. He had killed sufficient for his needs, and the others were left to fatten for another day." As the number of wild Queets salmon declined during this century, the Queets fishermen repeatedly chose to restrict their own fishing rather than plant hatchery salmon in the Queets. They considered hatchery fish inferior to the wild fish that had always sustained their people, and wanted to stick with what they had. "You can tell the difference between wild fish and hatchery fish the minute you cut them open," said one elderly Queets fisherman. "The wild ones are redder fleshed, and firmer. They fight harder too—as if they've got some urge to live that a hatchery fish doesn't have."

The problem facing the Queets during the winter of 1978 was that too few wild Queets salmon were returning to provide one family a livelihood, let alone a couple of dozen. If they were going to continue to live in the pattern of their ancestors, the Queets Indians realized there simply had to be more fish. They and their biologist Lestelle believed this could best be accomplished by changing logging practices and sharply curtailing the troll harvest on runs like the wild fish of the Queets, but the Queets Indians were not sanguine about this occurring. Despite a long string of legal victories, including U.S. District Court Judge George Boldt's famous Indian fishing rights decision of 1974, the Indians were still losing ground. Four years after Judge Boldt recognized the Queets Indians' right to half the Queets salmon caught, the trollers' share of Queets-spawned fish was still climbing, and the Queets Indians' share had dropped to just about nil. Reluctantly, the Indians decided to begin exploring the only other avenue open to them: planting hatchery fish.

They knew that the second federal hatchery built recently on the Quinault River had not been a smashing success, but they also knew that their cousins on the Quinault were able to fish more then they could. "Because biologists often assume, correctly or incorrectly, that hatchery fish have a higher rate of survival," Lestelle explained, "they assume that they can be fished at a higher rate. This means that between two runs of comparable size, hatchery salmon let you fish more than the wild ones." Lestelle advised against hatchery plants because of the damage they often do to the wild salmon, but the Queets Indians decided to make the first sizable releases of hatchery Chinook during the summer of 1979. "We're fishermen," said Jim Harp, who has hereditary rights to one of the best fishing grounds on the Queets, and whose father caught the largest salmon in modern memory on the Queets, an eighty-five-pound fall Chinook. "We can't survive without fishing," he continued. "If that means planting hatchery salmon, well then so be it."

I went fishing with Jim Harp one morning a couple of weeks after Lestelle's, Blackburn's and my jaunt on the upper river. It was a little before sunrise when we untied the boat in the cold shadow of the tribal fishhouse and shoved off quietly without oars. Harp, a large man with long salt-and-pepper hair and moustache, let the sixteen-foot aluminum skiff drift for a minute while he adjusted the position of his rifle, and then started up the outboard. The bow of the boat bounced like a dog's tail on a rug as we accelerated past pasture and stands of alder. Just before the next bend, Harp cut the engine and jumped over the side to help the boat over a shallow riffle where chum salmon spawn. Below, we wove our way through driftwood and brilliant patches of low fog toward the growing roar of the Pacific Ocean.

Jim Harp's station is located about a quarter mile from the narrow surging entrance of the Queets into the sea. Pulling his net, we found he had caught one fish overnight, a twenty-three-pound Chinook female that was already quite ripe, and still alive when we hauled her over the side. Harp deftly slipped the fish free of the gill net's nylon strands, and tossed her into the bottom of the boat. While he shook the silt out of his net (a beneficial effect of logging for salmon is that it allows the fish to see the nets better), I watched the salmon die. Clear early-morning sunshine and my shadow swung back and forth across her as she gasped, showing the tridentlike protrusions on the tip of her tongue, flexed her fins and finally expired, her mouth and gaze fixed. Finishing with the net, Harp paddled us over to the shore, where we lay down with our backs against a piece of driftwood and shared an orange and some coffee.

Within a few minutes, we were joined by others. First Chet Pulcifer came motoring out of the mists, a shadow among blinding bursts of sun, more sound than physical presence. Pulcifer, who has hereditary rights to the fishing ground opposite Harp, cut his engine and drifted in beside his driftwood-fouled net. Next came the Tribal Fisheries Patrol, checking for illegal net sets and whooping with pleasure in the morning. Finally there was Frank "Sheeny" Charles, the Mongol-eyed fish buyer whose ground is immediately behind Harp's on the same side of the river. Sheeny surveyed his net, and then strolled over and joined us against the log. At fifty-seven, he is one of the few members of the Queets band who still know how to make the big dugout canoes that were used by the Indians until the scarcity of cedar and the decreasing size of the salmon catch tipped the scales in favor of the small aluminum skiffs that are now standard.

Between spits of tobacco juice, Sheeny asked if either of us had seen the National League playoff game the night before between the Cincinnati Reds and the Pittsburgh Pirates. We discussed Cincinnati ace Tom Seaver's masterful performance in the early going, and Willie Stargell's three-run homer that eventually won it for the Pirates in the eleventh inning. Several wild coho hit Harp's net and set the floats on the top bouncing with their struggles. Sometimes the fish got loose, and other times they came right up to the net and turned away without touching it. Sheeny said the low flow of the river had been giving Indian fishermen working the upriver stations better catches than people like Harp and himself. Around 1 P.M. we headed back to the village of Queets. Harp's total for the day was the twenty-three-pound Chinook, and six beautifully bright coho weighing a total of sixty-five pounds.

On the way upriver, Harp pointed out two eagle trees that have been left isolated in the clearcut that extends from the mouth of the Queets to U.S. 101 on the north side of the river. The Quinault Tribe tried to force Mayr Brothers Logging to leave a buffer strip around the nesting trees in 1978, but had to back down when the Bureau of Indian Affairs threatened to sue the tribe if it interfered with logging on the reservation. Although exposed to the highway and within range of potential hunters, one of the 180-foot trees remains in use as an eagle nest site. Partially as a result of the eagle tree incident, the Quinault Tribe was finally able to force the BIA to adopt minimal logging standards for the reservation in 1979, but the tribe actually controls only a small fraction of reservation land today.

We raised Harp's fish up to the perpetually dripping fishhouse on a slow, screaming hydraulic winch that gave us time to examine two salmon whose bodies ended abruptly behind the dorsal fin in a tangle of white bone and red flesh. "Seals," said Harp, adding that both seals and sea lions will rob nets almost as far upriver as the village. Sheeny was on the phone, so Harp weighed his fish and registered the figure in a ledger while I shoveled ice from an old army surplus freezer that leaked all over the floor. As I was laying the last scoop around the fishes' heads, a pickup with the name of a Grays Harbor fire extinguisher company on the side drove up. Two whites in their late twenties got out, walked up the stairs, and then stopped short on the loading dock where a black rivulet of ice water ran across the concrete. "You folks need a fire extinguisher?" one of them asked, peering into the darkened interior of the fishhouse.

Behind them was arrayed the village of Queets. Small houses and large mobile homes lined the two-block-long street leading to the handsome modern community center at the other end of town. There was a bedraggled grocery store, several new cars and vans, an older car with no wheels resting on its brake drums, and a goat in a nearby yard eating the stuffing out of a mattress that had been propped against a tree to give it some shelter from the elements. Fish crows strutted through the broken glass in a half-dozen vacant lots, coolly disdaining the attentions of a white poodle with a green ribbon in its hair.

Somewhere in the distance children were screaming in delight at a game of tag.

I walked out onto the back deck of the fishhouse, which was about forty feet above the river. Leaning on the railing in the bright afternoon sunshine, I noticed nineteen dead salmon rotting on the muddy river bottom. It appeared that they had been thrown from where I now stood. When Harp joined me a moment later, I asked him about the fish. His mouth flickered under his moustache. He thought the salmon had been caught during the subsistence fishing period when no fish can be sold. Rather than give them away, he speculated, someone had thrown them out the back door. It was senseless and cruel, but the thing that got Harp was that some of the old people were not given fish. He looked at the bloated white bellies of the salmon, seeming to count them as I had done before, and then turned back into the cool cave within.

Peace and Power and Civilization

FOUR

IN THE OLD DAYS, the Chinook salmon of the Elwha River were known as *tyee*. The term meant "chief" in Chinook jargon, the crude pan-Indian trade language of the Northwest coast, and was applied to human and salmon society alike. Among people, it meant the political leader of a tribe; among salmon, it meant the largest fish, generally Chinook weighing thirty pounds or more.

The wild Chinook of the Elwha River, which flows off the north side of Mount Olympus into the Strait of Juan de Fuca, were easily the largest on the Olympic Peninsula. Spanish explorer Manuel Quimper purchased a number of "salmon of 100 pounds" from Indians nearby on July 25, 1790. Early American settlers remarked the exceptional size of the fish, as did the Department of Fisheries, which found "several males that would weigh 100 pounds each" on the river in November 1930.

Tyee apparently were encouraged by the basic nature of the Elwha River. Although no larger than the Queets, the Elwha contained many miles of ideal Chinook spawning grounds, especially between Lost River and Long Creek. To reach these shady riffles, salmon had to climb through a series of narrowing canyons, climaxing at the Goblin's Gate. "The strength of the rapids in this section of the river probably acted as a mechanism for the natural selection of larger fish," speculated the late Robert Mausolf of Peninsula College.

Long life was probably the way Elwha Chinook achieved the physique needed to fight their way into the upper river. Normally, sibling Chinook from the same redd reach spawning maturity over a period of several years. Salmon need a broad range in maturation to spread the effect of one good (or bad) year over many, but in the case of the Elwha Chinook the distribution was probably skewed on the long side. Because the smallest fish might not be able to make the climb to Lost River, the Chinook of the Elwha maintained the necessary age spread among spawners by living longer. Based on the record, it is likely that some Elwha *tyee* lived twelve or more years, compared to the four or five years common today.

All successful salmon runs develop this type of highly specific adaptation to the rivers they frequent. They know through the genetic legacy of their parents where to hide, what their prey looks like, when to run to the sea and when to return. Since every river is unique in its flow pattern and terrain, every run of wild salmon is necessarily different genetically from all others. The distinction may be obvious, as in the comparison of Elwha *tyee* to Chinook from nearby rivers, but even when the fish look exactly the same, important differences remain. "It's like a million different keys for a million different locks," said one biologist.

None of these genetic "keys" can be replicated, either through the lengthy natural process of selection, or the quicker, cruder man-made means. "New genetic combinations are created all the time, of course," observed another biologist, "but in terms of recreating a special run of one sort or another, it can't be done." Certain runs with certain characteristics may be most numerous at one point in time, but all are important for the long-range survival of the species. This is because each genetically distinct race may provide a set of characteristics needed in the face of future volcanic eruption, glacial advance, geomagnetic reversal, and so forth. "Genetic diversity is one of the main ways that salmon maintain adaptive flexibility," said Lestelle.

When the *tyee* ruled the Elwha, more than 8,000 Chinook spawned in the river annually, according to Washington Department of Fisheries estimates. Of these, 4,500 were the choicer spring run. The Elwha also supported sizable runs of every species of Pacific salmon found in North American waters. Sockeye ran up Indian Creek to Lake Sutherland, coho penetrated to the headwater tributaries, and chum filled the slow side channels along the main river. Most numerous of all were the diminutive pink salmon, which ran 275,000 strong every other year, according to Fisheries estimates. In 1909, the run of pink salmon in the Little River, a tributary of the lower Elwha, was so great that Harold Sisson's mother had to back her terrified horse across the ford.

Today there are no pink salmon in the Little River, and few *tyee* in the Elwha. To find the wild salmon that once graced this 320-square-mile river system, one must go to the state archives in Olympia. There, in a reading room adorned with pictures of the nation's vice-presidents up through Spiro Agnew, one can examine the records storage folder that contains the runs' remains. Filed under "Elwha Dam," the packet is comprised of a series of documents, beginning with a letter from James Pike, game warden of Clallam County, to Washington Commissioner of Fisheries J. L. Riseland. In an almost breathless tone that can still be detected seven decades later, Pike sounded the alarm.

"I have personally searched the Elwha River & Tributaries above the Dam, and have been unable to find a single Salmon," he wrote in a scratchy, fountain pen script in the fall of 1911. "I have visited the Dam several times lately . . . and there appear to be Thousands of Salmon at the foot of the Dam, where they are continually trying to get up the flume. I have watched them very close, and I am satisfied now that they cannot get above the Dam." Pike added that "the big run of Silver [coho] Salmon just commencing to come into the River" would be lost if the fish could not reach their spawning grounds.

The dam in question was a hydroelectric project then under construction in a narrow gorge about five miles upriver from the mouth of the Elwha. It was planned as an eighty-foot-high concrete retainer with a radical design that called for the dam to be hung from the canyon walls without a footing on bedrock below the river. Financed by a Chicago investment banking firm and overseen by a board of directors that included several prominent Seattle businessmen, the Olympic Power and Development Company's Elwha project was the greatest monument to venture capitalism yet seen on the peninsula. It was also in clear violation of the law.

Washington's first legislature had passed a law in 1890 requiring the construction of fish passage devices, such as fish ladders, on dams "wherever food fish are wont to ascend." This law, which was part of the state's wider fisheries authority concerning the length of the commercial fishing seasons, empowered the commissioner of fisheries to levy fines for violations and obtain court orders for the removal or modification of illegal dams. Federal fisheries law, which was passed piecemeal during the last two decades of the nineteenth century, also required consideration for the passage of salmon, but left enforcement at the discretion of the U.S. Army Corps of Engineers.

The impetus for these early laws was the desire to avoid the unhappy experience with the Atlantic salmon of the eastern United States. As Anthony Netboy noted in *The Atlantic Salmon: A Vanishing Species?* "The decline of the [Atlantic] salmon had begun in some localities in the 18th century, not only because of the damming of smaller streams, but because of the excessive pursuit of the fish with nets and spears and other implements. It was not, however, until the first half of the 19th century, when industrialists seized upon the water power of larger streams and some of their affluents, and blockaded nursery grounds, that the rivers began to lose their fisheries."

The New England states themselves had passed laws to protect the salmon as the nineteenth century unfolded, but without the desired effect. According to Netboy, there were 433 laws on the Maine books pertaining to fisheries and their preservation at the time that salmon virtually disappeared from the state's rivers. During the 1870s, R. D. Hume, who later made a fortune in salmon canning on the Rogue River of Oregon, witnessed a wild scene following the capture of one salmon in the Kennebec River near his native Augusta, Maine. Decades later, Hume remembered seeing:

> two of the wealthiest citizens argue for half an hour as to how a salmon of ten pounds should be divided so that each should get a fair proportion of the fat, and which should have the head part; and finally, after appealing to a large crowd of bystanders for their opinions regarding the question, at length settled the matter by cutting the fish on an angle, from belly to back, so as to give the one with the tail portion a fair share of the belly; and then paid $1 per pound for their portion, and went home with smiles on their faces and eyes glistening in anticipation of the glorious feast they were to have on the morrow.

Despite the warnings of men like Hume, the familiar pattern was evident in Washington from the outset. In 1899, the U.S. fish commissioner's report to Congress noted that "in Washington, while the throwing of sawdust into streams is prohibited, it is reported that the regulations have not been well enforced." The same report was appalled that laws regulating the commercial salmon fishing seasons were not enforced outside southern Puget Sound in the vicinity of the state capital. One early state fish commissioner even issued a public *mea culpa* for the nonenforcement of laws to protect the salmon. In 1911, a disgusted British Columbia commissioner of fisheries described Washington fishery law as simply a "dead letter."

The problem, of course, was that protecting the wild salmon inevitably meant limiting some private individuals' opportunity to enrich themselves. This the authorities were loath to do, especially when powerful financial interests were involved. Washington Fish Commissioner Riseland managed to ignore the Elwha Dam throughout an extensive publicity campaign, as well as the first year of actual construction. Not even the warning from the Clallam County game warden could provoke him to action. When Elwha Dam was completed in October 1912, it still lacked fish passage facilities. Then two things happened in quick succession: the radical foundation of the dam blew out to a depth of eighty feet, and Ernest Lister was elected governor of Washington.

A last-minute nominee of the Democratic party who was not expected to win, Lister went to Olympia with few political debts, and some ambitious plans. Although he was born to a wealthy Tacoma family and maintained close social and business ties with the commercial leaders of the area, Lister drew much of his political philosophy from John Rodgers, the state's early radical writer and Populist governor. Lister was an idealist who saw growth and development as the way to a better world and was determined to hasten its coming with a clean government that consciously served the common good. "You gentlemen," he told the legislature in his inaugural address, "are sent here by your constituents to get your share of the pie. I am sent here by all of the people to see that not too much of it is distributed."

Then as now, "the pie" was made up largely of public resources such as fish, timber, water and minerals entrusted to state management. Lister had little personal knowledge of the state's salmon resource, but he received some astute counsel on aspects of the situation from W. H. Kaufman, Whatcom

County assessor and Grange leader. In a letter to Lister of December 28, 1912, Kaufman gave the governor-elect a vivid picture of the operations of the salmon canning industry, which was then centered around Bellingham in Whatcom County:

> I came to this country in 1899, and the cannerymen had dominated county politics for some time prior, especially the assessor's [office] and board of equalization; so that up to the time I took office as assessor they had paid only HALF as much taxes as other people—having been able to keep outside of school and road districts, they paid neither school nor road taxes! Up to 1906 they paid NO TAXES WHATSOEVER, although the fishing privileges of this county alone are worth over $6,000,000. . . .
>
> By 1899 the Fish Trust—by log rolling, and wining and dining legislators—had obtained enough influence in the legislature to secure the adoption of the infamous "secrecy" joker, by which it is provided that the statistics of the Fish Commissioner's office shall be "confidential," "shall not be open for inspection of the public," nor "communicated to any person"—that includes county assessors, legislative investigating committees, the governor himself, ANYONE WHO MIGHT LET THE PUBLIC KNOW THE VAST PROFITS OF THE FISHING INTERESTS. . . . No more scandalous piece of graft legislation disgraces the records of any state. . . .

Kaufman had written a number of articles for the Bellingham *American-Reveille* to set forth "the facts in the case," but before long the cannery owners and their allies bought the paper and closed it to all coverage of their operations. Now Kaufman was asking governor-elect Lister to appoint a fish commissioner who was "fire tested." "We will get justice even with a fish commissioner as ineffectual as Riseland; but we will succeed more quickly and easily with a good man." Lister was impressed. Three months later, he named as fish commissioner Leslie Darwin, the former editor of the *American-Reveille* who had run Kaufman's muckraking cannery articles.

An imposing man with erect carriage, dark bushy eyebrows and a head of prematurely white hair, Darwin had strong opinions concerning the state's salmon. He had come to Bellingham at the mouth of the broad Nooksack Valley as a young man, prospected unsuccessfully in the 1898 Mount Baker gold rush, served as secretary to the state teachers' college, and then joined the Seattle *Times* to manage the editorial and business functions of the *American-Reveille*, which it had just purchased. During his seven years at the helm of the city's morning paper, Darwin watched Bellingham become the greatest salmon processing center in the world, shipping more than five million one-pound cans of salmon to Europe and Asia annually during the first decade of this century.

Like Kaufman, Darwin was appalled by both the canneries' tremendous wastage of fish (so many unused salmon were dumped overboard that human health risks were commonly incurred wherever canneries operated, according to state and federal reports from the period) and their gross profiteering at public expense. "It seems to me," he said later, reflecting on the central dilemma of the salmon's already evident decline in Washington, "to be a crime against mankind—against those who are here and the generations yet to follow—to let the great salmon runs of the State of Washington be destroyed at the selfish behest of a few individuals who, in order to enrich themselves, would impoverish the state and destroy a food supply of the people."

With Lister's approval, Darwin moved swiftly to reform the administration of his office and attack the canneries' use of dummy corporations to avoid paying the state tax on canned salmon, their frequent deployment of oversized traps and pound nets, and most especially, the "secrecy joker" that kept all cannery information hidden from public scrutiny. At the same time, he made some effort to enforce the wider environmental sanctions necessary for the salmon's survival, including the law requiring the construction of fish ladders at all dams. Writing to the bankrupt owner of a small mill dam on a tributary of the Elwha, Darwin put the matter bluntly: "Unless the dam is immediately equipped with a fishway in accordance with [the law], we shall have to proceed under statute to blow it out."

Regarding the much larger and more damaging Olympic Power dam on the mainstem Elwha, however, Darwin found the situation "perplexing." Although the dam, which was being rebuilt, still lacked fishways, Darwin never seems to have considered applying the law with the same rigor as in the case of the mill dam on the nearby Elwha tributary. The influential Olympic Power backers (among them, the salmon-trolling banker Joshua Green) and the governor's own infatuation with hydroelectric power (Lister was one of the first to propose a dam at Bonneville on the Columbia) encouraged Darwin to attempt a more exotic solution.

The Elwha Dam file in the Washington State Archives contains an August 1913 letter from Darwin to Olympic Power in which he proposed for the first time that the owners of the dam build a hatchery in lieu of a fishway. While acknowledging that "no officer of the state has any right to waive one of the state's statutory requirements," Darwin went on to say that the law could be circumvented if the hatchery physically adjoined the dam, which could then be considered a state obstruction for the taking of eggs to supply the hatchery. The science of artificial salmon propagation was entirely unproven at this time, but caught up in the sweep of the idea, Darwin declared enthusiastically: "my plan forever eliminates bother in the future."

Olympic Power was cool to the suggestion. "It would appear that you [Darwin] were making a very heavy demand on us," replied Thomas Aldwell, president of Olympic Power. Aldwell, who was a native of Toronto, Canada, had been promoting the dam since 1894, when he acquired the contested title to a 160-acre "homestead" on federal land in the Elwha gorge. His early life had been similar to Darwin's in many respects (he, too, came to the Northwest in the 1890s, served as manager of a provincial daily newspaper, and worked for the government), but when it came to personalities and politics, the two men were as different as the interests they served.

Aldwell saw "peace and power and civilization" in the development of environmentally exploitative industry and pushed the theme without respite for more than fifty years. He was deep into several unhappy railroad speculation schemes, the U.S. Army's unfortunate logging of the spruce above Lake Quinault, the development of the four pulp and paper mills that provide most of the employment in Port Angeles, his own commercial and residential developments and, of course, the dam. He himself saw his long and vigorous life as "an example of what any young man in this country can accomplish if he sets out to do so." Charles Clise, president of the Seattle Chamber of Commerce, called him "the type of pioneer whose vision and courage are still the bulwark of this state's growth and development."

Blessed with an ample portion of bravura, Aldwell cheerfully recounted in his autobiography, *Conquering the Last Frontier,* how as president of the Port Angeles Chamber of Commerce he helped dispense more than $120,000 in bribes and kickbacks to persuade industries to locate in Port Angeles. When money would not do the trick, Aldwell used other imaginative methods. In 1914, for instance, he went to Washington, D.C., to divert a parcel of land that was supposed to be the site of the city's hospital into the hands of his associates for private development. After Aldwell presented his case to the House Public Lands Committee, the conservative Speaker of the House Joseph Cannon commented nostalgically that "this reminds me of the days when Illinois was on the frontier." Progressive Republican George Norris opposed Aldwell's scheme on the grounds that the "lots should be sold at public auction," if at all, and the others seemed to agree. Seeing the case going against him, Aldwell played his hole card:

> I noticed that Congressman Norris was wearing an Elks' pin on his coat. I then told them that Port Angeles was the only Elks Lodge in the United States that had a name other than that of the town in which it was located. . . . I showed Norris my Elks' card, and it wasn't long before Norris began favoring the bill, as did

another member of the committee that had been opposing it. Going out to the floor, the other man who had helped approve the bill introduced himself to me as a Past Grand Exalted Ruler of the Elks.

Through similar appeals (Lister was an enthusiastic member of the Elks and Masons), Aldwell was able to stall the state for nearly a year, but on June 4, 1914, the fish commissioner delivered an ultimatum. "I am sorry that you have made no response to my last query to you relative to the hatchery at the foot of the Elwha Dam," he wrote. "Unless I hear from you in some positive manner in five days, I shall issue an order for you to erect a fishway. . . . It is out of the question for us to allow another run to beat its brains out against that dam." Presented with the matter in this fashion, Aldwell did an immediate about-face, signing an agreement with the state on August 14 which committed Olympic Power to donate land for a hatchery, and contribute $2,500 toward its construction.

The deal between Darwin and Aldwell was itself illegal, of course. State law still required the construction of fish passage facilities at every dam that blocked the migration of salmon. Olympic Power's Elwha Dam had been in violation of the law for five years, and should by rights have been removed at the company's expense. Darwin himself could have been charged with malfeasance in the case, based on the evidence in the State Archives. Instead, Lister convinced the legislature to change the law so that hatcheries *could* be built in lieu of fish passage facilities. With this legal nicety out of the way, the flood began. During the first few years of his administration, Darwin accepted seven hatcheries in supposed compensation for the substantial runs of wild salmon lost to dam construction on rivers such as the White Salmon, Chehalis and Elwha.

The Elwha hatchery went into operation in 1915. Initially, the state was able to collect as many as two million eggs annually from fish that were born before the dam was built, but within a few years the pool below the dam was nearly empty of fish. None of the wild salmon that used to spawn above the dam remained, and the hatchery had been unable to replace them. In 1922, the year after Darwin retired, the Department of Fisheries abandoned the Elwha hatchery and left the few remaining wild salmon to their own devices. A subsequent title search revealed that ownership of the hatchery site had never actually been transferred to the state as promised, and Crown Zellerbach Corporation (which bought the dam in 1919) has retained title to this day. Nearly all the hatcheries built by Darwin in connection with dams met similar fates.

On the Elwha, the immediate effect of the dam was to reduce the number of salmon by approximately 75 percent. All spring Chinook and sockeye were lost, along with most coho, pink and chum salmon. Only the fall Chinook, which had always spawned in the lower river, were relatively unaffected. In 1971 the Department of Fisheries calculated that the loss of the Elwha salmon runs had cost the people of Washington $500,000 annually. By this token, the total expense of the dam has been more than $35 million to date. Crown Zellerbach, for its part, reported a profit from the very first year of operation in Port Angeles, where it used the power from the dam to run the first of that city's large lumber mills.

The loss of these runs was only the beginning of the damage done by the dam, however. As time wore on it came to affect the entire river and even the coast that stretches east along the strait toward Puget Sound. Like logging, a dam changes the basic nature of a river by affecting the critical element of sediment load. In its natural state a river is a sort of corkscrew twisting on itself as it flows downstream. Entering a bend, the fast-moving water near the top pushes against the outside bank and erodes it, while the slower, sediment-heavy water near the bottom moves to the inside bank and deposits some of its load, be it sand, gravel or boulders. This process produces the beautifully mathematical meanderings that can be found in most of the world's rivers, and serves the fundamental purpose of dissipating energy in the river's unending quest for equilibrium.

Glacial torrents like the Elwha are, therefore, as much a

reflection of the sediment and debris they carry as of the water which does the actual work. "When a dam is built across a river and sediment settles in the still water of the reservoir," Luna B. Leopold of the U.S. Geological Service has written, "clear water will be released to the channel downstream. But the channel was accustomed to water carrying sediment. The clear water causes the channel to change its shape and slope. These changes in channels downstream from dams cannot be accurately predicted because of our lack of knowledge, but the changes are causing considerable difficulty to engineering works."

For the surviving salmon of the lower Elwha, the dam's worst consequence has been the disappearance of the gravel they need for spawning. As the bright green waters of the river have cut deeper and deeper in an effort to consume their excess energy, the riverbed on many of the best riffles has been transformed into a boilerplate of boulders and bedrock. Forced together by their constricting spawning grounds, the Chinook now dig one redd on top of another in a group frenzy that more closely resembles the habits of pink salmon and further wastes their efforts to continue their race.

An even larger problem that has only recently become apparent is the erosion of Ediz Hook. This three-mile-long spit, which forms the natural harbor of Port Angeles, is losing more than 13,000 cubic yards of material to the strait annually, and has been designated a "major problem area" in the Corps of Engineers National Shoreline Study. The reasons for the accelerating breakup of Ediz Hook, according to the Corps, are the Crown Zellerbach dam on the Elwha and the industrial water line supplying ITT-Rayonier's mill in Port Angeles, which have interrupted the natural supply of gravel to the spit.

Between 1967 and 1972 the federal government, City of Port Angeles and Crown Zellerbach spent $1 million to prevent the spit from breaching. Then in 1973, the Corps of Engineers began a fifty-year project to maintain the spit with rock and gravel quarried on the Elwha and trucked to the spit. The project, which is expected to cost taxpayers $4 million, has further reduced the survival chances of Elwha salmon by altering the composition of the spit and the species that live on it, for as the Corps's environmental impact statement noted: the "increases in the population of rockfish could increase predation on migratory juvenile salmon."

Ultimately, the dam on the Elwha had consequence for wild salmon all over Washington through the policies it fostered in the Department of Fisheries. Despite its biological failure, Leslie Darwin's deal on the Elwha became the model toward which his lesser successors strove. The immediate attraction of the hatchery lieu law from the standpoint of Fisheries was that it increased the department's funding. The drawback, however, was that the state gave up most of its power to stop a dam for the sake of the wild salmon, as well as the interest in doing so, since the bulk of Fisheries' energy was increasingly directed toward building the hatchery system that is today the largest on the Pacific Coast.

FIVE

I WAS WATCHING HUNDREDS OF PINK SALMON scatter the last, lurid light of evening across the Graywolf river when I heard the sound again. It was a faint, quavering cry, and as it rose and fell above the roar of the river, it was impossible to tell if it came from one throat or one thousand. Harsh and somehow urgent, it seemed to be echoing from the heart of the mountains.

The Graywolf, which drains the high valley between Blue Mountain and the Graywolf pinnacles east of Port Angeles, is noted for its peculiar auditory mirages. Solitary travelers seem particularly susceptible to the "river voices," but groups of people and even animals have heard them as well: I once saw a deer browsing on the bench above Divide Creek prick its ears and listen intently to these same faraway sounds.

Fifty years ago this steep valley rang with the howling of the wolves that gave the river its name. The now extinct Olympic

Peninsula timber wolves favored the Graywolf above all others and made their last stand against the government-paid killers in its upper reaches. Straining to hear faint sounds in the deepening dusk, I could imagine the greenish-orange embers in their eyes a little too well, and I hunkered down into my big, smoky-smelling mackinaw.

The sun had left the valley floor at 3 P.M., and now, six hours later, my wait was nearly over. In front of my camp lay what is probably the single richest spawning grounds on the Olympic Peninsula for pink salmon, *Oncorhynchus gorbuscha.* As soon as it was dark, I planned to wade the river and observe the fishes' nocturnal cavortings. I was carrying a flashlight, but stealth demanded that I travel in complete darkness until I had reached my destination at the center of the glide.

It was late August, and the Graywolf summer pink run was swelling to the first of its three climactic waves. I had been following these pinks (which come into the river earlier than any other pink run on the peninsula) since before dawn, when I spotted a six-pound male lying between two boulders the color of rotten ice. He had a high, knife-edged hump flying like a burgundy banner above the water, hooked snout and a rainbow across his tail that caught fire as the sun cleared the opposite ridge, charging the river with color and revealing thousands of diaphanous dew-covered cobwebs on the branches of the trees.

Farther on, I found several dozen pairs of pinks fighting their way up a riffle into a narrow crack of cloudless sky. Here the flat-sided males were less adept than their sleek, black-lipped consorts. Several times I saw males washed down with the current when females passed easily into the small patch of smooth water above. With a fall of 3,000 feet in seventeen miles, the Graywolf is one of the swiftest rivers in the West, dancing white and foaming between the mountains and always moving down. Because it is not as glacial as the Dungeness (which it joins in the foothills of the Olympics), the Graywolf is so clear in late summer that one can actually see the air ripped into it wherever it surges over rock or log.

Pinks will pick out isolated spawning pockets when necessary, but their tribal nature encourages them to congregate on the river's few large spawning grounds. When I arrived at my present camp, I found the river alive with wild humpy males chasing each other in wide gyres across the smooth, 150-yard-long glide where the river flowed at a depth of two feet over a beautifully graveled bed. Redds extended in bunches from the edge of the lower fall-away up to the pool at the base of the riffle above. One popular female with a white belly and broad black stripe down her side sent her half-dozen suitors into a tizzy every time she rolled on her side to excavate the redd. As each puff of silt drifted away on the current, one or more males raced downstream several hundred feet, spun around like tail-skidding dirt-track speedsters, and dashed back.

Another ripe dame with pink crescents on her gills and an iridescent green head was run over by one of her own suitors in the confused jostling around the redd. She and the other females seemed willing to indulge the most extreme behavior by the males, but let one of their own sex become involved in the act, and the situation changed dramatically. When one female dug too close to the redd of another, which seemed to be happening everywhere simultaneously, the proprietress would rocket after the offender. Their chases were much faster and more gracefully executed than those of the males, and when they caught each other they tore savagely at each other's fins and other exposed parts. Like the males, however, they were seldom able to discourage their challengers, with the result that the same fish would repeat the game of Advance, Chase and Retreat for days until one of them no longer had enough life left to continue.

On the heart of the glide a mass of salmon was wheeling in an endless circuit, drifting sideways to expose their broad sides when hostile, and gliding past each other like fingers into a glove when not. Viewed from the shore, the pinks appeared as a shifting lavender stain on the sunny riverbottom. There were probably 100 redds on the glide, and several times that many fish. Upriver, another group of fish had holed up in the pool, where they were leaping at lazy intervals. Most of these fish (which I took to be part of the second wave) were not yet ripe, but among them were also some consumed and seemingly spastic fish bumping along the shoreline, and two white carcasses that glowed in the depths like lights in a swimming pool at night.

Owing to the still sizable Alaskan and Siberian runs, pinks are the most numerous salmon on the face of the globe. In 1926, I. F. Pravdin observed a massed run of Asiatic pinks in Kamchatka that was nearly a mile long, and made a roar "somewhat similar to the noise of boiling water in a gigantic cauldron." Besides their small size, prominent hump and white belly, several behavioral characteristics set pinks apart from other salmon. They always return to their natal streams as two-year-olds, and in Washington, which is near the southern extreme of their range, they are the only salmon that run exclusively in odd numbered years. And apart from chum salmon, they are the only salmon that immediately seek salt water after hatching.

Although not generally numerous elsewhere on the Olympic Peninsula, pinks have long thrived in the northern rivers that flow into the strait. Here the rivers are agreeably short, the steep valleys somewhat fortified against predators, and the rivers less likely to flood and scour the eggs out of the redds. In striking constrast to the Queets and the other rain forest valleys on the west side of the peninsula, the area around the Dungeness receives less than seventeen inches of rain a year. This climatological quirk is caused by the central mountains of the Olympic Range, which interrupt the flow of moisture off the Pacific and cast a rain shadow across the region. The Dungeness is one of the few places where cactus and ponderosa pine grow naturally alongside salal and Douglas fir.

Glancing down at my watch at 9:30, I saw a star reflected in the pool below, and decided it was time to go. I played the flashlight across the curving tail of the glide where I would be walking to avoid disturbing the fish too much, and then switched it off. The darkness welled up like blood from a bad wound. I could make out the black line of trees along the far bank and the mountains silhouetted against the starry sky, but nothing else. Concentrating on my feet, I found the gravelly riverbed strewn with large round rocks. Planting my staff, taking a step, planting my staff, taking a step with the other foot, I slowly waded thirty-five yards out into the rushing, shin-deep water, imagining each caress of the current to be a salmon.

Finally, when I judged that I had reached a point near one of the most active redds, I switched the light back on. There were many more salmon on the glide now, and almost all were in motion. Some dashed away from the yellow beam, others seemed dazed by it. A tremendous fight between two females erupted to my right where the wake from their repeated thrashings rocked along the shore for the entire length of the glide. A small female who had not yet spawned slipped by me so closely that I could see that her dorsal fin was capped with a series of jewel-like shields at the terminus of each ray that glowed pink on the upper edge, and gold on the lower. Beyond, six large Chinook moved upstream in single file through the melee like sharks among pilot fish. Several of these Chinook had large patches of white fungus on their heads from trying to get through the hatchery weir downriver.

Pink salmon are given to group sex, which can involve as many as six males spawning at the same time with a single female. Typically, spawning occurs when the female swims slowly over the nest, and then lowers her anal fin into the redd, stimulating the nearby male or males. As her consort joins her on the redd, both fish gape and quiver violently while the eggs and sperm are shed simultaneously into the waiting bowl of gravel. I did not get a chance to observe the penultimate moment in the life of pinks that night, but I did see what might be described as a moment of compassion. Off to my left a hideous old male whose face had been broken away just in front of his eyes was holding near a still-prime female on her redd. The female, who had several active suitors, not only tolerated, but almost seemed solicitous toward her spent and dying companion, and it occurred to me that he was probably a former mate.

On the way back, I stopped again near a large boulder and turned on the light for the last time. Salmon all around me flew off in unison like arrows from a squad of archers, but two males remained. One of them hung right in front of me, rolling his back toward me whenever I shone the light directly at him. Just as I was admiring how cleverly he was diminishing the intensity of the light, the other fish, who had a prominent white stripe down the crest of his hump, swooped down on me from behind. Feeling a sharp tug at my leg, I found this bold cavalier had locked himself onto my right boot, and was trying to shake me. As I raised my staff to dislodge him, the other fish attacked my left leg. It was then that I noticed that I was standing in the middle of their redd, and I stumbled away toward camp, which trembled before me in the fading beam.

Forty-two thousand summer pinks returned to the Dungeness and Graywolf rivers in 1979. This was considerably less than the run's historic high of 400,000 fish, but still better than the 8,000 fall pinks that returned to the lower river one month later. The reason for the difference in size between the two pink runs in the Dungeness system is largely due to the availability of water. The early run, which is genetically distinct from the later run, enters the river in July when snow melt has swelled the flood, and made passage to the headwaters relatively safe. The fall run, by comparison, enters the river in September and October when it is fed almost exclusively by irrigation seepage, and spawns immediately at the mouth. In the old days, the Dungeness could accommodate both in profusion.

Captain George Vancouver, who commanded the second European exploring expedition along the north coast of the peninsula in 1792, was so impressed with the beauty of the Dungeness that he named it for a sentimental favorite that flows into the English Channel near Dover. "The country before us exhibited everything that bounteous nature could be expected to draw into a single point of view," he wrote. "The land . . . was well covered with a variety of stately forest trees. These, however, did not conceal the whole of the country in one uninterrupted wilderness, but pleasingly clothed its eminences, and chequered the valleys . . . which produced a beautiful variety of extensive lawn, covered with luxuriant grass, and diversified with an abundance of flowers." Vancouver's lawn was actually a series of prairies that the Klallam Indians kept cleared with fire, and which baked into a desolate waste every summer while the damp forest luxuriated all around.

White settlement began on the Dungeness a half century later at Whiskey Flats, which took its name from the proprietors' policy of selling liquor to the Indians. About this time the Klallam Indians were forced to abandon their three villages at the mouth of the Dungeness and move down onto the beach. It was here that the Klallams suffered the last epidemic of the white diseases that had turned their land into "a slaughterhouse of human beings" as early as 1791. After plagues of "intermittent fever" and venereal disease, the Klallam were finally struck with smallpox when a sailing ship bound from San Francisco to Seattle lost most of its crew to the disease en route. As the ship drifted down the Strait of Juan de Fuca, the survivors threw the clothes, bedding and bodies of the dead overboard. These items washed ashore and were picked up by the Indians, who died like flies in the winter of 1855.

The Treaty of Point No Point, signed that year, gave the United States title to the land of the Klallam. In exchange, the tribe was to receive a reservation, money and the right to continue to live their traditional salmon fishing life. Although the promised money was never forthcoming, the whites became increasingly anxious to remove the Indians from the area. Finally, after the Klallams murdered a dozen Tsimshian Indians camped on Dungeness Spit on the night of September 21, 1868, federal troops were sent to burn the Klallam villages at Port Townsend and Diamond Point, which was quickly turned into a leprosarium. All Indians who could be found were towed in their canoes down Hood Canal behind the government cutter to the reservation at Skokomish. The few Indians who managed to remain in the Dungeness area were forced to pay $500 in gold for 210 acres of logged-off land at the place they named Jamestown.

Meanwhile, early white settlers in the Dungeness, like Shetland Island sea captain Thomas Abernathy, began building their crude log cabins and clearing the forest of Douglas fir, noble fir and western red cedar. Some of the timber was cut and sold for shipment to San Francisco, but most of it was simply burned. "The timber of the eastern portion [of the peninsula] has been largely destroyed, either by axe or by fire, mainly by the latter," a U.S. Geological Service report observed in 1902. That same year, on September 12, the entire Olympic Peninsula experienced its famous "Dark Day," when 110 forest fires raged simultaneously from British Columbia to Central Oregon. Smoke from forest fires was so heavy that no more than a twilight gleam pierced the clouds all day, and many "thought the world was coming to an end, and prayed for deliverance," as an Olympic Peninsula schoolteacher recalled.

Potatoes, oats and peas were planted among the stumps, and early yields were so heavy that the Dungeness quickly became one of the principal exporters of agricultural products in western Washington. New settlers pushed the clearing to the edge of the prairies around Sequim and into the hanging valley in the foothills of the Olympics ten miles from the strait. Whiskey Flats changed its name to Dungeness, and a group of farmers built a three-quarter-mile-long dock at the mouth of the river to facilitate the loading of freight and passengers. No longer could one see a woman "with her voluminous skirt and petticoats that swept the floor, hat with flowing veils, and kid gloves, being carried by a barebacked Indian" across the tide flats.

Irrigation became increasingly important for farming in the Dungeness Valley as logging and ploughing sped evaporation and run-off. Although not as grandiose as Thomas Aldwell's scheme for the Elwha, the idea of diverting the Dungeness for irrigation became a similarly consuming passion for Dungeness farmer D. R. Callen. When the first water from the river flowed onto the parched farms around the Sequim prairie in 1896, the settlers made "offerings" to the irrigation company he founded, one of which featured local children reciting a poem composed for the occasion ("A laurel wreath to honor those good men / Who brought about this glorious end, / So in the future there may be those / Who sees this land blossom like a rose"). Soon half a dozen irrigation companies were draining the river into an elaborate network of gravel troughs and wooden aqueducts, and the valley had become a leading dairy center with a combined herd of 9,000 cows.

Few of the low dams that diverted the Dungeness into irrigation ditches were equipped with ladders for salmon passage. Salmon could jump some of these at high water, but at other times they blocked all migration. Protective screens over irrigation intake pipes were even rarer. As a result, millions of salmon fry were lured into the deadly maze of ditches, from which there was generally no escape. Adult salmon seeking to spawn were also trapped in the irrigation systems. Jerry Angiuli, a member of the Clallam County Planning Commission, remembered how after "flood irrigating" in the 1940s he had to "go through the fields picking up dead salmon because the cows would leave an area of grass the size of a desk around the carcass. . . . There were hundreds every year, mostly humpies [pinks] and silvers [cohos]." A few years later, according to Angiuli, an irrigation diversion downstream from his family's farm on Cassalery Creek blocked the salmon and they disappeared.

Elsewhere, the shrunken streams provided salmon with less area to perform the vital functions of their lives. Many salmon were unable to find a place to spawn, and of those that did, many lost their eggs when the river dropped more. Fry were limited by the lack of adequate rearing area, and all salmon, large and small, suffered from the fact that there was not as much room to run from their enemies. The water that remained heated up faster, thereby reducing the amount of oxygen it could hold and fostering the speedy growth of salmon diseases. Warm water dulls the salmon's senses, and above 55 degrees Fahrenheit (about the temperature of cold bath water) it prevents them from spawning. Water returning from irrigation ditches was warmer still, and often contained manure, pesticides and other poisons. In good years, irrigation generally took about two-thirds of the Dungeness, but during extreme droughts virtually all the water was removed from some sections, leaving pools and trickling rivulets in a broad bed of gravel.

With the passage of the Reclamation Act in 1902, this tale was repeated on a much grander scale all over the arid West. During the first three decades of this century, the U.S. Bureau of Reclamation irrigated more than three million acres of Washington, Oregon, California, Nevada, Wyoming and Colorado. The addition of water made much of this land intensely productive and allowed the cultivation of new crops, such as the Yakima Valley apples for which Washington is now so well known. A triumph of the early Progressive movement, the Reclamation Act required the farmers who benefited from the projects to repay the government, and stipulated that no one person could own more than 160 acres of land under federal irrigation. Advocates of reclamation, such as Nevada Congressman Francis Newlands, saw public irrigation as a miraculous font of free riches, but in fact there were great costs, both economic and environmental.

Because of bureau policies and subsequent changes in the law, farmers receiving bureau water have generally been able to avoid (or at least postpone) repaying the government for the cost of the irrigation works. They pay a monthly fee to cover operational costs, but only a small fraction of the outstanding debt, which bears little or no interest. On the Bureau of Reclamation's forty-year-old Columbia River project, for instance, the difference between the farmers' payments and the actual cost amounted to a 96.7 percent public subsidy in 1980, according to a U.S. Department of Interior report. Ironically, the people who benefited from these subsidies were not the small farmers Newlands wanted to help. Because of the Bureau of Reclamation's chronic failure to enforce the 160-acre limit, a great deal of publicly irrigated land has come under the control of large agribusiness ventures such as Jubil Farms Inc., an 8,000-acre operation in the Sacramento Valley that is controlled by a Japanese trading company.

One of the Bureau of Reclamation's first jobs was the Newlands Project on the Truckee River in western Nevada. At the time that the bureau built Derby Dam twenty miles east of Reno, the Truckee was the home of the world's largest cutthroat trout, *Salmo clarkii*. Long a staple of the Paiute Indians, the Lahontan trout gained considerable renown among sportsmen after early explorers, such as Lieutenant John C. Frémont, noted their "extraordinary size" and called their flavor "excellent, superior, in fact to any fish I have ever known." A record forty-one-pound Lahontan trout was taken in 1925, but a little more than a decade later, the fish had disappeared from the earth. The reason? The Bureau of Reclamation dam would not release enough water to allow the fish to reach their spawning grounds above Pyramid Lake.

In Washington, the Bureau of Reclamation's work centered on the Columbia Basin in the eastern portion of the state. Here eight unladdered dams were built on Columbia tributaries from the Tieton River to Salmon Creek. On the Yakima River, the bureau's dams wiped out the sockeye that had been the single largest run in the river and played a major role in reducing the total salmon population from 600,000 to 9,000 fish. During the 1930s, the bureau decided to dam the Columbia itself near an immense glacial outwash known as Grand Coulee. Hailed as the greatest engineering feat ever undertaken by man, Grand Coulee Dam was also the single most destructive human act toward salmon of all time. When this unladdered colossus was completed in 1942, it closed more than 1,000 miles of spawning rivers and streams in the upper Columbia, killing the famous "June hog" Chinook that had previously been the mainstay of the great Columbia fishery.

Another hidden cost of the Bureau of Reclamation's work has been the loss of existing farms put out of business by the new subsidized competition. With tremendous production and the accompanying economies of scale, farmers on federally irrigated land were able to offer larger lots and lower prices than almost anyone. Selling to the mushrooming national supermarket chains, they helped amalgamate many regional produce markets into one national market. Washington apples and California lettuce were two of the many irrigated crops that came to dominate local produce. Less obvious to the shopper, but equally important, was the shift to irrigation-grown alfalfa as the base of large scale Western dairying. Inevitably, some of the smaller local agricultural areas that had lost their markets began to atrophy and fall prey to urban sprawl. Among the farming valleys that used to supply Seattle, one of the first lost in this manner was the Dungeness.

Instead of "blossoming like a rose," the Dungeness grew a variety of common urban blight. The cooperative creamery was closed in 1954 when the small dairymen could see the handwriting on the wall. A few larger dairies survived, along with some cabbage seed farms and other assorted agricultural operations, but by the 1960s much of the valley was being transformed through the magic of real estate offerings. "For Sale/Small Acreage/Easy Terms," "Acreage View Tracts For Sale," "Open House/Condominiums/House Sites," the bright signs among the quaint abandoned fields proclaimed. Many of the retirees who moved into the Dungeness area added signs of their own: "Keep out," "Beware of Dog" (in fluorescent orange letters on black), "Watch for Flying Golf Balls," "For Sale," "View Lots" (amid bare, eroding soil and stumps), "Hobbies Ahead," "No Trespassing/Violators Will Be Prosecuted" (beside a mailbox painted with red and yellow flowers in a meticulous hand).

"Here's how it works," Jerry Angiuli said, putting his feet up on the desk in his Sequim tire store. "The realtors like to sell five-acre ranchettes. A guy and his wife go out to look at the property on a sunny day when the mountains are out and the strait is blue, and he's got to have it . . . The first year is OK—especially if he retired early and spent some time on a farm as a kid—because he's busy building his house and having the lawn put in. Then he's got a house and four and one-half acres of weeds. So the second year he builds a fence and buys a cow. Then he finds he's got to have a stall to breed her, irrigation and a tractor to plough the land, and the next thing you know he's got $30,000 into his 'hobby' farm. Then one of his friends says, 'Hey, there's great fishing out at Sekiu. Let's go out for a few days.' But he can't do it, because someone's got to take care of the place, and the next thing you know he starts getting real mad and decides he's going to subdivide his place into little lots. . . . When someone tells him he can't do that, he calls his lawyer and starts screaming about his rights."

As the residential population in the Dungeness area burgeoned, its water consumption more than offset the declining use of water for irrigation. Drainage patterns were altered by the increased drilling of wells, and flooding was made more likely by the speedy run-off from paved surfaces. In 1975, the Washington Department of Fisheries estimated that a dozen separate runs of wild Dungeness coho and chum salmon had been exterminated by diversions for human and agricultural use. Two years later, fisheries had to send a bulldozer down into the dry bed of the Dungeness to scour a narrow channel so that the wild summer pink salmon could reach their spawning grounds in the upper Dungeness and Graywolf rivers. This last-ditch effort saved most of the early run, but nothing could be done for the later fish that spawn in the lower river.

Irrigators, developers and water speculators claim a "legal right" to more water than actually flows in the Dungeness, thanks to the ruling of an accommodating Clallam County judge fifty years ago. Washington law has long required that "a flow of water sufficient to support game fish and food fish populations be maintained at all times," but as a recent report by the U.S. attorney in Seattle concluded, "this policy has not been implemented." The U.S. attorney's report, which was presented as evidence in a 1978 U.S. District Court case, blamed the existence of "potentially very destructive" irrigation practices in Washington on the State Department of Ecology. "Although the [state] departments of Fisheries and Game have submitted 34 requests [for legal recognition of the salmon's right to water on various rivers] in the last 10 years, the Department of Ecology has acted on only one. Meanwhile applications for water rights other than fish are being filed, and these have priority by the time they are established."

Much of the development on the Dungeness has taken place within the flood plain, that is, the area normally flooded every few years. This had led to more diking along the Dungeness, and further reduced the salmon's chances of survival. In 1973, Clallam County asked Dungeness Farms for permission to divert the river so some new homes would not be flooded at high water. "They put the diversion in in 1974," recalled Polly Ball of the county's Shoreline Advisory Committee, "but the first high water pushed the river right over the diversion, which left the old channel high and dry and prevented the salmon from using what I understand was one of their best spawning grounds." The departments of Fisheries and Game have jurisdiction over permits for structural flood control projects, but they did not even check into the matter far enough to see that no engineer had ever approved the project. The U.S. attorney's report cites severe short-staffing and institutionalized timidness as the causes of the departments' failure to act in situations like the one at Dungeness Farms. "The departments are concerned that if many [river degrading] projects are denied, their authority might be reduced," it observed dryly.

Harry McBride, a Department of Fisheries biologist assigned to keep track of the Dungeness pink salmon, shrugged when I asked about this. He was standing by the open gate in the Dungeness hatchery weir, clicking a hand counter as pink salmon hurried past. It is true, of course, that the federal government itself is the largest owner of illegal irrigation dams in

Washington, primarily through the Corps of Engineers and Bureau of Reclamation. "The Department of Fisheries has done a lot of good work on the Dungeness," he said, referring to projects such as the installation of diversion intake screens during the 1940s and 1950s, the gravel-cleaning operations on the lower river during the 1960s and erosion control on Gold Creek during the 1970s. "Maybe we might have done a better job," another Fisheries officer told me, "but you know you can't get too far out in front of the public."

Pink salmon shot through the sights of McBride's orange cowboy boots in spurts. Their partially exposed tails snapped like the playing cards we used to clip to the spokes of our bikes as kids. McBride said he saw pinks pass through the weir "trailing all kinds of gear." With a couple of exceptions, the Department of Fisheries has not allowed a non-Indian sport fishery on these summer pinks since the 1960s, in order to insure that enough fish survive to spawn the next generation, two years hence. Legally, the Klallam Indians were the only people who could fish the river for pinks. In fact, however, the river is commonly fished by the Klallams and a much larger group of non-Indian fishermen, some of whom are sportsmen, some subsistence fishermen and some commercial poachers.

As I was departing, I asked McBride if the river was closed to pink salmon fishing then, and he said yes. My next stop was the Dungeness Forks Campground, which is located at the point between the converging Graywolf and Dungeness rivers. Most of the half dozen parties in residence seemed to be fishing. Walking down to the rocky shore of the Graywolf, I found a man in his thirties showing his son how to gut a pink female he had snagged with a three-hook setup. The hooks had caught the fish in front of its still silvery tail which now bled on the rocks. Neither the Department of Fisheries nor the U.S. Forest Service, which has jurisdiction over the area, had posted signs notifying people in the campground that the pinks were closed for conservation of the run.

Farther up the river, I found the tails of three salmon that had been severed with a knife, and another pink salmon female that had been gutted and abandoned to the soft ball of maggots now unfolding on her tongue. Around dark, a crew of seven or eight hardy-looking types arrived in camp and set out for the river with snagging gear and beers in tow. "Lots of salmon up here," one of them called amiably as they passed my tent. Noting four pinks laid out on the grass by their trucks in the morning, I stopped and learned that they were Forest Service timber cruisers. Just then, another member of their party returned with the rest of the morning's catch: three female pinks weighing four or five pounds apiece.

That same week, I checked the price of salmon in a Port Angeles supermarket. A slender, four-pound coho (which was likely hatchery produced and troller caught) cost $4.50 per pound, or $18 for a fish that would barely feed two hungry men.

SIX

A SHORT, ANIMATED MAN WITH A LOUD VOICE was sitting by the window reading a history of his life written by one of his granddaughters. He was wearing an old Washington Department of Fisheries shirt with a rumpled "superintendent" patch on the sleeve, jeans that were too short, some serious-looking long underwear and a pair of bedroom slippers. His face was splotchy and unevenly shaven, but his eyes were clear and firm.

Ernest Brannon arrived in Washington from Chicago when he was eight years old. Always having the desire to fish, he was happy to live not too far from a river, which was the Green River out of Auburn, Washington. When not helping his dad, he would go fishing. Many times he would go to the Green River hatchery to help. He would do anything just to be working with fish—"I don't know who wrote this," Brannon interjected with a wink.

When he was 16 years old they put him on the payroll at $90 *a month starting July 1, 1922. He bought a second-hand bicycle out of his first pay check to ride to work. He quit school in his second year of high school as he had to help finance a big family. After serving at Green River hatchery number one for a year, he was asked to go to Green River number two, about 40 miles above the original hatchery near Kanaskat.*

The egg take was so large in 1924 that it was necessary to send eggs to Green River number two. The road ended at the gauging station, and the hatchery was about a half mile above this. With the help of just one man, he had to slide 1,516,000 eggs—"that's thirty-six baskets," Brannon said, peering over the top of his reading glasses for emphasis—*up tracks covered with heavy snow to the hatchery on a homemade sled.*

It was rather lonesome there. The hatchery was on the Northern Pacific Railroad tracks on a hill and the only company they had was the trains going by each day. In the winter he had to go for groceries on snowshoes. Sometimes the [Tacoma municipal water inspector] brought the mail out to him—"I'd snowshoe to Kanaskat," Brannon recalled, "and then catch the freight back. It'd slow down on the grade before the tunnel, so I'd have time to throw my things off and jump after."

It took him a while to find his place again in the plastic-covered text. Finally he pressed his big forefinger against the page and continued. *On December 2, 1929 he came to the Dungeness salmon hatchery as superintendent. The hatchery was built in 1902 . . . and . . . the house had no water or lights. He soon put water in the house, and another room and a bathroom was also added*—"When I went to the Dungeness, the director [of Fisheries] said, 'Ernie, don't try to rack the Dungeness; it can't be done.' There were no eggs in the hatchery at the time. The previous superintendent hadn't been doing anything but drawing his pay.

"I went out immediately and started gaffing the little coho salmon and picked up 500,000 to 600,000 eggs the first year. This is the rack I put in," he said, picking up a photograph of a weir made of wooden slats snaking across the rushing river.

Beneath it was another photo showing the same weir armored with several feet of river ice and snags. "Now the director told me not to worry about racking the Dungeness. I've been retired how long? Five years? I built that rack in 1932 and it's still there today!"

The first years that Brannon spent at the Dungeness hatchery were also memorable for his marriage to Helen (the department gave them two kerosene lamps as a wedding present), and his discovery of the nearby Elwha River. The first Fisheries representative to set foot in the Elwha since the state abandoned its hatchery eight years before, Brannon found something surprising: there were still *tyee* in the lower river below the dam. "This year I fished 10 different days, catching 181 female Chinook and 215 male Chinook with only a gaff hook," he reported to Olympia. "Several of these males would weigh 100 pounds each."

Brannon also noted there were times when the "power dams would cut the water nearly off." Adult salmon did not apparently suffer greatly from the practice ("they would lay in the holes while the water was down and not move around any"), but juvenile salmon were seriously affected. "We found a few salmon that were stranded from the water being shut off and I estimate we picked up 50 young salmon and trout from four to six inches long that had died because of no water. This condition existed between the . . . intake for the new [industrial] water supply and the outlet where they spill water, a distance of about a mile."

The number of young salmon killed when the dam shut off the water was certainly larger than the numbers reported by Brannon, for the vast majority of the mortalities would have buried themselves alive. The normal response of young salmon to a falling water level is to dive into the gravel substrata, rather than swim unprotected into the current. Juvenile salmon will continue to dig to a depth of several feet as the water recedes, and have even been known to follow underground watercourses into wells and springs. On the Skagit River, the Seattle

City Light dams have killed as many as 239,000 young salmon in a single night when they ran a high flow until the end of the peak consumption period around 11 P.M., and then reduced the flow sharply until the next morning.

Impressed by the salmon production potential in the lower Elwha, Brannon urged some kind of action. His superiors, however, were much less enthusiastic about the remaining Elwha fish. During the term of Governor Roland Hartley, a lumber mill owner, the Department of Fisheries had already allowed Crown Zellerbach to build a second unladdered, uncompensated dam six miles up the Elwha at Glines Canyon, along with an Aldwell-inspired diversion of 150 cubic feet per second of river for the Port Angeles pulp mill that has come to be part of ITT-Rayonier. Supervisor of Fisheries Charles Pollock did nothing except to authorize Brannon to collect wild Elwha eggs for the Dungeness hatchery.

Throughout the 1920s and 1930s, the Department of Fisheries tended to approach the Elwha situation like the death of a distant relative: It was all somewhat sad, but there was nothing they could do about the outcome. In 1937, for instance, state Representative Francis Perkins volunteered to introduce legislation that would require restoration of the Elwha salmon killed by the dam. Director of Fisheries B. M. Brennan declined the offer, claiming his hands were tied by the 1915 law allowing hatcheries in lieu of fishways (which did not in fact become law until three years after the gates of the Elwha Dam were closed for the first time) and the state's agreement with Aldwell for the abandoned hatchery (which in fact had never been lived up to by Aldwell or Crown Zellerbach). "This contract, that was entered into and signed by the State of Washington, is so binding that there seems to be little or nothing that can be done further with protecting fish life in the river," Brennan said, adding with a yawn, "it is also best to proceed slowly in such a matter. . . ."

Elsewhere in the state during this period, not a single major dam was provided with either a fishway or hatchery mitigation. The complete failure to enforce even Darwin's liberalized hatchery lieu law coincided with the first big push to develop the Northwest's potential hydroelectric power. Dams were allowed to kill significant salmon runs in the Puyallup, Skagit, Skokomish and Yakima rivers as Tacoma City Light, the state's first municipal utility, and private power groups like Washington Water Power vied for the best hydroelectric sites. The private power interests enjoyed an advantage during the laissez-faire Republican administrations of the 1920s, but were never able to raise enough capital to carry out really big projects, such as the 1925 plan to build a private power dam at Priest Rapids on the Columbia.

Spokesmen for the salmon industry generally sided with the Democratic public power advocates in these early battles over dam construction in the Northwest. "We all remember when the railroads were very nearly the government in this country," Miller Freeman wrote in the July 16, 1925, Seattle *Star.* "This has been in a measure corrected, but a new evil has arisen overnight. From my contacts during my investigation in the East, I have concluded that the Federal Power Commission is a creature of the [monopoly] power interests." Freeman, who was publisher of *Pacific Fisherman*, wondered "would it not be well for the public to slow up a bit in its insistence on development of natural resources so far in advance of our needs?"

No such brake was applied during the flush days of President Harding and Governor Hartley, and dam construction in the Northwest actually increased during the ensuing Depression as the federal government undertook power development on a scale undreamed of by the most ambitious capitalist. Bonneville Dam, completed in 1935, was planned by the Corps of Engineers as part of a ten-dam hydroelectric complex on the mainstem Columbia. There was no need for the power at the time from either Bonneville or its companion Grand Coulee, but President Franklin Roosevelt was playing political alchemist in the hope that a fat enough public subsidy to private industry—in this case, cheap taxpayer-supported irrigation and electricity—could convert water into jobs.

Shortly after Roosevelt's death, an expanded version of the Corps's plan began to take shape. The Federal Power Commission licensed dams on the mainstem Columbia at Rocky Reach, McNary, Priest Rapids and Chief Joseph to a variety of public power groups in the early 1950s. Dams were also authorized on the Cowlitz River, the last unspoiled Columbia tributary of consequence in Washington, and the Deschutes River, which occupied a similar position on the Oregon side of the Columbia. Asked about the dams' impact on salmon, General Chorpening, head of the Corps, told Congress that "with the experience gained in the operation of Bonneville Dam, there will be no difficulty . . . in the proper handling of the fish problem."

Bonneville had in fact been equipped with an array of experimental fishways (the first such dam in Washington since Darwin left office nearly twenty years before), but salmon fishermen knew from the Corps's own reports that Bonneville was killing 15 to 20 percent of the combined Columbia River run every year, and that half a dozen more dams, each subtracting 15 percent, would leave no salmon in the river at all. The catch of salmon had already dropped from a historic high of 42 million pounds in 1883 to 7 million pounds in 1954, largely as a result of dams and overfishing by the commercial salmon industry itself. Sensing that a moment of true crisis was at hand for the salmon of the Columbia, the fishermen and the industry they supported decided to make a stand over the Cowlitz, a beautiful river which drains the area between Mount Rainier and Mount St. Helens, and meets the Columbia at Kelso.

The fact that the permit for Mayfield Dam on the Cowlitz had been issued to Tacoma City Light only made the contest more interesting, for during the 1930s and 1940s the public power interests turned against their former allies in the fishing industry and sought to avoid all laws for the protection of salmon. Tacoma City Light led the way in 1926 when it built Cushman Dam on the Skokomish River without fish ladders or a hatchery. "Five thousand Tacomans gathered at the base of the [transmission] towers . . . cheered as aerial bombs signalled the event," according to Tacoma *News-Tribune* coverage of the dam's dedication. Milo Bell, retired professor of Fisheries at the University of Washington, recalled that "the Department [of Fisheries] tried for years, and could never get anywhere with Tacoma City Light. They wouldn't even meet with us." At the time Tacoma was awarded the license for Mayfield Dam, it owned and operated four dams on major salmon rivers in Washington. Not one of them had either fishways or partial hatchery compensation for the runs destroyed by the dams.

In Tacoma, the municipal utility was a symbol of civic pride. It sold the cheapest residential electricity in the United States, and even cheaper bulk rate power to the heavy industries such as Kaiser Aluminum, Boise-Cascade and ASARCO that make up its economic base. With its lumber mills faltering because of the overcutting of available timber, Tacoma was becoming increasingly dependent on the utility. Its continued growth was seen as synonymous with the city's continued growth, and it enjoyed the support of the majority of the city's 150,000 residents, and their only newspaper, the *News-Tribune*. "Forget your worry, sportsmen, about losing some of the Cowlitz River and the salmon races that run in that stream when the great Mossyrock and smaller Mayfield dams . . . rise to move Tacoma ahead to better things industrially and economically," wrote popular sports columnist Elliott Metcalf. "We all know that when time marches on, he goes ahead and that's what is happening at Mossyrock and Mayfield. It is inevitable as death that the power productive Cowlitz will be harnessed for the good of all, not set aside for the minority, or few."

Actually, the opposition to Tacoma City Light's plans for the Cowlitz came not from "the minority, or few," but from the majority of the citizens of the state. Commercial and sports fishermen were determined to stop Tacoma City Light (as were the Cowlitz County towns in the vicinity of the proposed hydroelectric project), but the greatest champion of the wild salmon of the Cowlitz proved to be the State of Washington.

Under conservative Republican Governor Arthur Langlie, who was noted more for his antagonism toward public power than his love of fish, the Washington departments of Fisheries and Game were finally given the go-ahead to enforce the dam statutes with the full authority of the law. This was to be the first (and only) time that the State of Washington ever tried to prevent construction of a major dam for the sake of wild salmon.

Citing the authority of the Dam Sanctuary Act of 1949, which prohibited high-head dams on the lower Columbia in Washington, state Director of Fisheries Robert Schoettler filed suit against the Tacoma utility, thereby firing the first shot in what came to be a very bitter fight. For eight years Fisheries was able to prevent construction from starting with a series of state court victories, but after a lackluster presentation by new state Attorney General John O'Connell (who had advocated the dams' construction before his election), the U.S. Supreme Court overturned the previous rulings. In its June 1958 decision for Tacoma City Light, the Supreme Court ruled that the issuance of a special purpose license by an agency of the federal government endowed the recipient with immunity from state law. Tacoma City Light began construction on the dam immediately, while opponents began an initiative campaign to put the issue directly before the voters of the state. Initiative 25, which was essentially a reiteration of the Dam Sanctuary Act of 1949, was passed by a 52 percent margin of the state's voters while Tacoma City Light worked on Mayfield's footings.

When O'Connell declined to press the case, Tacoma City Light itself asked the Washington Supreme Court to rule on the legality of Initiative 25. And so after twelve years of litigation, the issue was finally settled on May 24, 1962, when the State Supreme Court reluctantly ruled that the will of the people could not impede the progress of public power. "Initiative 25 is superseded and is inoperative when it comes into conflict with the exercised 'paramount jurisdiction' of the [federal government]," concluded the majority opinion, which went on to tongue-lash the public utility for its conduct in the case: "Tacoma City Light . . . has proceeded to erect one of the dams and is proceeding with the other in violation of the expressed desires of a considerable segment of the people of the state of Washington, the will of the legislature, and the will of the people of the state."

In response, Tacoma officials claimed they were the victims of "nonstop discriminatory harassment." Said one Tacoma city councilman in the spring of 1962, "Seattle [City Light] builds dams, Puget [Power] builds dams, Bonneville [Power Administration] builds dams and nobody says a word. Tacoma tries to build a dam and the whole state goes crazy. You can't figure it!" Men like Utility Director C. A. Erdahl and E. K. Murray, the utility's head outside legal officer, also felt that Tacoma had taken a bad rap on the salmon issue. It was unfair, they contended, for Tacoma to be blamed with destroying the fish when the city had promised to build a hatchery that would replace the salmon lost. Tacoma had recently helped build George Adams hatchery in partial compensation for the damage done by its dams on the Skokomish, and on the Cowlitz, too, there would be "power *and* fish," as the Tacoma City Light publicity slogan proclaimed.

The Cowlitz hatchery was designed to be the largest and best equipped Pacific salmon hatchery in the world. Built to the specifications of the Department of Fisheries and paid for entirely by Tacoma City Light, the facility was comprised of thirty-six large self-cleaning ponds, eighteen starter raceways, a hatchery building, incubation facilities, frozen feed storage lockers, a laboratory and a visitors' area. "This wealth of concrete and steel, pumps, valves and water quality controls represents the fruit of years of experience and practical knowledge gained by Fisheries' engineers, fish culturists and biologists," the department's official history of the hatchery system commented with pride.

When it became apparent that the Federal Power Commission would allow Tacoma to abandon the fish passage facilities already installed on Mayfield Dam, the hatchery was designed to "handle the entire run of salmon in the Cowlitz." Wild adult spawners were trapped at the base of the dam during construction, and from these runs the department determined the number of spring Chinook, fall Chinook and coho that Tacoma City Light would have to pay to replace through artificial propagation. Before it was over, the Department of Fisheries had the satisfaction of running Tacoma's total construction costs for salmon mitigation to more than $20 million, more than the utility paid for the turbines and generators in the two Cowlitz dams.

The larger aim of sustaining the runs eluded them, though. During the first decade of operation, the Cowlitz hatchery failed to meet its compensation goals three-quarters of the time. An additional $2 million was required to correct what the department later called "mediocre" design, and the hatchery's operational costs were similarly increased by the many drugs needed to treat the chronic and killing diseases that annually reach epidemic proportions among Cowlitz hatchery fish. Worst afflicted are the choicest salmon in the river, the spring Chinook. Although descended from wild stocks that once made up one of the strongest Columbia tributary runs, the Cowlitz spring Chinook have reached the point where they have to be inoculated three times after they return to the hatchery to keep them alive long enough to spawn. Farther up the Columbia, summer Chinook, sockeye and steelhead have fared even worse: in 1978 the U.S. Department of the Interior began studies to determine whether the salmon of the Columbia, once the most numerous in the world, should be placed on the threatened or endangered species lists.

If Darwin's failure to stop construction of the original Elwha Dam had seriously undermined state authority to preserve the wild salmon resource, the Cowlitz court orders toppled it. The construction of dams was now a legal inevitability; all the state could do was seek hatchery mitigation of the losses. Fisherman and conservationists had waged as bitter and protracted a campaign against the Cowlitz dams as the state had ever seen, but they were beaten by the power that Miller Freeman warned about three decades before, the Federal Power Commission. Although born out of the early Progressive campaign for government regulation, the commission was charged solely with the task of fostering dam construction and actually precluded by statute from considering alternatives to power development.

No federal agency with responsibility for fish and wildlife had the authority to do anything but comment on Federal Power Commission actions, and when the U.S. Supreme Court ruled that state laws did not apply to any group that received a Federal Power Commission license, the door was thrown wide. The commission was free to decide for itself what succor it would give the wild salmon. In the wake of the Cowlitz experience, this most often meant more hatchery production. On the Elwha, for instance, the relicensing of Elwha Dam allowed the state to secure a modest settlement from Crown Zellerbach for another hatchery on the lower river. The contract, which was signed April 25, 1975, stipulated that the company would pay 26 percent of the cost of building the Elwha rearing channel and stop the radical fluctuations in flow that have been so damaging to young salmon, in exchange for release from any future claims by the state.

Thor Tollefson, director of Fisheries under Governor Dan Evans, proclaimed a major victory, but Crown Zellerbach, quietly tending its affairs in San Francisco, had much the look of the cat who ate the canary. The firm, one of the largest paper products companies in the world, had purchased a state pardon for its criminal actions on the Elwha for $145,000, or less than one-third the profits it received from its Port Angeles operations in their first year back in 1921, according to *Moody's Industrial Manual*. The "compensation level" set in the contract did not include either of the two choicest runs destroyed by the dam, and the total number of fish that could be raised annually was only about 10 percent of the runs lost. And among that 10 percent, the fish were certain to be smaller than their wild predecessors.

The phenomenon of the decreasing size of salmon has been underway since the first records of the fish. In 995 A.D., Norse explorers along the Atlantic coast of North America reported salmon that were "larger than their relatives that we knew from Greenland." One thousand years later, Roderick Haig-Brown observed: "I sometimes think that all of the problems of Canada's Atlantic salmon are reflected in the almost unbelievable decrease in the size of the fish. [An early writer] reports of the Grand Codroy River: 'salmon up to 40 pounds have been caught.' . . . The present average weight for the river is about four pounds . . . and the largest fish taken during the years 1972–4 was only 24 pounds." Among Atlantic salmon, this diminution is thought to be the result of overfishing, which eliminates most of the older fish and repeat spawners.

Among Pacific salmon, hatcheries have probably been the most powerful force for smaller fish. Because of the cost of feed, hatchery fish are often raised on an accelerated schedule and released into rivers as soon as possible. This tends to make the succeeding stages of their lives correspondingly brief, and means that they weigh less at maturity than wild salmon. By capturing wild fish and using their eggs for artificial propagation, state and federal hatchery operators have steadily downgraded the potential of the stocks. This has been especially true when they targeted on the largest fish and did not plant the fry they produced back in the river where the eggs were collected, as was the case with Ernie Brannon's work with the Chinook of the Elwha. Brannon felt he was practicing "selective breeding" to create a large hatchery fish, but in fact he was draining off the last of the *tyee* for no proven gain. On the Dungeness, the same end was accomplished by Brannon's "rack," which prevents all Chinook of more than twenty pounds from going upriver to spawn naturally.

Although many wild Chinook escaped (one of Brannon's daughters secretly let the wild salmon through the weir at night), Brannon was relentless and resourceful. He took as many as seven million eggs in a year, and along the way developed much of the gaffing method used by Fisheries today. "I'd wade up and down the Elwha two and three miles," he said, his words coming faster and sharper. "I'd come pretty near up to the dam, and where I couldn't wade I'd float my canoe in there. I'd gaff all the big fish I could find, and then put their eggs in the canoe. When I got back downriver, I'd empty the eggs into a 10-gallon milk can full of river water, and then load them into the truck. That and rolling boulders around in the river is what give me my shoulders!"

Brannon's boulder rolling was part of an effort on his part to improve the riverbed, and help it retain a little more gravel. "You can have a real effect on a section of stream if you set your mind to it," he said. "I tried to create the kind of gravel pockets the fish liked, and I think it helped." Despite Brannon's efforts though, the size of the Elwha Chinook steadily decreased. The last really big fish that Ernie Brannon caught was a seventy pounder landed in 1946, the first year the Dungeness hatchery had a walk-in freezer. Brannon took the fish home and interred it alongside a somewhat flat cougar as tourist fare. Every summer for the next thirty years the "giant fish" was hauled out again and again so people could have their picture taken with it. By the time that Brannon retired in 1973, the fish had been freezer burned to the consistency of styrofoam and had lost half its original weight.

Brannon and his wife live today in a dramatic eyrie on a cliff overlooking the Elwha. The walls of their home are papered with commendations he received during his fifty-one years of service with the Department of Fisheries. "When I spoke before the legislature, I said, 'it says on my citation that I was a high school graduate—I want to repudiate that!' " he recalled. "I was a high school dropout." Brannon's wife laughed: "Yes, and it caused a lot of trouble to have it changed," At the same time, Brannon is intensely proud of his son, Ernest Brannon, Jr., who is an associate professor of fisheries at the University of Washington. At seventy, Ernie, Sr., walks with a short rolling stride, regularly beating men half his age up the trail. Regarding the past, he will acknowledge that some mistakes were made, but only in the third person. "It's wrong," he said, speaking of his own sometime practice of taking eggs from a stream without corresponding plants. "They shouldn't rob a stream when there's a good run of fish in it."

Despite the billions of eggs collected on the river over the last three-quarters of a century, the Department of Fisheries has never been able to establish a hatchery supply of eggs for the Elwha fall Chinook. For this reason, the department continues to gaff heavily in the few pockets of spawning gravel that remain to the fish in order to supply its artificial rearing channel. I watched the process one fall morning among a crazy group of Chinook at the head of a breaking riffle. Taking my position on the bank around 9 A.M., I counted eleven fish of various sizes and colors racing around the sun-dappled redd. The fish were like magnets of opposite pole, driving each other apart every time they swung together. None of them noticed the bearded gentleman in black hip waders who had just set a large plastic bucket on the opposite shore.

The man from the Dungeness hatchery waded the knee-deep path along the head of the riffle to a point about fifteen feet above and off to one side of the redd. Swinging his twenty-foot-long gaff pole around by levering it across his knee, he slowly inched the forged hook over the hollow of freshly dug gravel where a silver female lay with her burnished, blue-bronze mate. His first lunge missed, but moments later the female jumped straight up out of the water, the hook through the meat of her back. The gaffer quickly wrestled her to the shore with the rope that held the hook after he had thrown aside the awkward pole, and beat her in the head three times with a rock. He then slit the skin in front of her tail so his fingers could hook in, and returned the way he had come.

On the other side, he milked the twenty-pound female's eggs into the bucket with a stroking motion. Dirty gulls waited silently along the water's edge while the rusty stain of blood at the bottom of the redd ebbed slowly on the current. Except for a couple of quick forays by skitterish males, the dead female's redd was empty of fish the rest of the morning. "There's a seventy-pound buck somewhere on this river," the Fisheries gaffer, Jim Garrett, told me. "We've seen him a couple of times, but we haven't been able to get him." When he was finished, he discarded the carcass, picked up his gear and headed upriver. Heading the other way, I found one Chinook carcass that might have weighed thirty pounds, and many in the neighborhood of eighteen pounds. I also found the gaffer had beaten me to every redd.

The five miles of free-flowing Elwha that remain today comprise something of a river in miniature. Downstream from the gorge and the dam, the Elwha cuts out through a series of forested islands into a broad-shouldered valley. The long asphalt ponds of the state's Elwha rearing channel are located on a sizable bench at river mile three. Overhung with a beautifully intricate web of red and yellow twine to ward off kingfishers and mergansers, these ponds rear young salmon that have been incubated elsewhere, usually at the Dungeness hatchery. Across the river and downstream 100 feet is the opening to a long meandering channel that runs through a tunnel of heavy vine maple. This side channel contains some of the best gravel left on the Elwha, but because of the water diversions upriver, it is dry.

Long-time Elwha Valley resident Harold Sisson remembers when "this section here was full of fish," and thinks "it could be again." Sisson, a logging contractor who owns the property, said, "All you'd have to do is bring in a Cat and clean out some of the debris so you could put a controlled water intake pipe on the upper end on the river." Sisson offered to give the Department of Fisheries a free long-term lease to use the channel, but was rebuffed. "They're not interested in anything that won't look impressive in an aerial photograph," Sisson snorted. A few minutes later, though, he told me that the Department of Fisheries had purchased a nearby area of springs used by wild chum salmon for spawning. The department, he said, had held the land undeveloped for a number of years simply to maintain the habitat of the lower Elwha.

Below Harold Sisson's 160-acre farm, the Elwha curves out onto a wide alluvial fan of low-lying land. To the north across the ten-mile-wide Strait of Juan de Fuca, the dark mountains of Vancouver Island loom. The Elwha meets the blue strait between Observatory and Angeles points at Freshwater Bay. This half moon of partially protected water was named by Spanish explorer Manuel Quimper in 1790. Forced to anchor by contrary winds, Quimper and the men of the *Princess Real* traded with the Indians for salmonberries, and filled the ship's water casks with "delicious water, taken from a beautiful stream [the Elwha]." Unlike the Dungeness, the mouth of the Elwha is unprotected by an encircling spit; the green river simply disappears into the blue strait.

Within the last few years, two supertanker oil ports and transcontinental pipeline terminuses have been proposed near here, one at Low Point ten miles west of Freshwater Bay, and one at Port Angeles five miles east of the mouth of the Elwha. One of the pipeline groups has since bowed out, but the other now needs only final approval by the State of Washington to proceed. This is the Northern Tier Pipeline Company, a consortium of the land companies of the Burlington Northern and Milwaukee Road railroads, U.S. Steel, Westinghouse and a number of independent entrepreneurs. Northern Tier wants to build a 1,557-mile pipeline from Port Angeles to Clearbrook, Minnesota, capable of delivering 800,000 barrels of crude oil a day.

The proposed Northern Tier pipeline would cross a dozen major salmon rivers in western Washington (the Dungeness among them), as well as Puget Sound itself. Because of the extreme sensitivity of salmonids to petroleum (as little as three parts per million prevents migration), many fisheries biologists feel that the pipeline could endanger most of the salmon of Puget Sound. It is also possible that the great Fraser River runs, which migrate along the strait before turning north to Canada, could be affected by the pipeline and the tremendous growth in tanker traffic needed to supply it. The U.S. Environmental Protection Agency has expressed doubts that the proposed oil port will be able to comply with the Clean Air Act, as well. This is a source of major concern for the Olympic National Park, since federal law requires the natural values of the park to be preserved, and the United Nations recently designated the Olympic National Park an International Bioreserve Area.

Citing a U.S. Department of Energy report, opponents of the pipeline plan charged that there really was no need for the oil Northern Tier would deliver to the upper Midwest. The real purpose of the pipeline, they concluded, was to give U.S. Steel and Westinghouse a market for their products while sewing up the future right to transport oil, coal slurry or whatever. Northern Tier responded that the project would benefit the public by generating an estimated $10 million in state taxes during the construction period in Washington alone. Northern Tier also claimed that the pipeline was vital to the national security of the United States because other pipelines serving the upper Midwest pass through Canada.

Northern Tier was still grinding forward (thanks to special dispensations from President Jimmy Carter and Washington Governor Dan Evans) when the Corps of Engineers released a report on the safety of Elwha Dam in late 1978. The Corps found the sixty-eight-year-old dam "structurally unsafe" because it had never actually been anchored in bedrock at the base. Despite years of rebuilding and the fact that the reservoir behind had nearly been filled in to prevent leaks, several hundred cubic feet per second of water still coursed under the dam at all times. Declaring that the dam had "high downstream hazard potential," the Corps urged immediate action, either in the form of major repairs or provisions for "a controlled breaching of the dam."

Most of the people endangered by the dam were Elwha Klallam living along the lower mile and a half of the river, much as their ancestors did when they met Quimper with berries and water. The Elwhas remembered the blowout of the dam as "the time when there were salmon in the trees," and blamed the rebuilt dam for the flooding that has forced some of them out of their homes every year for decades. They were particularly enraged by the revelation that Crown Zellerbach, the dam's owner, had received a similar private report on the dam's safety ten years before, but had done nothing, not even so much as install an adequate warning system. "I guess they don't care if a few Indians drown," said Frank Bennett, chairman of the Elwha Tribal Council.

Crown Zellerbach and the Washington Department of Ecology quickly agreed to a schedule of repairs for the dam, but others saw the situation as an opportunity to install fish passage facilities at least on the lower dam. Rex Van Wormer of the U.S. Fish and Wildlife Service endorsed the idea, and a professor of fisheries at Peninsula College in Port Angeles, Robert Mausolf, came forward with a plan to pass fish upriver over the dam with an aerial tramway. The Washington Department of Fisheries expressed some mild sympathy for these proposals, but it could not do anything about them because of its recent agreement with Crown Zellerbach regarding the Elwha rearing channel.

Thus, as the State of Washington considered whether to allow an oil port and pipeline to be built on the north side of the Olympic Peninsula, it was still perpetuating the problems caused by the area's first major industrial energy development seven decades before.

The Atmosphere They Breathed

SEVEN

AT THE BEND IN THE RIVER where you can first see the boiling white wall of the Salmon Cascades, the fish were meditative and still. Dancing waves of sunlight played along their backs, and dragonflies swooped above them in the shimmering spray as they held their position near the bottom. I watched for nearly fifteen minutes before one of them broke the trance, drifting slowly backward after its shadow, and then kicking forward past a boulder the size of a baby whale into the next pool.

There were three dozen salmon in this long, broken hole, which extended upriver to where the canyon walls began to narrow. They were chasing in pairs, rolling right under the surface and testing the emerald green current in short, powerful bursts. Those ready to continue their pilgrimage crossed to the south side of the river and ran in close to the sheer stone walls where foam was continually evanescing into black water. Here they held up again, and sometimes could be seen edging forward, waiting for the moment when they would lengthen like a wire under tension, and make their run at the wall.

The salmon were invisible for the next twenty yards until they leapt from the exploding upwell at the foot of the cascades. Silhouetted against the blinding torrent, they appeared cool gray with an iridescent pink stripe on their sides. Big males with the beginnings of a hooked jaw, more slender females and jacks as small as six inches long all took their turn, often jumping several at a time. Some leapt only a few feet before being overpowered by the charging water; others leapt more than a dozen feet in a high arc that spent their forward momentum too soon and were also swept back; still others leapt high and true, but off to one side or the other so that they struck the rock walls and sometimes lodged in the round, cauldron-shaped holes in the cliffs.

The fish that made it—and almost all would eventually make it—leapt a dozen feet or more into the pounding tumult at the heart of the cascades with their tails frantically beating the misty air in the classic flight of the coho salmon. Having gained this point, they drove to the left where a great quantity of water jumped and jostled in a violently precarious backwell. Now and again a fish would throw itself against the ten-foot-high waterfall immediately above, but more often they threaded their way back to the right into a trough between the two largest torrents. Many were hurled back here as well, disappearing with only a quick glimpse of tail or head showing through the foam like pictures of the damned.

Some, however, achieved a respite of sorts in a shallow basin at the head of the trough that constantly bubbled up at the center like an old-fashioned drinking fountain. Exhaustion showed plain in the countenances of these fish, some of which bobbed with their heads out of the water like human runners collapsed in agony at the end of a race. Another stretch of cascades remained, but the worst was over. The boulder-strewn rapids ahead were more river than waterfall, and after resting for a few minutes the fish pressed on, running from the cover of rock to rock with relative ease, until they finally reached the sandy pool where the successful salmon lolled nose down, like zeppelins about to land at Lakehurst.

These were the summer coho, *Oncorhynchus kisutch*, of the Soleduck River, and this was their special rite of passage. In order to spawn, they must run in fifty miles from the ocean on the first heavy rains of fall, and then climb the fifty yards of white water and falls that make up the cascades. Vision is crucial in making the climb (coho hardly ever jump at night), but the quality that guides them back to the spawning grounds that they left as fry four years before is their uncanny sense of smell. Adult salmon recall and follow the odor of their natal streams, their vegetation and aquatic residents, including other salmon (which they can distinguish by species and sex solely on the basis of smell). In the Soleduck, which drains a portion of the northwest corner of the Olympic Peninsula between the Elwha and the Queets, the smell that draws them over the cascades is the sulphur stink of Sol Duc Hot Springs six miles upstream.

Elsewhere in the North Pacific, hot springs play an important, albeit different role in the life of the coho. In Siberia and Kamchatka, for instance, coho habitually choose rivers with hot springs in them so the water won't freeze before they have had a chance to spawn. In the first published account of Georg Steller's discovery of the Pacific salmon, Stepan Krashnennikov recounted that "they [coho] swim upstream as far as possible toward the warm springs and remain there until far into autumn, and even until the middle of the winter. . . . I myself was near these springs [on the Kamchatka River] at the end of February, fishing for them." Thousands of years ago when the salmon recolonized the Olympic Peninsula in the wake of the retreating glaciers, it may have been these hot springs that first drew the coho to the Soleduck.

Today, the summer coho run past the surreal green and white algae growing around the mouths of the hot springs and on into a rugged valley covered with a silver forest of immense, fire-killed snags that stand above the old growth like guard hairs on a thick coat of fur. As fall progresses, elk come down these mountains to browse the salmonberry bushes along the braided, stream-sized channels where the summer coho are slowly ripening in pools protected by log jams or overhanging trees. Many salmon predators come as well, drawn by the sight of coho literally flying through the trees as they leap to loosen their eggs.

In addition to their jumping ability, which excels that of all other coho on the peninsula, the Soleduck summer coho were until recently recognized as the last stable wild coho run on the Washington coast. While wild coho runs along most of Washington, Oregon, California and British Columbia were declining by an estimated 50 percent over the last two decades, the Soleduck summer coho held steady with an annual spawning escapement of a little less than 2,000 fish a year. Because their spawning grounds lay within the protection of the Olympic National Park, and the Quileute Indian fishermen at the mouth of the river had long let them pass undisturbed, there seemed no reason why this one wild coho run could not continue to hold its own. Both the park and the tribe were, in fact, committed to this goal when the Washington Department of Fisheries unilaterally decided to kill the run for the sake of artificial production at its Soleduck hatchery.

The state's plan was to sacrifice the wild fish for hatchery production of summer coho. Director of Fisheries Gordon Sandison acknowledged that the number of wild coho spawning above the Salmon Cascades would decline "by as much as 50 percent" as a result of Fisheries' actions, but argued that the sacrifice was necessary to prevent an even greater calamity to the river's fall coho. In 1970, when the state's Soleduck hatchery went into operation, fall coho in the Quillayute system (which is formed by the Soleduck, Bogachiel, Calawah and Dickey rivers) numbered 13,700 and was one of the largest runs on the peninsula; eight years later this run had dropped to 3,600. During the same period, the total catch of hatchery and wild coho in the Quillayute fell to a third the average catch of wild fish alone before the hatchery was built.

Because of the Soleduck hatchery's inability to sustain a significant run of fall coho during these same years, the curtain of hatchery fish that has sometimes obscured the condition of the wild runs is absent on the Soleduck. Here one can see in stark outline the pattern that has been repeated to one degree or another wherever hatcheries have been built on the Pacific. "The history of fish culture for a long time was that you put in a hatchery, and the wild runs disappeared," said Harry Wagner of the Oregon Department of Fish and Game in 1979. Loyd Royal, long-time chairman of the International Pacific Salmon Fisheries Commission, added, "It has to do with the basic biology of the situation, and how the resource is managed. . . . The faster you build hatcheries, the faster the wild runs will disappear."

By the mid-1970s the crying need of the wild fall coho was for hatchery propagation of the fish to be suspended, but with $465,000 already appropriated by the legislature for hatchery expansion on the Soleduck, the Department of Fisheries was not interested in schemes to reduce the hatchery operations. The department needed a way to take some of the pressure off the wild fall coho, while at the same time expanding total hatchery production of coho in the river. Shifting hatchery efforts to the summer coho of the Soleduck was the approach adopted by the state, and so in 1977 Fisheries announced a plan to build a new satellite hatchery for summer coho, Bear Springs II, in addition to increasing production of the fish at the main Soleduck facility. Fisheries confidently promised 26,000 additional coho for Washington fishermen as a result of Bear Springs II.

Similar promises had been made for the Soleduck hatchery itself. Built at a cost of $3 million, the Soleduck station is one of the state's newest and best-equipped "full-service" hatcheries, featuring twelve concrete ponds and nearly ideal 46-degree spring water for incubation and rearing. It has been responsible for an increase in the spring Chinook runs in the Quillayute, and produced two extremely strong returns of coho before the bottom fell out in 1975. Tagging studies have shown that a higher percentage of Soleduck hatchery spring Chinook are caught by Washington coastal fishermen than the small wild Quillayute spring Chinook run, which contributes most heavily to the Alaska fishery.

At the same time, the record of the Soleduck hatchery gives a clear picture of how modern hatchery practices routinely cause serious problems for wild salmon. The relatively successful spring Chinook stock used at Soleduck, for instance, may have aggravated problems with an incurable bacterial kidney disease in the Quillayute system. This race of spring Chinook, which is a cross between Cowlitz and Umpqua river fish, was known to be heavily infected with the disease before the transfer to the Soleduck was made, but the state was more concerned with producing fish that would not be caught by Canadian fishermen. "We wanted to create a run that would turn left, instead of right, when it got to the ocean," the head of the state's hatchery system explained. This did not occur, but the disease remained, infecting nearly 100 percent of some lots.

Bacterial kidney disease, commonly known as BKD, is caused by one or more strains of bacteria that attack the kidney, liver, spleen and heart of salmon, producing blisters and pus-filled lesions. As the disease advances, the kidney breaks down and the body cavity becomes distended with fluid. BKD has claimed as much as 30 percent of some lots at Soleduck before release, but the total death count is undoubtedly higher. Many pathologists believe that the disease takes its greatest toll when the fish migrate from fresh to salt water, and their kidneys must make the high-stress transition to life in a different medium. Later, BKD can kill adult salmon (like the Cowlitz spring Chinook) before they have a chance to spawn.

Between 1972 and 1977, Fisheries planted BKD-infected fish from the Soleduck hatchery in a dozen Olympic Peninsula rivers. No examination was made to see if the wild salmon in the rivers had been exposed to the disease, but in a number of cases the department "suspected that BKD was present in stocks released from the Dungeness hatchery in the 1950s," according to a department document. Most of the Cowlitz-Umpqua plants in rivers like the Clallam, Pysht, Sekiu and Dosewallips were made in a way that encouraged interbreeding between hatchery and wild fish, and therefore encouraged the spread of the disease, since BKD is believed to be transmitted from the mother to her eggs. (There is also considerable evidence that the disease can be transmitted or encouraged by the feed that is given hatchery fish, according to the Department of Fisheries.)

In 1978, the Soleduck hatchery experienced its first outbreak of BKD in summer coho, following tagging for migration studies. The disease had never been observed in wild Soleduck summer coho, but once again the department chose to release the fish. One group, which had not been tagged and apparently carried the disease in a dormant state, was released on June 15 inside the Olympic National Park in defiance of Park Superintendent James Coleman's orders and violation of federal law. During the ensuing flap over jurisdiction, the state revealed that the 150,000 summer coho released above the Salmon Cascades had suffered from an outbreak of another common hatchery malady, cold water disease, which occurs in both coho and Chinook stocks at the Soleduck hatchery.

Spokesmen for the Department of Fisheries apologized for violating the park's orders, but defended the plants as an environmentally responsible action. They maintained that the fish had been successfully treated for cold water disease and "were considered in good condition when they were released." The state also downplayed the significance of the presumably dormant BKD in the fish. Fisheries' head pathologist, James Wood, pointed out some recent successes with moist pellet feed and experimental drugs, which proved particularly effective on a batch of BKD infected fish transferred from the state's Skagit hatchery to the Nisqually Tribe. Noting that there was no visible indication that the summer coho had the disease when they left the Soleduck hatchery, Wood went on to speculate that

BKD existed in wild Quillayute salmon before the state brought in the Cowlitz-Umpqua fish. "This plant will have no impact on the wild stocks whatsoever," he said. "And if it could harm people, we'd know about it by now, because a lot of them have been eaten."

Not all parties accepted the Department of Fisheries' judgment in this regard. The same year the department made its illegal plant of summer coho inside the Olympic National Park, another group of fish from the Soleduck hatchery suffered a severe outbreak of BKD after they had been passed as fit for planting and transferred to a Quinault Tribal hatchery. Concerned about spreading the disease, tribal biologists had the Cowlitz-Umpqua spring Chinook tested by the U.S. Fish and Wildlife Service. The results, which constituted one of the first independent tests for disease in Department of Fisheries hatchery fish, found that 88 percent of the fish from the Soleduck hatchery were infected with BKD. When subsequent tests determined that the disease did not occur in wild Queets spring Chinook, the Fish and Wildlife Service recommended that the fish be destroyed. Before the summer was out, the Quinault Tribe had buried more than half a million of the state's hatchery fish.

Besides questions of health, hatchery salmon can affect wild salmon through direct competition. Research has repeatedly shown that when large numbers of hatchery fish are pumped into a stream they displace their fitter, but less numerous wild cousins. In work at the University of Washington research station at Big Beef Creek on Hood Canal, Brian Allee found:

> When fish which were reared under hatchery conditions were planted where naturally reared fish were prior residents, the hatchery fish appeared to crowd out the wild fish. It seems likely that the lack of dispersion or emigration on the part of hatchery reared fish was a primary reason for their greater contribution to the final resident population. This behavior resulted in relatively higher population densities than wild fish, which presumably had based spacial requirements upon food availability, [could tolerate] . . . Hatchery fish as a result showed poorer growth.

The relatively poor ability of hatchery fish to capture (or even recognize) food is one of the major behavioral differences between hatchery and wild salmon attributed to environment and its effect on the learned behavior of the fish. In the hatchery, the life of the salmon is likely to begin on the screening of heath trays, followed by fiber-glass holding tanks, rearing ponds and a tank truck; water flow is stable, cover nonexistent, and pelletized food is thrown out to them by the handful from a bucket at one end of the pond. Experiments with both Pacific and Atlantic salmon have shown that the hatchery environment very quickly establishes behavior patterns much different from those of wild fish of the same age, including a pack tendency and heightened aggression.

On the Qualicum River of Vancouver Island, hatchery coho have been observed to drive off native cutthroat trout, apparently because their deportment was incomprehensible to the wild fish. "Socially, hatchery fish are somewhat deprived from full utilization of their evolved signals of communication," observed Gordon Glova of the British Columbia Department of Fisheries and Environment. Unable to confront the hatchery coho on a one-to-one basis because of their pack behavior, and unable to evoke the appropriate response to a fish of their size with their standard signals, "the larger trout abandoned their stable territory in pools, and became somewhat nomadic, with reduced feeding opportunities." Glova found that within a few weeks 40 percent of the wild fish were gone from the system.

Once in a stream, hatchery fish often residualize, or remain in fresh water for as long as a year. Large scale residualization of hatchery fish has been observed on the Cowlitz, Kalama, Queets, Toutle, Lewis and Elk rivers in recent years, and is suspected to occur to one degree or another in every river where a hatchery is currently in operation, especially when fish are planted as fry. According to Loyd Royal, "residualized fish become competitive with wild fish populations, hence any survival is probably deductible from that of the wild population. . . . The evidence is clear that such a practice can be detrimental to . . . the wild population of all species involved."

All species can be affected because of the young fishes' habit of feeding on the same nymphs and larvae. R. C. Johnson of the Washington Department of Fisheries found in the early 1970s that success of chum and pink salmon returns was inversely related to hatchery coho production in Puget Sound, and plants of coho, which occupy the dominant position in the pool feeding order, have also been shown to diminish the survival of wild steelhead. On the Soleduck, therefore, Fisheries' planting of summer coho above the Salmon Cascades could be expected to harm the wild Soleduck steelhead, which are the last strong segment of the wild steelhead runs that once made the Quillayute the most famous steelhead river on the peninsula.

When imported stocks are used for hatchery propagation, as is the case with the Cowlitz-Umpqua fish at Soleduck, more difficulties arise. Like Charles Darwin's Galapagos finches, different runs of wild salmon have evolved a host of specific adaptations to the individual characteristics of the rivers in which they live. The common interbreeding between hatchery and wild fish in the wilds can dilute or destroy these genetic traits and produce fish that cannot survive as well as their predecessors. A number of studies in Canada and the United States have shown that hatchery fish spawning in the wilds produce fewer progeny than the truly wild fish in the same stream, and Royal has suggested that the heavy planting of Chambers Creek steelhead by the Washington Department of Game has shifted the run timing of wild steelhead to less productive periods.

Recent work at the University of Washington's Big Beef Creek station has also raised some interesting questions about hatcheries and the loss of genetic diversity in salmon stocks. Steven Schroder found when working with Big Beef Creek chum salmon that subordinate chum males normally fertilize 30 percent of wild chum eggs, even though the dominant male proved capable of fertilizing all of the eggs if the other males were not present. This supports the general view that the vitality of wild salmon depends, at least in part, on a wide genetic mix within each individual run. Hatcheries commonly follow the opposite practice, fertilizing the eggs of many females with one male's sperm. This may explain why some stocks of fish "wear out" after a number of years of artificial propagation.

Judging by recent developments in the older and more advanced field of agronomy, the genetic homogeneity that widespread planting of hatchery fish tends to produce may be the most pernicious long-term effect of the artificial propagation of salmon. Reflecting on the problems that have been increasingly associated with monocrop development, *California Agriculture* noted recently: "It is now recognized that the narrow base of our highly selected crop plants make them dangerously vulnerable to disease and pests. Genetic engineering is still in its infancy. We must not yet abandon basic genetic resources, particularly . . . wild species and primitive varieties of plants that carry the genes for traits we may desperately need in the future."

Fisheries biologists like Cornelius Groot of the Canadian research station at Nanaimo argue that genetic diversity is particularly important for salmon because of the inherent nature of their migratory existence. "You see, one difference with agriculture is that you have some control over the plot in which you sow the grain. We [in salmon culture] still have to make use of a partially natural environment . . . over which we have no control, and which is constantly changing. Because of that, we need to [maintain] the variety and range of genetic material." While the genetic effects of hatchery plants may not be recognized for some time, the potential for immediate impact through competition with wild fish is vividly illustrated in a recent study on the Madison River in Montana. There wild trout populations increased 180 percent after the release of hatchery fish was discontinued.

Still other studies have demonstrated that significant differences in size and strength exist between hatchery and wild salmon, but this measurement is best made with a rod and reel just after a steelhead has taken your lure. A cousin of the Atlantic salmon, the steelhead or anadromous rainbow trout, *Salmo gairdneri*, has a reputation as a ferocious fighter. Early explorers in Kamchatka reported seeing steelhead catch and eat swimming rats. Although heavier boned than the true Pacific salmon, the steelhead is said to be agile enough to pluck berries off overhanging bushes with its leaps. Steelhead are the rarest of the peninsula's salmonids, and wild steelhead are even rarer, making up less than a quarter of the total steelhead run on hatchery rivers like the Bogachiel.

I have seen the wild steelhead of the Soleduck move like liquid electricity on their spawning grounds, and fished for them on the lower of the river's mythic seven drifts, but the wild steelhead I remember best is the first one I caught on the Skagit River. In many ways it was the perfect steelhead trip. Up a little after 4 A.M. that day in late December, I found the bedroom window spattered with recent rain. Driving south toward the Skagit, the only signs of life in the night landscape were the well-lit milking parlors with their long lines of stolid Holsteins. My destination was the town of Darrington, where I was to join my companions for the final drive to our launching point above Rockport. Among the five of us, we represented just about every possible grade of steelheader: Roy and Eddie were professionals who fished the river almost every day it was open as guides and boatmen for recreational fishermen; Harold was a lifelong steelheader who in his eighties had recovered from excruciatingly painful bursitis attacks to stand in the cold water and fish again; Don, a publishing executive in his fifties, was a one- or two-trip a year fisherman; and last as well as least, I was a novice on my first trip ever.

We all had a cup of coffee at an early-morning restaurant, then headed up the valley as the first light of dawn flushed the snowy peaks that surround the Skagit and its major tributaries, the Baker, Sauk and Suiattle rivers. Pulling into the boat launch above Rockport around 7 A.M., we counted sixteen trucks and empty boat trailers ahead of us. Roy's flat-bottomed boat offered the comforts of a charcoal stove and several flasks, but the ride upriver soon proved chill. Reclining on the indoor/outdoor carpeting on the bottom of the boat, I asked Harold how to catch steelhead. "You'll need this," he said, handing me a rod and reel. Next he opened his tackle box, which looked like a confectionery of fluorescent orange berries, vivid green spinners, licoricelike slugs of lead and barbed hooks. Choosing an item or two, he set the box aside and rigged my line. Noting the steam boiling off the river in various places as he worked, Harold commented, "Nice and cold out here. This line will freeze up if you don't watch it." The remedy, Harold said, was to dip the tip of the rod into the water between casts.

At the head of a long glide where a bald eagle perched in the crown of a 100-foot-tall cottonwood, Roy cut the engine and let us drift. Dispersing to the four corners of the boat, we cast our lead-weighted lures out across the characteristically green water of the Skagit. The idea, I soon learned, was to bounce the lead along the bottom so that the lure seemed to swim a foot or so off the riverbed. There was a constant danger of hanging up on a snag or boulder, but it could not be avoided since the fish like to lie on the bottom behind obstructions. "Got to hit the steely on the head with it," called Don from the bow. "If you're not on the bottom, you're not fishing," drawled Roy. The eagle watched us pass without comment, but an antsy flock of goldeneyes scattered before us, only to circle back in behind when we were past.

Harold caught the first fish a little after nine on a glide full of big submerged boulders just below where a plunging tributary joined the river. The fish showed in front of the boat almost as soon as she was hooked, a burgundy and silver shadow that hesitated for a moment, drifting on the current, and then tore at the hook in its jaw like a poodle into tissue paper. "Six-pound female," Roy said, reaching for the landing net. Harold brought the fish in on the next pass and threw it bouncing on the bottom of the boat. Cutting her open, we found her egg skeins had already broken, even though she had not yet begun to dig a redd. Eddie struck next, hooking a five-pound male that rolled in the leader and put up even less of a fight than Harold's fish. Both of these were produced at the Department of Game's Skagit hatchery by the look of their dorsal fins, which are badly chewed in fish that have been held together in high numbers.

Running back upriver, we started our drift again at the head of the glide where Harold had his strike. I cast fifty feet or so out into a nest of big boulders, and then noticed that I had failed to brake the reel correctly with my thumb, causing it to resemble an accident in a spun glass factory. I was deep into the task of unraveling the mess when Roy hollered, "Look at your pole, man," and whipped the tip straight up into the air. This set the hook in the mouth of the steelhead I hadn't even noticed on my line, and ignited the sea-run rainbow's first dash. Since the knot on my reel prevented me from giving out any line, I stumbled after it the length of the boat while my companions scattered like chickens. Seconds later, the fish turned back in a rush, heading straight for me. I picked up line until it passed under us on the right. "Put your rod in the water," Roy advised, shoving the tip in as far as the third joint to prevent the line from fouling on the bottom of the boat while I gave back all the line I had gained.

On the rocketing return across the head of the glide we caught our first glimpse of the fish when a flash of silver about thirty feet from the boat announced the beginning of the next run. This time, however, I was able to play her across the bow of the boat and draw her slowly up and in. "Don't want to hurry that fish," Roy said with growing pleasure. "That's a nice one there," Harold added. "It might run a dozen pounds." After the next pass the fish drifted with the slackening line close to the boat, and I saw I had a large, cleanly minted steelhead on my line. She made two more runs up the glide, one of which was punctuated by a furious leap, but on the third drift back we netted her. "Twelve pounds, Harold," Roy said after he weighed her on his hand scale, adding, "*that* is a wild steelhead."

EIGHT

IN THE BEGINNING, what is now the Washington coast was known with simple dread by its navigational coordinate, 47 degrees north latitude. It was here on one of the craggiest, most unprotected portions of the North Pacific rim that the Spanish galetta *Sonora* sent a well-armed landing party ashore for fresh water on the morning of July 14, 1775, and lost them all before they could drag their longboat out of the surf.

While the ship's commander, Don Juan Francisco de la Bodega y Quadra, watched with horror through the glass, a wave of Indian warriors rushed out of the forest and overpowered the Spaniards in bitter hand-to-hand fighting on the beach. Subsequent European explorers along the Northwest coast avoided the area until 1787 when the *Imperial Eagle*, an English trading vessel flying the Austrian flag, lost a longboat and crew in a similar manner near the mouth of a river at 47 degrees, 43 minutes north latitude.

The following year, Captain John Meares of the English merchantman *Felice* was offered the severed hands of some of the dead crew of the *Imperial Eagle* while trading with Indians 150 miles away on the west side of Vancouver Island. Although successful in obtaining sea otter pelts for the rich China trade, Meares became increasingly apprehensive about the Indians as he sailed south from Nootka Sound toward the 47th parallel. His fears were borne out on July 15, when a longboat from the *Felice* was attacked while cruising the coast near the mouth of the recently discovered Strait of Juan de Fuca. As Meares described the ensuing scene:

> The Indians behaved with a spirit and resolution that resisted the usual terror of fire arms among primitive people; for the contest was close, and for some time our men fought for their lives. One of them had been singled out by an individual savage for his victim, and a fierce engagement took place between them. The native was armed with a stone bludgeon, and the sailor with a cutlass. They both manifested, for some time, equal courage and dexterity; but if an intervening oar had not broke a blow, armed with all the force of his enemy, our brave countryman must have sunk beneath it. It, however, failed of its object, and gave him an opportunity, by a severe stroke of the cutlass, to deprive the native of an arm. [The Indian], notwithstanding such a loss, contrived to swim from the boat, indebted for his life to the noble mercy of his conquerer, who disdained to kill him in the water.

Farther south, Meares stood out to sea, but unfavorable winds carried him close enough to the coast to catch a glimpse of the island fortress that served as the central stronghold of the Quileute, the most consistently hostile of the tribes that inhabited the area around 47 degrees north latitude. An isolated group of Chimakuan among Salish and Nootkan tribes, the Quileute occupied some of the richest village sites on the coast. Apparently never numerous, these survivors of an older order held their territory by dint of individual ferocity and the natural ease with which the islands at the mouth of the Quillayute River could be defended. While many tribes (including the powerful Haida of the Queen Charlotte Islands) welcomed the Europeans for their trade iron, copper, cloth and beads, the Quileute wanted no foreign intrusion, white or otherwise.

They and the band called the Hoh could have been involved in the battle with the *Sonora*, and almost certainly were responsible for the severed hands of the crew of the *Imperial Eagle*. Although one captain, American Robert Gray of the *Columbia*, traded with them at sea in 1793, no white attempted to set foot in the realm of the Quileute again until 1808, when the Russian brig *Saint Nicholas* went aground near Destruction Island. According to the journal of Timothy Tarakanof, purser aboard the *Saint Nicholas*, the Quileute attacked within minutes of the twenty-one Russians' coming ashore. Over the next week, the Indians chased the Russians south along the coast to the mouth of the Hoh River, skirmishing all the way. At the village of the Hoh, the Indians sullenly agreed to ferry the whites across the river, but as Tarakanof recounted, ". . . when the larger boat reached the middle of the river . . . the savages . . . pulled out a stopper which had been stuck in the bottom of the boat, threw themselves in the water [with their paddles] and swam for shore."

With one member of their party killed and the captain's wife taken prisoner as a result of the Indians' canoe stratagem, the Russians retreated up the Hoh in the first winter rains of 1808. "The ninth, tenth and eleventh days came and went with the rain pouring down incessantly," wrote Tarakanof. "Not knowing whither we went, we wandered in the forest and on the mountain, endeavoring only to be hidden from the natives." Near starvation, the sailors under Captain Sturman Buligan finally appropriated an upriver Indian band's winter camp, complete with its store of dried salmon, salmon eggs and seal oil. This sustained them until the next spring, when they retraced their steps and surrendered to the Quileute on the advice of Mistress Buligan, who refused to rejoin her husband after a comfortable winter in captivity with the Quileute. Three years later, thirteen survivors of the *Saint Nicholas* were ransomed by the American brig *Lydia* for a bolt of cloth, locksmith saw, mirror, knife and a measure of black powder and lead shot per prisoner.

The Quileute were then acknowledged by all as the masters of nearly 1,000 square miles of the Olympic Peninsula, including the Quillayute, Soleduck, Bogachiel, Calawah, Dickey and Hoh rivers. They hunted whales, seals and sea otter along the rocky Pacific coast, and from their extensive river systems they took great numbers of all species of salmon. The prairies between the Bogachiel, Soleduck and Calawah rivers provided the bulbs of the beautiful flowering camas and tiger lily, as well as herds of elk and deer that came to browse, and from the formidable forest came salmonberries, crab apples, and the cedar logs for long houses, canoes and carvings. They measured time by the succession of natural provender ("beginning of steelhead spawning" was January, "the time for getting salal berries" was July), and within that cycle they were generally self-sufficient.

Reflecting on the cycle of their lives, the Indians of the Northwest coast produced a series of paradoxes to explain the visible world, and man's place in it. Many tribes like the Quinault told the story called "The Boy Who Went to the Salmon Country," which described how a member of the tribe was carried to an underseas world where the roles of salmon and man were reversed, and he himself was a salmon. The boy was told by his salmon family to go and kill some humans for dinner. When he had done this, the boy was shown the correct way to return human bones to the water so that the people could revive and come back to life after death. The knowledge of this was the key to the perpetuation of the salmon, and when the Indian boy finally returned to the village, many adventures later, he brought with him tremendous numbers of fish and was thereafter known as the Salmon Bringer.

The central lesson of this mirror world, with its emphasis on proper human action as the key to the salmon's abundance, is further elaborated in a tale recounted by Philip Drucker in *Cultures of the North Pacific Coast:* "The salmon dwelt in a huge house, similar to those of the Indians, far under the sea. In their home, the salmon went about in human form. When the time came for the annual runs, they put on their salmon skins and converted themselves into the fish that were the staple of the area. The run was thus conceived to be a voluntary sacrifice for the benefit of mankind. . . ." To complete the metaphysical connection between man and salmon, many Northwest Indians thought of themselves as fish. Coho, chum and Chinook salmon were, for instance, all family crests of the Tlingit tribe's Raven clan, along with the hawk, puffin, starfish, moose, mouse, martin, whale, frog and wood worm.

Transformation between outward forms was the greatest manifestation of spiritual power, or *tamanaos*, to many Indians, and so it is not surprising that they turned their famous artistic powers to the portrayal of this moment. One mask carved by the Bella Coola Tribe of British Columbia illustrates the relationship between salmon and man with striking design and craftsmanship. The outer part of the mask is wrought of four pieces of alder and portrays an immense, almost jowly Chinook salmon with a band of copper (the most valuable substance to the Indians) for eyebrows, a spotted forehead and four rays with salmon carved in profile projecting out all around. Inside, and hidden, is a wondrous human face that seems about to speak; this is the Salmon Bringer. Made to be worn at the winter dances, this mask served as a sort of living text to reenact the legends it represented. Edward Malin described the dance's climax in *A World of Faces:* "By releasing all the strings except the top [and pulling on that one], he [the dancer] was able to thrust open all the parts of the mask with an explosive vigor, revealing the face of the Salmon Bringer. In the semi-darkness of the firelight with its muted flames and dancing shadows, this must have been a spectacle to remember!"

For many tribes, the most important ritual of the year was the first salmon ceremony. When the first salmon of the run was caught by tribes like the Quinault it was carried head first into the fisherman's house and butchered with a mussel-shell knife. The heart was later burned, so that dogs would not eat it, and the bones were scrupulously returned to the river. Although it varied considerably across its range from Siberia to what is now Southern California, the first salmon ceremony seems to have always embodied the basic ethical connection between man's actions and the abundance of the salmon. In the north, where it was elaborated and elevated (the Kwakiutl Tribe of Vancouver Island had three separate ceremonies and a collection of arcane proscriptions, one of which forbade the eating of coho eyes after dark), the ceremony achieved a liturgical clarity that gives a glimpse of what the fish looked like to their foresworn brothers. The first salmon ceremony of the Tsimshian Tribe of Southeast Alaska contains a recitation of ceremonial names: "Quartz Nose, Two Gills on Back, Lightning Following One After Another, Three Jumps. . . ."

It was "the time of heavy salmon spawning" when the Quileute first heard of the white man's desire for peace. The Russians and Spaniards their fathers had fought were gone, and so too were the English. Only the Americans grew. Now these people, with whom the Quileute had had brief but comparatively amicable relations, wanted a treaty of peace. The Quileute sent no representatives to the Treaty Council of the Chehalis convened by the Americans in February 1855, but several months later they did meet with U.S. Indian Agent Michael Troutman Simmons somewhere on the coast. Illiterate Big Mike Simmons, an early Puget Sound settler, conveyed the general terms that had already been agreed to by the Nisqually, Puyallup, Duwamish, Muckleshoot, Yakima, Shoshone, Nez Perce, Walla Walla and Umatilla tribes.

Through a translator, Simmons proposed the ceding of nearly all Quileute land to the United States in return for certain privileges and payments. If they accepted the treaty, the Quileute would receive the promise of peace from the United States, a reservation "sufficient for their wants" to the south in what was then the territory of the Quinault, $25,000 in cash payments over a twenty-year period, a school, blacksmith and carpentry shop, and the "right of taking fish at all usual and accustomed grounds and stations . . . in common with all citizens of the territory." There was an implied threat of war in all that talk of peace, but Simmons was at pains to give the Quileute the impression that these were not the terms of defeat. He pointed out that the proposed settlement was larger than many that had been accepted elsewhere, and purposely downplayed any unpleasant implications in the text on the orders of Isaac Stevens, the first territorial governor of Washington and chief treaty negotiator for the United States.

At the Treaty Council of Point No Point, Stevens himself struck the note of paternal reassurance that was characteristic of the American approach during the treaty negotiation period. Asked by Indians if the treaty would restrict their fishing for salmon, Stevens proclaimed: "Are you not my children and also the children of the Great Father? What will I not do for my children, and what will you not do for yours? Would you not die for them? This paper [the treaty] is such as a man would give to his children, and I will tell you . . . this paper secures your fish. Does not a father give food to his children?" Initially, most of the Indians believed the effusive little man with the pipe stuck in the band of his tall black felt hat, but before summer, tribes such as the Nisqually were in open clamor over the now apparent intent of the government to move them from their homes and fishing grounds along the river to the infertile hillsides above, where they were being encouraged to practice agriculture. When Stevens broke his promise to the Yakima by opening their land for white settlement in July 1855, a brush war between Indians and whites burned like a fast fuse over Stampede Pass into Puget Sound, and ignited the Northwest Indian War.

How-yaks, the chief appointed by Simmons to speak for the Quileute, undoubtedly knew of the early Indian victories on the Yakima and Puyallup rivers in the fall of 1855, but like most of his people, he was intensely local in outlook. The problems of distant tribes in no way friendly to the Quileute did not concern him as much as the changes he saw taking place around him at home. He knew that the people in the Quileute villages were richer than ever before in ceremonial titles, coppers, slaves and the like, and he also knew that the reason was that there were fewer and fewer people. The white man's diseases had cut the number of Quileute warriors in half since the first battles with the Spaniards, and now the tribe could see the sails of many tall ships running off the coast. If the white man's peace would protect the Quileute's way of life, as Simmons said, then it was good, and How-yaks said he would sign the treaty and make the journey to Olympia to do so.

It is characteristic of the Northwest Indian War that one of the most feared warrior bands in the territory signed a treaty of peace with the United States on the same day that hostile Indian forces, fighting against the constraints of almost identical treaties, made their biggest military showing. While Nisqually, Puyallup and Muckleshoot warriors, said to be following Leschi, slipped across Lake Washington in canoes to attack the sloop-of-war *Decatur* at Seattle on January 25, 1856, How-yaks was sixty miles away in Olympia being entertained by Governor Stevens. Later, he and representatives of the Quinaults signed the Treaty of Olympia, which ended the insurgents' chance for an alliance with the coastal tribes and more than offset the temporary psychological advantage they gained in their raid on Seattle.

Within six months, the difficulties of waging an extended guerrilla war had all but crushed the Indian rebellion in western Washington. The Nisqually and Puyallup were led onto the now somewhat larger reservations, and their leaders executed, Leschi on the gallows, and his brother Quiemuth shot in his sleep while being held prisoner in Governor Stevens' own office. The Quileute must also have heard about these developments far away on the other side of the Olympic Mountains, but their own lives were unchanged, as How-yaks had promised. They ruled the Quillayute and Hoh country, and no one said otherwise until a decade later when coastal Indian Superintendent C. H. Hale reported to Washington, D.C.:

> In no other portion of the constituency has there been any manifestation of hostility, except with the band of the Quileute Indians living north of the Quinault Agency and included as parties to the Treaty of Olympia. Nearly a year ago three Indians of this tribe murdered a white man near the Strait of Juan de Fuca. In the discharge of my duty, I . . . demand[ed] the murderers. . . . The tribe refused to accede to the demand, and made threats of attack upon the Agency and the destruction of Government property. . . . These Indians . . . know but little of the whites and suppose they can easily set at defiance the authority of the government. . . . It is believed that no white man has ever been permitted to visit their village and its locality is only approximately known.

Two years later, Makah guides and informants led a detachment of U.S. Army regulars into La Push, where a dozen Indians were arrested for a variety of offenses ranging from selling slaves to the alleged murder of another white man several years before. One of those arrested for murder was the powerful shaman and subchief known to the whites as Doctor Obi. After languishing in the brig at Fort Steilacoom for several months and observing that there was "nothing to hope for but death at the hands of a jury here" (as a member of the U.S. Indian Service noted at the time), Doctor Obi escaped from prison and made the 200-mile journey back to La Push. Although charges against him were effectively dropped when the Indian Service refused to undertake his recapture, Doctor Obi appears from this point on to have been an implacable enemy of the whites.

He shot their cattle, and when secrecy permitted, he shot them too. He tore down fences, so that Indian animals could get into white gardens, and also worked his mischief in reverse, so that the Indians would have cause for grievance. Every act of defiance enhanced his power until, in middle age, he was the most feared medicine man among the Quileute. The inevitable clash between Doctor Obi and coalescing white authority came in 1882, when white settler Dan Pullen laid claim to the actual village site of La Push. As Pullen began to evict the Indians and force them to move down onto the beach, the shaman went into a rage and attacked the white at the door of his own house with a club, screaming that he was going to kill him. Once again the government sent an expedition to La Push to apprehend Doctor Obi, who was taken to Neah Bay to answer to the petition from the thirty-two white residents of the Quillayute valley asking for his removal from the territory as a perpetual troublemaker.

Startled into action by the unexpected rise of Doctor Obi, the Indian Service decided that poor past surveillance of the Quileute could be corrected if a government station was established at La Push. Since the Quileute had always refused to send their children to the existing boarding school at Neah Bay, the government determined to open a school at La Push, and hired Alanson Wesley Smith to serve as combined schoolteacher and agent. Smith, a Methodist, arrived in the fall of 1883 bent on redeeming the Indians through the "adoption of all the culture traits which his life as a Dakota Territory farm boy, the son of a school teacher and ardent Salvation Army leader, had taught him," as George Pettitt wrote in *The Quileute of La Push.* He wanted to remake his charges, and set about it on the first day of school when he renamed virtually everyone in the village, producing the strange collection of historical, biblical and heavily Anglicized Indian names that has characterized the tribe since: Henry Hudson, Robert E. Lee, Leven P. Coe, Buckety Mason and Hoh Joe Cole.

Smith's closest friend in the area was Dan Pullen, who later married his sister, Harriet Smith. On Pullen's suggestion, the newcomer filed claims on the land immediately south of the village along the coast in his wife's name, a section of rich river bottom land just east of the village in his brother's name, along with another nearby parcel for himself. Indian resentment against these land claims and Smith's practice of whipping delinquent children in school was great enough to force the teacher to carry a gun at one point, but even without Doctor Obi, the Quileute could see that the most immediate threat to their existence was Dan Pullen's claim to the site of the actual village. "We can never have peace among the Indians there until he [Pullen] is removed," Indian Agent W. L. Powell wrote to the commissioner of Indian affairs in 1885. "It is a wonder to me that they have not killed this man, and if all I hear about him is true, I think they would be justified in doing so. . . . I have a delegation of some 20 Indians here, who have many complaints to make of their treatment."

The problem was that Pullen claimed a legal right to the site of La Push by way of the Treaty of Olympia. This "paper," it was now explained to the Indians, extinguished the tribe's claim to the Quillayute and Hoh valleys. The tribe was supposed to move to the reservation at Quinault, and the fact that it had not done so in no way gave its members legal title to their ancestral homes. The situation was confused, however, by the fact that the government had never made the payments to the Quileute promised in the treaty, and had to some degree recognized the legitimacy of the Indians' claim to La Push by establishing the government school there. Relations between Indians and whites continued to deteriorate until the Indian Service, which was still unwilling to undertake the forced removal of the Quileute, finally persuaded Congress to create a small, one-square-mile reservation for the tribe at La Push in 1889.

The new reservation was greeted with favor among the Indians until it was discovered that the order signed by President Benjamin Harrison contained the following stipulation: "provided: that this withdrawal shall not affect any existing valid property right of any party." Pullen, who built an austere Victorian mansion overlooking the ocean, declared that the "prior right" clause gave him clear title to La Push and stepped up his efforts to force the Indians out, with the tacit approval of Smith. That fall, while most of the Quileute were in the Puget Sound area picking hops, Pullen set fire to the Indian longhouses, and burned them to the ground. When the Quileute returned to La Push, they found their homes had been leveled, planted in new grass, and fenced with barbed wire.

Unarmed, and without provisions of dried salmon, the Quileute chose not to fight. After the initial confrontation, during which Pullen threatened to shoot any Indian who tried to reclaim the village, the tribe quietly moved into improvised quarters on the beach for the winter. There were those among the Quileute who called for vengeance, but sometime between Dan Pullen's burning of La Push and the U.S. Army's massacre of the last independent Sioux near Wounded Knee, South Dakota, three months later, the last will to fight left the body of the Indian people. They were beaten, and thereafter they had to struggle simply to stay alive. Everywhere in the West, the traditions, beliefs, art and accumulated wisdom of the native Americans were disappearing like dew from the grass on a hot day, and so was the world that made them.

This was not coincidence, of course, for many of the immense changes brought about by white society in the land now known as the United States and Canada were performed as acts of war against the Indians. In the early days of the United States when the western frontier was Kentucky, American efforts to force the Indians out centered on the appropriation or destruction of the game necessary for the Indians' survival. Writing of Davy Crockett, the legendary frontiersman who served two terms in Congress in the 1820s, Vernon Louis Parrington noted: "His 105 bears in a single season, his six deer shot in one day while pursuing other game—two of which were left hanging in the woods—serve to explain why the rich hunting grounds of the Indians were swept so quickly bare of game by the white invaders. Davy was but one of thousands who were wasting the resources of the Inland Empire, destroying forests, skinning the land, slaughtering the deer and bear, the swarms of pigeon and turkey, the vast buffalo herds. Davy the politician was a huge western joke, but Davy the wastrel was a hard, unloving fact."

Farther west, along the Red River of Texas and Oklahoma, the North Platte River of Nebraska and Colorado, the Missouri River of the Dakotas and the Yellowstone River of Wyoming and Montana, the Americans and their national government carried the policy of resource wastage to an unprecedented level in the virtual extermination of the American buffalo. At the beginning of the nineteenth century there were an estimated 60 million bison in North America; 100 years later there were 35,000 left in the two surviving herds. The Indian tribes that depended on the buffalo for food and almost every other item in their lives were told by the United States government that they would be fed if they went to the newly established reservations, and then were denied the promised food when they complied. "I am expected to see that Indians behave properly whom the government is starving—and not only that, starving in flagrant violation of the agreement," Major Raland MacKensie, commander at Fort Sill on the Red River, wrote to his superior General Philip Sheridan in 1877. Sheridan, however, had no sympathy for either the buffalo or the Indian. "Let them kill, skin and sell until the buffalo is exterminated, as it is the only way to bring lasting peace and allow civilization to advance," said the man who also coined the phrase, "the only good Indian is a dead Indian."

The Quileute first felt the pinch of white pressure on their livelihood with the passing of the sea otter in the 1880s. Once the Indians' most valuable trade item with the whites (Meriwether Lewis called their lush, silver-tipped pelage "the most delicious fur in the world"), these small sea mammals were hunted to extinction along the Washington coast by white marksmen. These pelt hunters fired marked bullets at the animals from towers built on the shore, hoping that the surf would wash the carcass ashore. The next marine resource taken from the Quileute were the California gray whales that ran along the coast during their pelagic migrations. The Quileute had traditionally harpooned a score of whales every year from their sleek, ocean-going canoes, but after fifty years' predation by Yankee whaling fleets (which followed the California grays along their entire range from the lagoons of Baja California to the iceberg-strewn Sea of Okhotsk) the whales had all but disappeared. The Quileute killed their last whale in 1904. Sealing showed a similar pattern. The Quileute took 8,000 fur seals in 1881, but were soon unable to compete with the aggressive, rifle-armed white sealers Jack London described so vividly in *The Sea Wolf.* The last year the Quileute hunted seals was 1932, when they took sixty-five skins.

Salmon had always been the principal staple of the Quileute, and with the passing of so many of the tribe's other resources, the fish became absolutely paramount in Indian life; now, more than ever, the salmon was the man, and the survival of one was dependent on the survival of the other. To ensure that the crucial runs would continue, the Quileute attempted to maintain strict control over the resource. In 1881 when James Swan visited La Push, he reported that the Indians would sell smelt, "but of salmon they would neither give nor sell. The fall run of [Chinook] and [coho] had just commenced to come, and while they would give us all we could eat of their own cooking, in their own houses, they refused to sell or give a single fish to be taken away." Tribal tradition also controlled the time and duration of fishing, for as Sextus Ward, a Quileute who was three years old at the time of the Treaty of Olympia, later recalled: ". . . ordinarily each village would have at least one trap and . . . in addition to the traps the Indians caught fish with spears and nets. . . . When the Indians had obtained enough fish they would remove the weirs from the river in order that the fish they did not need could go upstream and lay their eggs so that there would be a supply for future years."

Formal regulations adopted by the Quinault Tribe for the control of fishing in 1907 were the model of the region, requiring among other things a seventy-five-foot open channel between nets and a Sunday closure while State of Washington regulations required neither. Washington Fish Commissioner Riseland acknowledged in 1912 that the Quinault had "the best fish protection of any river in the state of Washington," but he and other state representatives found Quinault and Quileute control over their salmon obnoxious in much the same way czarist Russians loathed the spark of independence the salmon inspired in their Siberian subjects. Stepan Krashnennikov observed in 1755 that "the Kamchadals are so fond of this fish [salmon] that they manifest great joy when they eat the first one they catch. Nothing makes the Russians who live in this country more unhappy than this Kamchadal custom. The Kamchadal fishermen who are so pleased with themselves never take their masters the first of these fish; they never fail to eat it themselves, in spite of all threats."

The trouble resumed for the Quileute in 1912 when a white settler named Samuel Morse built a salmon cannery at the mouth of the Dickey River, about a mile up the Quillayute from La Push. Morse brought in white fishermen to supply him, and staked off choice portions of the river for their use. When the Indians protested, the U.S. District Attorney informed them that the Corps of Engineers had classified the Quillayute a navigable waterway, thereby giving exclusive jurisdiction over it to the Department of War. By this simple stroke, the Quileute were denied control over the river, and the salmon. Shortly thereafter, Washington State adopted legislation requiring all salmon fishermen to purchase a state license, and then refused to sell licenses to Indians on the grounds that they were not United States citizens. This altogether eliminated Indian fishing on the Quillayute until the Indian Service stepped in to block state enforcement.

Unable to press the issue on the reservation itself, the Washington Department of Fisheries turned its efforts to discouraging Indian fishing outside the reservation. In 1914, activist Commissioner of Fisheries Darwin officially warned the superintendent of the Neah Bay Indian Agency that the Quileute Indians would be arrested if they continued to fish at their traditional spots on the Soleduck, Bogachiel and Calawah rivers. Elsewhere in the state, similar pressures from the whites and their government were restricting the time Indians could fish and forcing them to abandon their choicest fishing grounds. Addressing the state legislature in 1915, Charles Buchanan, Indian agent at the Tulalip Reservation on Puget Sound, observed that the salmon runs had

> naturally lessened with the advent of the white man; more recently, the use of large capital, mechanized assistance, numerous

> great traps, canneries, etc., and other activities allied to the fishery industry have greatly lessened and depleted the Indians' natural sources of food supply. In addition . . . the stringent application to Indians of state fish and game laws have made it . . . increasingly precarious for him to procure his natural food. . . . One by one [the Indians'] richer and remoter fishery locations have been stripped from him while the law held him helpless and resourceless.

Buchanan's comments did not receive a warm reception from the legislature. The assembly that convened in the spring of 1915 was virtually the same group that Governor Lister had described as being "sent by [their] constituents to get [their] share of the pie." None of the state's officials had been elected by Indians (who couldn't vote). They tended to see the native American as part of their pie, rather than part of their constituency. Lister himself, who was a comparative liberal, advocated that the Indians be stripped of all existing reservations so that the land could be turned over to white homesteaders. The idea that magnanimous America had allowed the Indians to retain too much land and wealth had long been popular in white society, having rationalized the illegal seizure of Indian lands everywhere from the salmon rivers of Maine to the Wallowa Valley of Eastern Oregon. In Washington, the closing of the frontier saw this basic impulse for self-aggrandizement transformed into the firm popular belief that the Indian enjoyed an unfair competitive advantage over the poor, downtrodden white man. Leslie Darwin spoke for a virtually unanimous state government when he wrote in the Department of Fisheries annual report for 1913:

> After an examination of the various Indian treaties . . . , this Department became convinced that the Indians off the reservation have no rights superior to those of the Whites.
>
> Practically every Indian has an allotment of land, and a home of his own. This is very much more than is possessed by the average fisherman of this state. It would seem unfair, therefore, to tax the White person for a license and not require one of the

> Indians, particularly where the Indian engages in competition with the White man.
>
> But much more objectionable yet is the insistence of the Indians upon their right to disregard the closed season which our laws establish. . . .

Darwin went on to report that Fisheries had arrested Indians at their usual and accustomed salmon fishing stations in Whatcom and Chehalis counties during the previous year. Referring to the case in Whatcom County, where the Indian was acquitted, Darwin complained that "the bad affect of the [court's] decision was apparent from the fact that last year, in order to fill the hatcheries on the Nooksack to their capacity, it was necessary to ship eggs in from other places."

One could hardly ask for a clearer example of the bias of "state fish and game laws" to which Buchanan referred. In the eyes of the Department of Fisheries, the fact that the whites had built the largest salmon cannery in the world near the mouth of the Nooksack, illegally overfished the runs with gill nets, traps and seines, driven the Indians off the prime fishery locations, dumped unrefined industrial wastes into the adjacent marine waters and killed still more of the river's salmon through hatchery operations was all somehow beside the point.

It was the Indians, the state concluded, who were responsible for both the decline in the wild runs *and* the failure of the state's hatcheries.

the ponds, juveniles had managed to find a passable breach in the dam. Inching my way along a log that became more deeply submerged the farther I went, I saw coho fry charging about, tossing and shaking a fir needle like dogs with a bone. Others were making passes close under the surface, or simply holding their position in the slow, smooth current. Several of these little fish moved in close enough behind my legs for me to see their delicate orange tails billow like pleated summer skirts.

On the way back to the boat, which we left on the bank of the river, Bill Grubb found sixty or so coho fry trapped in a pool no larger than the average kitchen table. They had come in at high water when the river overflowed its banks, and now they were slowly exhausting the food and air in their shrinking realm. Aware that they would die before the river rose that high again, Grubb borrowed my wife's scarf, rolled up his sleeves and hoisted himself out onto an alder that overhung the pool. Seining the pool in one slow motion, he captured a dozen coho fry and then handed the quivering cloth back to Lane, who ran to the edge of the creek and liberated the fish with a laugh.

While Grubb made pass after pass with his improvised net, Lane, Jim Porter and I took turns carrying the wild fish to freedom. Viewed up close, these two-inch-long coho were like jeweled miniatures from the treasury of the czar. Their eyes were concentric circles of perfect jet and gold, their bodies the same soft gray as the bottom striped with darker parr marks the color of shadows on sand, their anal fins traced with a fine but brilliant line of white, and their tails flushed with coral. When I opened the scarf in the creek, the little fish squirmed into the deepest folds of the cloth to lie still. Finally forced into the burbling waters of the stream, they shot away with a burst, and then glided invisibly into the shadows.

Coho are generally regarded as the most adaptable of the Pacific salmon, capable of seeking hot springs in Kamchatka where cold is a problem, or alternatively waiting for the winter rains to open the blocked mouths of California creeks where lack of water is a problem. On the Olympic Peninsula where

NINE

WE WADED THE MOUTH of a clear, unnamed stream and climbed the sandy bank on the other side. Finding no trail through the thigh-high grass, we followed the creek as it meandered north into the surrounding hills. Coho and steelhead fry darted among the waving red alder roots growing up out of the streambed, and an old salmon nest was visible in the gravel at the base of the first beaver dam.

Beyond this gushing, ramshackle affair, we walked along fallen logs out into the cathedral of leaning trees that surrounded an extensive series of ponds. There was a monumental stillness to the scene that was broken only by the occasional jumping of a fish, or the rattling cry of a kingfisher from the far shore. The stream that feeds these ponds is artesian in origin, and in April it was clear enough to let us minutely examine the fungus, moss and lichen-covered debris on the bottom.

Although it appeared that adult salmon could not ascend into high winter flows are a limiting factor, they have evolved a special relationship with springs like the one on the lower Soleduck River. Fisheries biologist Phil Peterson recently found in studying two springs on the nearby Clearwater River that some 8,000 coho fry entered the springs from the main river in the fall. They spent the winter there protected from flooding, and then headed for the sea in the spring. Peterson noted that 10 percent of a marked group of hatchery coho released upstream ended up in the springs, but speculated that a higher percentage of wild fish may depend on them, especially since logging has accentuated the naturally heavy seasonal flow on the peninsula.

No one knows exactly how many springs there are on the Soleduck, but it is likely that Bear Springs, where the Washington Department of Fisheries built its satellite hatchery to produce Soleduck summer coho, once supported a significant part of that rare and perishing wild run. Construction of the Bear Springs facilities put an end to that, however, just as similar state hatchery projects closed a half dozen other springs to wild salmon on rivers like the Satsop, Skokomish and Toutle during the late 1970s. "I've told them that if they put a hatchery in there," Grubb said gesturing back at the spring with an oar as we slipped into the big, boiling Soleduck, "they should go ahead and put the gun in their mouth and get it over with. . . . What we are seeing is a simple case of resource suicide."

Grubb is a handsome, long-haired man who seems propelled by a tight coil of intensity within. He and his lanky colleague Porter had both been fisheries managers for the Quileute Tribe at the time that the state started talking about its plans for Bear Springs. They participated in the tribe's singlehanded battle against the facility, and later, Porter, who is a third generation descendant of peninsula homesteaders, brought an action against the project in his own name as a citizen of Clallam County. "If we are going to save our wild salmon, we are going to have to come to grips with the factors that are destroying them. As a part of that, we have to realize that hatcheries are a large part of the problem," said Porter, whose views have been attacked as fanatical by Washington Director of Fisheries Gordon Sandison.

It is not surprising that the only opposition to the Bear Springs hatchery came from the Quileute and their allies, for the Indian-white conflict over salmon in Washington had long since escalated beyond who would get the fish, to what kind of fish would be available to catch. As early as 1899, the state fish commissioner complained about "trouble with Indians on our hatchery streams," and in 1916 when the federal government built the first salmon hatchery on the peninsula at Lake Quinault, the Quinault Tribe protested vehemently. At Indian insistence, the Lake Quinault hatchery weir was removed after it was shown to be killing fish in 1921, and the hatchery itself was later shut down. The Indians' objections to the hatcheries were based on their belief that hatchery fish were physically inferior, and that their introduction weakened the wild runs that had always sustained their people.

The whites did not agree. "The majority of people are of the opinion that the hatchery is a requisite for the future of the salmon," wrote the superintendent of the Quinault hatchery in 1919. "This is especially true of all cannery men, who are apparently cooperating to the fullest extent with [hatchery] work. Many of the Indians are unable to see the benefit of the hatchery, and at the present time, owing to the [restrictive] new regulations governing fishing [imposed by whites], these are more prejudiced than in previous years." Sixty years later, it is clear that it was the Indians, and not the whites, who correctly assessed the situation. On the Elwha, the Chehalis and other Washington rivers, early hatchery work produced a heavy drain on the salmon resource.

The reason for many early hatchery failures was, in fairness to the Department of Fisheries, as much political as biological. The same unwillingness to take responsibility for the effects of white development that led the state to blame the Indians for the salmon's decline also made it demand that the unproven science of salmon propagation be pushed into production long before it was ready. The first salmon hatchery in the United States had only been built in 1871, and there was as yet no systematic knowledge of even the simplest requirements for successful operation when the first hatchery went into operation on the Columbia some time later. It was not until 1893 that R. D. Hume, pioneering cannery man and hatchery operator, discovered that "the turning out of large numbers [of fry] in a small stream attracts their enemies of all kinds, besides giving the fish an insufficient supply of food, from which lack many perish from starvation."

The alternative to large fry plants was to feed the young salmon until they smolted and were ready to go to sea, but as Fish Commissioner A. C. Little acknowledged in 1899: "It is a fact at the present time it is not well known what would be the best food for young fry, that is obtainable at a price that warrants feeding a very large number of them." As a result of the legislature's reluctance to provide operational funds for hatcheries once they were built (one early fish commissioner refused to build any more until some money was forthcoming), the Washington Department of Fisheries was forced to rely more and more on hatchery methods that it knew had little merit. Between 1900 and 1935, fry plants by the state increased from 25 million to 90 million while the state's commercial salmon pack fell from an average of 48 million to 15 million pounds.

In Canada during the 1930s, fisheries biologists demonstrated that the substantial releases of hatchery sockeye into British Columbia's Fraser River had produced no increase in either the commercial catch or the number of fish spawning in the wilds. Canada reacted by closing all of its Pacific salmon hatcheries, and a number of federal facilities in the U.S. were also terminated. The Washington Department of Fisheries, however, continued to expand its hatchery network, building hatcheries on the Lewis River and Issaquah and Minter creeks, and planning others until "the Second World War shelved construction of new hatcheries," as the department's official history notes.

There was no proof that Washington hatcheries were performing better than those elsewhere, but biological concerns were not paramount in the minds of the state's leaders at the time.

Clarence Martin, who was elected governor of Washington in Roosevelt's 1932 landslide, was interested in jobs, plain and simple. Six hundred thousand people, nearly half the state's population, received relief during the first years of Martin's administration, and the number grew as the Great Depression dragged on. It was a desperate time made more so for the governor by the resurgence of the Wobblies and their allies from the Seattle General Strike of 1919, for as Norman H. Clark wrote in his bicentennial history of the state: "The predictions of Karl Marx seemed nowhere more accurate than in the desolate manufacturing economy of Washington State." To counter the threat of the radical left, the previously conservative Martin championed the New Deal, and brought large-scale deficit spending to state government to maintain the state payroll and expand public assistance.

A wealthy businessman from a small town in eastern Washington, Martin believed that development of the sort symbolized by Grand Coulee Dam, rather than economic reform, was the answer to the state's woes. He wanted more Eastern investment, more industry and more government subsidies, and like Lister before him, he did not entertain objections from the Department of Fisheries regarding these goals. When the subject of salmon arose, Martin's background growing wheat for his Cheney mill gave him complete confidence in the seemingly analogous prospect of growing salmon in hatcheries, and the Department of Fisheries, which received a large part of its budget for hatchery work, happily followed his lead. Director of Fisheries B. M. Brennan certainly knew of the Canadian hatchery discoveries (he was later director of the International Pacific Salmon Fisheries Commission), but he could not accept them, since that meant acknowledging that developments like Grand Coulee Dam would destroy great sources of free food at the very time when people in the state were literally starving.

And so the Washington Department of Fisheries continued to build hatcheries even as the choice upper Columbia spring and summer Chinook runs were lost through the failure of the federally financed hatcheries that Martin helped obtain. Research published in the 1950s showed that the best state facilities were able to return their seed a little better than half the time. In their classic *Artificial and Natural Production of Silver Salmon at Minter Creek*, Salo and Bayliff found that 58 percent of the experimental coho releases at Minter Creek over a nine-year period were self-sustaining. The rest of the time eggs had to be brought in to maintain production. The source of these additional eggs was ultimately the wild salmon, which the authors observed had declined substantially in Minter Creek as a result of state hatchery operations.

Artificial and Natural Production of Silver Salmon at Minter Creek also found, however, that when the hatchery worked it could produce many more fish than the stream had before. Salo and Bayliff, who were employed by the department, calculated that returns could be increased still more if certain hatchery practices, like the planting of unfed fry that Hume had warned against sixty years before, were discontinued. For Robert Schoettler, who became director of Fisheries in 1950 when his predecessor Alvin Anderson died suddenly in office, this promise of large returns justified the hatchery program. Schoettler knew it was a gamble, but he saw no choice. "In the past sixty years salmon have made their contribution to progress in Washington State," he wrote in the department's annual report for 1950. "Paradoxically, it was a contribution that now imperils their future. The peak of the state's . . . salmon harvest was from 1910 through 1917, when more than 12,300,000 cases were packed commercially. From 1938 through 1945, the yield was only 2,350,000 cases—one fifth as much."

Schoettler did everything he could for the wild runs (directing the suits against Tacoma City Light over the Cowlitz; helping build twenty-five fishways on existing dams and waterfalls), but he knew he was not winning the fight. If the salmon runs were going to be maintained, let alone built back up, Schoettler felt a way had to be found to increase the production of the areas that still remained available to the fish. Hatcheries seemed the only way of doing that, and so the department built more stations for artificial propagation on the Toutle, Elkomin, Nemah and Washougal rivers, as well as a saltwater facility at Hoodsport on the east side of the Olympic Peninsula. Heeding the counsel of academic advisors, Schoettler ordered stiff reductions in egg takes (Salo and Bayliff found that smaller plants produced much higher survival rates) and emphasized the rearing of young salmon until they reached the smolt stage. These policies were just beginning to show some scattered successes when one hatchery operator suddenly seemed to have found exactly what Schoettler and other concerned observers had been seeking.

The man was Lauren Donaldson, professor of fisheries at the University of Washington. Donaldson was interested in introducing a hatchery run of salmon to the University of Washington campus in Seattle to see if he could breed fish that would thrive in polluted urban waters. By the mid-1950s, he had established a small run of Chinook and steelhead that were larger for their age than anything that had ever been observed in the wilds. The result of systematic selective breeding, Donaldson's fish were thick-bodied and extremely fecund (one rainbow produced 23,000 eggs, more than twenty times the number a wild fish could carry in one spawning). His fish were shorter lived and smaller at maturity than wild fish (which reach forty-five pounds and live as long as nine years), but when he laid one of his two-year-old fish weighing ten pounds out on the campus grass next to a wild fish of the same age weighing a few ounces, who could doubt that man had bettered nature?

An affable man with a flat, square-chinned face, Donaldson did more than anyone else to popularize the notion that salmon degrading developments did not inevitably mean the impoverishment of the resource, and of the people who depended on it. He praised the state's efforts to enforce environmental laws and prescribed expanded hatchery work as the key to meeting future salmon needs. With financial support for his programs from various public and private utilities, the U.S. Atomic Energy Commission and the state departments of Fisheries and Game, Donaldson was an early proponent of such hatchery developments as fish farms and ocean ranches. In 1958, Director of Fisheries Milo Moore undertook a massive program of fish farms, or natural lakes and lagoons where hatchery salmon were confined and raised in large numbers. To prepare the selected areas, the department poisoned all native species of fish, including wild salmon and trout. On the Quillayute, the department killed the wild sockeye and coho of both Lake Dickey and Lake Pleasant. A total of twenty-five fish farms released 13.5 million fry and smolts in 1961, the year the first returns from the program showed that almost nothing was coming back. Within five more years, Moore's program was abandoned because, as new Director of Fisheries Thor Tollefson said, "techniques enabling high production of good quality young salmon in fish farms at a reasonable cost have yet to be found."

Fish farming cost the people of Washington millions of dollars and dozens of wild salmon runs in less than a decade, but it did not diminish the state's enthusiasm for salmon hatcheries. State Senator Victor DeGarmo of the Senate Fisheries Committee was one of those who called for the continuation of fish farms, and attacked the state biologists who admitted that their program was not working. "We need more common horse sense," DeGarmo told Stanton H. Patty of the Seattle *Times*. "I'm 100 percent for the fish farms. They're the cheapest way to put out fish. Let's get going. We don't need any more research." Other legislators criticized the department's reducing its egg take and called for the construction of conventional hatcheries, which had been showing some surpluses since the introduction of a pasteurized feed developed by the Oregon Department of Fish and Wildlife known as the Oregon moist pellet.

DeGarmo and the others drew their support from the state's increasingly disgruntled non-Indian commercial fishermen. Before the turn of the century, it had been possible to take 10,000 coho in a single haul on Puget Sound, and a fishwheel might average 100 tons of salmon a season on the Columbia. There was big money in salmon fishing when hundreds of canneries lined the rivers of the state, but even in these glory days the effects of the white fishing industry were apparent. Between 1883 and 1892, R. D. Hume observed that the choicest Chinook in the Columbia declined sharply through the combined efforts of the fishwheel operators, pound net men and gill-netters. Many Columbia River fishermen were, of course, keenly aware of the trend in the salmon runs, but they saw no cause for reducing their catch, even though it was acknowledged by all that thousands of fish were thrown overboard every year when the canneries could not, or would not, buy the fish. "[T]he increase of propagation, rather than curtailment of fishing, is the true policy to pursue," declared a typical pamphlet published by the Washington Fisherman's Association.

Realistically, though, there was no way to increase either hatchery or wild propagation under existing policies, and so the fishermen fell upon each other, seeking to steal the shares of competing fishing groups. The Indians were hit first by all classes of white fishermen, and then on the Columbia the Oregon gill-netters clashed with Washington pound net operators, bringing the territory and the state close to undeclared civil war in the summer of 1887. After blasting for the construction of a Canadian railroad loosed a disastrous slide into the Fraser River at Hells Gate in 1913, Washington fishermen (who caught the majority of the Fraser fish in the Strait of Juan de Fuca and off Point Roberts) refused to accept a mutual curtailment of fishing for the future of the runs. "Evidently using logic familiar to the parents of many five year olds," Daniel Jack Chasan wrote in *Up for Grabs*, "Washington State preferred the bigger share of a small pie to an equal share of a larger one."

By the 1920s, the fratricide among fishing interests centered on an effort by net fishermen to eliminate their fixed gear competitors by law. Measures were put on the ballot in Oregon and Washington to outlaw fish wheels, pound nets, set nets, traps and the like. Gill-netters argued that the tremendously efficient traps were a menace to the salmon. Cannery men who owned traps responded that the gill-netters caught three times as many salmon, and did so with first pick, since they were concentrated at the mouth of the rivers. Gill-netters charged that thousands of juvenile salmon were killed in the traps, and the trap owners responded that it was the dams and irrigation projects that were killing the young salmon. After half a century of debate, Oregon and Washington both passed initiatives which eliminated the fixed gear fishery and left their share to be divided among the remaining fishermen.

The net fishermen's great victory in 1934 bought them about ten years, but by the time Tacoma City Light was awarded its Federal Power Commission license for the dams on the Cowlitz, things were becoming very tight. There were now too many net and troll fishermen for the remaining runs, and the fishermen were beginning to bankrupt each other. While the size of the Puget Sound gill-net fleet doubled in the late 1950s and early 1960s, the combined Puget Sound catch fell from an average of nearly six million to three million fish. More fishermen with better gear covering more of the water found fewer fish. "It's impossible for a fisherman to make a living on Puget Sound now," said Anacortes purse seiner Joe Suryan in 1963. Harold Dodd, a Northern Puget Sound fish buyer, added, "We're in trouble. If the canneries ever pulled their financing out from under the fishermen, the industry would go broke."

"More Fish" was the cry of the state's 1,500 commercial fishermen, and to the State of Washington that meant only one thing—more hatchery fish. "If no more stream losses were to occur, natural production of salmon would probably be maintained at a relatively high level," observed a Department of Fisheries policy paper from the early 1960s, which added with emphasis, "there is every reason to believe that *this situation will not continue* with stream losses occurring at their present rate." Since the department was charged with enforcing state laws to prevent those very stream losses, its prediction was as good as fact. The dilemma that faced the state in 1962 was one born of reliance on hatcheries coupled with widespread failure to enforce statutes for the conservation of the resource, except where they impinged on the weakest elements in society, which usually meant the Indians. Faced with the real specter of commercial extinction, the fishermen and the state agency that served their interests saw no alternative but more of the same. By 1966 when Director of Fisheries Tollefson announced that the state would triple its hatchery releases within ten years, the state was already moving in for the kill on the Indians.

The arrest of Indian fishermen by the state had continued since Darwin's warning to the Quileute in the fall of 1914 (Benjamin Harrison Sadilto and David Hudson were among the Quileute elders who were arrested and convicted in state court for fishing at their traditional stations), but the Indians were quickly becoming adept at the use of the separate, and superior, federal court system. In 1939, for instance, the state arrested a Yakima Indian named Sampson Tulee for fishing without a state license. Convicted in state court, Tulee appealed to the U.S. Supreme Court, which ruled in his favor in 1941. Noting an earlier case involving the Yakima Tribe where a federal court found that salmon fishing was "not much less necessary to the existence of the Indians than the atmosphere they breathed," the Supreme Court declared:

> [W]e are impressed by the strong desire the Indians had to retain the right to hunt and fish in accordance with the immemorial customs of their tribes. It is our responsibility to see that the terms of the treaty are carried out, so far as possible, in accordance with the meaning they were understood to have by the tribal representatives at the councils and in the spirit which generously recognizes the full obligation of this nation to protect the interests of a dependent people.

On the Quillayute, the Indians recaptured some control over the river in 1946 when they won a federal court decision giving them exclusive jurisdiction over the river within the boundaries of the square mile they finally wrested from Pullen for a reservation. State pressure on Indian fishing outside the reservation continued, however, as the Department of Fisheries closed the Hoko River just north of the Quillayute to all Indian net fishing in 1950. Once the Makah Indian fishermen had gone home, the state opened the river to fishing by non-Indian sports fishermen. Director of Fisheries Schoettler justified this arrangement on the grounds that it was too expensive to enforce the regulations on Indian fishing. The Makah Tribe, whose main seat is Neah Bay where the Strait of Juan de Fuca meets the Pacific Ocean, sued and won a major victory when the U.S. Ninth Circuit Court of Appeals ordered the state to halt the practice.

Similar situations were occurring all along the West Coast of the United States and Canada, but Washington was the first to seek the complete elimination of Indian fishing. Armed with state court injunctions against Indian fishing on the Puyallup and Nisqually rivers "for conservation purposes," Fisheries and Game began arresting all Indian fishermen on those rivers in 1963, during the second term of Governor Albert Rosellini. Speaking for the state, Assistant Attorney General Joseph Coniff told the U.S. Senate that "the unregulated Indian net fishery of the nature which has been described is totally incompatible with any intelligent management program designed to conserve this great natural resource." The state acknowledged that the Indians caught only 6 percent of the salmon (compared to 12 percent for white sportsmen, and 82 percent for white commercial fishermen), but steadfastly maintained that it was the Indians who were overfishing the runs. U.S. Commissioner of Fish and Wildlife and former Assistant Director of the state Department of Fisheries Clarence Pautzke expressed the common white view this way:

> While percentagewise the Indian catch in the Pacific Northwest is not of major significance, the locations where the Indian fishery is carried out make it of extreme importance insofar as the proper management of anadromous fish are concerned. . . . The Indian

catch usually takes a disproportionately high percentage of the spawning runs. . . .

The following year the state sought and received a ruling from Pierce County Superior Court Judge John Cochran which completely nullified the Indians' treaty fishing rights. The judge declared that the tribe in question (the Puyallups, who signed the Treaty of Medicine Creek and are recognized by the federal government as a legitimate, functioning Indian tribe) no longer existed. Judge Cochran issued a permanent injunction against Indian fishing on the river, and the state continued making arrests. Drawing support from national figures such as actor Marlon Brando and comedian Dick Gregory, who were both arrested by the state while fishing with Indians, the Puyallups and Nisquallys kept on trying to fish until violence flared once again between the two old antagonists. As *Uncommon Controversy* described the scene: "An Indian boat was spilled by state officers, and several nights later a force of state patrol officers attempted a raid at Frank's Landing [on the Nisqually]. The Indians resisted, and state patrol officers were called in. On October 13, [1965] in a well-publicized protest at the same spot, Indians put a canoe into the water. Officers attempted arrests for illegal fishing, and an emotional battle of paddles, sticks and stones ensued."

The Indians heatedly argued that the state was violating the treaties for the benefit of the very white fishermen who were, in fact, responsible for the overfishing. "At night it looks like a floating city out there," said Puyallup Tribal Chairman Frank Wright of the white gill-net fleet operating off the mouth of the Puyallup River. "These commercial men have nets 1,800 feet long and they go row after row down the straits here by Whidbey Island and whatnot and they take all those salmon before they come to us and they say, 'Well, the runs of the Puyallup is depleted and you will have to let them go by. . . ." Retired Lummi Tribal Chairman Forest Kinley added, "You just take a look at the state of Washington. . . . There has been overfisheries in front of [Indian fishermen] on every one of these rivers.

This harassment has gone on all my life." Rising to the Indians' pleas for aid, as well as the State of Washington's clear challenge to its authority, the federal government entered the fray directly in 1970 when it filed a massive suit against the state on behalf of seven treaty Indian tribes.

In the *United States v Washington*, presiding U.S. District Court Judge George Boldt was asked to make a broad examination of the salmon conflict between the Indians and the state over the last century and to rectify some of the many wrongs alleged to have occurred to all parties. A conservative who was appointed to the federal bench by Richard Nixon, Boldt spent three years hearing arguments and collecting an immense body of testimony, which included specially commissioned reports on everything from the anthropology of the Indians to the biology of the surviving salmon. Then on February 12, 1974, he brought the gavel down hard, delivering an opinion that was at once an interpretation of the treaties of the 1850s, a judgment on how the people of the state had lived up to the agreements that bought them what is now Washington, and a series of orders designed to radically transform salmon fishing in the West.

In his initial findings of fact, Boldt concluded that the departments of Fisheries and Game had systematically discriminated against Indian fishermen by allowing white commercial and sports fishermen to catch all the harvestable salmon before the fish got to the Indians. Boldt flatly rejected the state's contention that "unregulated" Indian fishing was the cause of the salmon's decline. "Notwithstanding three years of exhaustive trial preparation, neither Game nor Fisheries has discovered and produced any credible evidence showing any instance, remote or recent, when a definitely identified member of any plaintiff tribe exercised his off reservation treaty rights by any means detrimental to any species of [salmon]. Indeed," Boldt wrote, "the near total absence of substantive evidence to support these apparent falsehoods was a considerable surprise to this court."

Turning to the treaties themselves, Boldt found "there is

nothing in the written records of the treaty councils or other accounts of discussions with the Indians to indicate that [they] were told that their existing fishing activities or tribal control over them would in any way be restricted or impaired by treaty. The most that could be implied from the treaty context is that the Indians may have been told . . . that non-Indians would be allowed to fish at Indian fishing locations along with Indians." Since there was no Chinook jargon term for the crucial phrase "in common with," Boldt decided on the basis of *Webster's American Dictionary of the English Language* of 1828 that "in common with" meant "divided equally with." To insure that the Indians got the fish they were entitled to, Boldt ordered the State of Washington to manage salmon and steelhead so that 50 percent of the runs traditionally fished by treaty tribes could be caught by the Indians. Meanwhile, Boldt retained jurisdiction over the parties while preparing for the case known colloquially as phase II of the Boldt decision, which was to examine the even more politically explosive issues of the ownership of hatchery fish and responsibility for destruction of the environment.

Washington's white fishermen were livid. It was immediately clear to them that turning 40 percent of the state's annual salmon catch over to the Indians meant reducing the non-Indian share by 40 percent. The Boldt decision was a direct attack on what they considered to be *their* right to fish, and they claimed it meant bankruptcy for nearly half the commercial gill-netters, purse seiners and trollers in the state. Having blocked all previous efforts to limit their number, the burgeoning white commercial fleet (which doubled again between 1965 and 1974) quickly set about sabotaging Boldt's ruling with the help of their friends in state government. Before the year was out the Puget Sound Gillnetters Association obtained a state court injunction against part of Boldt's ruling, which forced Boldt to enjoin the state from interfering. In early 1975, the Department of Game unilaterally cut the steelhead allocation to treaty Indians on the theory that the Indians had no right to fish produced in the state's hatcheries, and once again Boldt was forced to intervene.

The Ninth Circuit Court of Appeals upheld Boldt's ruling in its entirety in June 1975. Plainly piqued at the intransigence of the State of Washington, the court said of the state's actions: "Except for some desegregation cases . . . [Judge Boldt] has faced the most concerted official effort to frustrate a decree of a federal court witnessed in this century. . . . The record in this case . . . make[s] it crystal clear that it has been the recalcitrance of Washington officials—and their vocal non-Indian commercial and sports allies—which produced the denial of Indian rights. . . . This responsibility should neither escape notice nor be forgotten." Unrepentant, many white fishermen simply ignored the regulations designed to give the Indians a shot at the fish, and the State of Washington did little to stop them: only a fraction of the violators were charged, and of the 300 citations issued, only one resulted in a penalty.

Illegal fishing had long been a feature of the white commercial fishery, but during the fall of 1976 freebooting reached an all-time high. Encouraged to defy Boldt's ruling by gill-netter spokesman Phil Sutherland and state Assistant Attorney General James Johnson, white fishermen went for every fish they could get. Within four nights on Puget Sound, 247 white vessels were observed fishing illegally. The climax came on the night of October 24, when a state officer shot a white gill-netter, William Carlson of the *Alaska Revenge*, while attempting to make an arrest for illegal fishing off Foulweather Bluff. Carlson, who was fishing to try to make a mortgage payment on his boat, was paralyzed by a shotgun blast in the neck. The next day white fishermen descended on Olympia en masse to express their outrage over the shooting and the federal court ruling, which they now saw as the heart of their problems. Shortly thereafter, the state dropped all charges against Carlson, who received $250,000 in damages. Never again did it seriously attempt to enforce Boldt's orders.

Treaty Indian fishing interests, on the other hand, were subject to increasing attention from state authorities after Gordon Sandison's appointment as director of Fisheries in 1977. That the state's intent was sometimes simple harassment is clear from incidents like the one in the spring of 1977 when a Lummi Indian fish processor was charged with the criminal wastage of salmon after white suppliers refused to deliver ice. According to Robert Cumbow, who was Fisheries' chief information officer at the time, this decision was made because "the gung-hos were urging Sandison to show the white fishermen which side he was on." Shortly thereafter, the state cancelled its belated program to reduce the size of the white salmon fishing fleet because Boldt ordered it to allow Indians to bid at the public auctions where the boats were resold. The $3.5 million buy-back program had used federal money to pay white fishermen as much as forty times what their boats were worth on the open market, according to a story by Scott Maier in the *Argus*. "The program set out to reduce the fleet, but it had the opposite effect," said Dave Swift of the Puget Sound Gillnetters Association. "Instead fishermen sold junkers and geared up with better boats."

The next summer the Washington State Supreme Court ruled that Fisheries and Game could not enforce any aspect of Boldt's ruling. This gave legal sanction to the state's de facto stance. With the Indians' share of the salmon still below 15 percent and the state refusing to obey his orders, Boldt seized direct control of the Indians' share of the salmon. This extreme judicial technique, which made a federal judge in Tacoma essentially responsible for promulgating and enforcing fisheries policy in Washington, was followed by a federal court order from Boldt to all of the state's non-Indian salmon fishermen, directing them to cease fishing. Calculating that the U.S. Coast Guard did not have the boats or the manpower to make the order stick, the white fishermen kept the illegal harvest going full bore, catching an estimated 183,000 salmon, which were sold in "a carnival atmosphere, [with] laughing and joking," according to one observer.

Allied as they never had been in the past, white fishermen made the bald-headed judge with a fondness for bow ties the target of a clamorous personal, professional and political attack. "Save Our Salmon—Can Judge Boldt" bumper stickers proliferated, and slanderous speculation about his relationships with Indian women was commonly heard. Long-time Washington Congressman Lloyd Meeds, who had suggested that the Boldt decision was law and ought to be lived with, was forced into retirement. White fishing interests also played a major role in electing Congressmen Jack Cunningham and Slade Gorton, both of whom pushed for legislation that would unilaterally revoke the Indian treaties of the 1850s. Gorton was particularly well known as an Indian fighter, having directed the state's legal battles against the tribes for the last decade as Washington's Attorney General, and personally argued the state's unsuccessful appeal of Boldt to the U.S. Supreme Court.

Despite all the squirming though, the weight of Boldt's decision was being felt in Washington. Year after year, many treaty Indian tribes increased their share of the catch to 20 percent, 35 percent, and even in some cases, more than 50 percent. Ironically, the Indians who had to deal with federal rather than Washington State authorities were the ones who had the greatest difficulty during the late 1970s and early 1980s. While the state was finally managing to give many Puget Sound treaty Indian tribes a fair shot at the fish, the federal government itself was to blame for the fact that some coastal treaty tribes' share had dropped to virtually zero. Since the United States' adoption of a 200-mile limit of sovereignty off its coast in 1977, the U.S. Department of Commerce had allowed trollers to severely overfish many wild runs of coho and Chinook. In 1980, the Hoh Indians had no fall fishing because the trollers had not even left them one fish above the spawning requirements of the wild Hoh coho.

The Hoh Tribe sued the Department of Commerce to force recognition of their situation. They wanted Secretary of Commerce Juanita Kreps to manage the salmon runs on a river-by-river basis (instead of areawide aggregates), and provide the tribe with the 50 percent of the fish Boldt's decision had recognized as their right six years before. Of particular concern to the Hoh was the way Commerce's management consistently penalized the wild runs and the Indians who depended on them. "Under this system," said Rich Mattson, Hoh tribal biologist, "tribes with hatchery runs might get somewhat more than 50 percent, while tribes that rely heavily on natural runs would get consistently less than 50 percent." The Hoh won the case in August 1981, but once again the resource appeared to lose. Rather than further curtail the trollers' season, it was decided to cut back on the number of fish allowed to spawn. This meant that the trollers would fish, and the Indians would fish, and there would be less fish in the future.

Out at La Push once, I remember flipping through a book of photographs with Chris Morganroth, the Quileute fisheries manager. When we came to a color shot showing scores of Soleduck summer coho jumping in a rainbow at the Salmon Cascades, Morganroth paused. "I suspect pictures are the only place you're going to see a run like this again," he said.

Into the Oxbow

TEN

WE DRIFTED WITH OUR PADDLES laid across the oaken gunwales of the kayak. A cow and a chainsaw sang a duet in the distance. Several insects traced passionate circles on the smooth water around us, and the air had the stillness that sometimes precedes rain. I raised the binoculars and scanned the alders on the right bank of the river where the russet-throated green heron had just disappeared. The bird, which feeds on young salmon, was undoubtedly in plain view, but I could not pick its statuesque form out of the jumble of foliage.

In another moment, my wife, Lane, picked up her paddle and began to stroke. Her pace was calm and deliberate, for there was no need to hurry. I joined her after a few beats and we soon accelerated across a rising sand shoal into deep water on the right where the absolutely clear river ran shady and black. Following the meander back around the other way, we approached a red clay cliff hidden just below the main highway through the valley, a paved two-lane road that runs from the gas station that is Humptulips out around Point New to the nonexistent metropolis of Grays Harbor City, and eventually into Hoquiam.

The previous spring we had seen cliff swallows dancing here along the glassy surface of the river to gather material for their nests. They alighted and took off in a constant roll of flight, while barn, rough-winged and violet-green swallows dove and flitted across the river from the woodland and pasture beyond. As a brisk breeze began to rise, the swallows became increasingly daring, with double back loops, tight spirals and clipped-wing, high-speed dives visible all around. Twice we saw pairs of smaller rough-winged swallows grapple in midair, and fall together over the river in tumbling union.

Now, three months later, those swallows and the fledglings they raised were gone, headed for their winter grounds in Central and South America. The cliff, which resembled a high adobe wall that had undergone a heavy automatic weapon attack, was silent and bare. "Clear sky," Lane said, pointing to the one pale pool of blue remaining among the clouds that began rolling in off the Pacific a couple of hours before. The peninsula had been enjoying a glorious Indian summer for weeks, but with the autumnal equinox three days past, Lane and I agreed that fall might be about to begin. Ahead, an old fisherman's red wool coat was the only point of color in the sere scene. We inquired about his luck as we drifted past. "Naw," he said, shifting on his stool, "I haven't even had a bite. We need a good rain to bring the salmon in."

Several thousand fall Chinook had, in fact, already entered nearby Grays Harbor, according to the Department of Fisheries. The majority of these fish were still holding in the large pear-shaped estuary formed by the confluence of the Humptulips, Wishkah, Hoquiam, Chehalis, Johns and Elk rivers, but the eagerest fish had already begun their move. We knew this from the newspaper-wrapped bundle stored beside me. It contained a six-pound fall Chinook jack that had been given to us earlier in the day near the mouth of the Humptulips. Driving past Jessie Slough, Lane and I had stopped to inquire about the river and fell into conversation with Gilley and Jimmy, two Lower Chehalis who are part of a new contingent of Indian fishermen who have begun to fish the river again in recent years.

"Sure there're snags," Gilley averred with a grin. Both he and his companion seemed enthusiastic but skeptical about our expedition. "So you're going to paddle the Hump in a kayak?" Jimmy asked again. "You need a fish," Gilley declared. "Here, I'll give you this jack. Isn't that a nice fish?" I agreed and offered to pay him for it. Gilley, who had a light skin and generally Caucasian features to go with his raven-black hair, declined with a wave of his hand, saying, "Your money cannot buy this fish. Do you understand what I am saying?" He paused, and then added, "Get a motel with a nice kitchen and fix this fish up right." I snorted and asked if he and Jimmy would like to help drink a six-pack of beer we had with us. "Well, all right," he said, making a pattern in the air with his knife as he bent down to clean the fish on the dock.

We cooked our gift salmon on a gravel bar about six miles up the Humptulips River from its mouth on Grays Harbor. Pulling the kayak up into a little protected cove at the beginning of a great oxbow, we pitched our tent and began digging a fire pit beside a large old drift log. A quick survey of the bar revealed an ample supply of smaller, snapping-dry driftwood, along with curious clumps of clay that had fractured in their drying so that piles of tidy rubble were all that remained to show their former shape. Once the fire was going well, we took it apart and covered the flat round rocks in the bottom of the pit with a layer of wet alder leaves. The salmon, which Lane had stuffed with green beans, onions and tomatoes from our garden, was then placed in the pit and covered with more leaves and the reassembled fire.

Thirty minutes later, we pulled the backbone away from the extremely tender flesh and sat down to eat a pile of piping hot salmon and vegetables with our fingers. There is still much contention today regarding which of the Pacific salmon is the *ne plus ultra* for flavor and texture. Many support the "white salmon" (which is a race of white-fleshed Chinook abundant at one time in the tributaries of the Lower Columbia); others champion the red-fleshed "Alaska king salmon" (another race of Chinook); still others prefer the fat, silvery coho caught by the troll fleet along much of the coast; and on the Olympic Peninsula most people will testify that the Quinault sockeye or blueback is the choicest salmon man can eat.

Our fish was a red-fleshed Chinook, and as such closer to the Alaskan ideal, although its size was a tenth of a good sixty-pound Yukon king. Watching the puffs of steam rising from each morsel as I broke it open and popped it into my mouth, I was willing to become a partisan. The fish was succulent yet firm, rich yet mild, combining its own gentle flavor with that of the vegetables and butter to fine effect. We ate about four pounds of salmon between us while a number of sport salmon fishermen passed along the shore, casting without success into the deepening gloom.

There were five more fishermen working the pool the next morning when we shoved off, continuing our journey down the Humptulips to North Bay. Our craft was a royal-blue and silver kayak made of a canvas and rubber skin stretched over a folding hardwood frame. The entire sixteen-foot-long boat can be taken apart and folded into three bags, but the most useful quality of the *faltboote* produced by the Klepper firm of Germany is the way it behaves in the water. Faster than a canoe and more stable than other kayaks, it is capable of handling an extremely wide range of nautical conditions. The two-man boat we were using, Murray and Rosa Morgan's *Romur III*, had been paddled everywhere from the Danube River to the Bering Sea off Kotzebue during fifteen years of service.

Dip left; swivel the feathered, double-ended paddle; dip right; return the paddle to its original angle with a twist of the wrist; dip left. . . . Adjusting our weight and testing the current on the glide above the first bend, Lane and I renewed the rhythm that has carried us so many watery miles. The idea with long-distance paddling is to get yourself up to speed and then maintain it with a relatively small expenditure of energy, much as a bicycle racer "spins." Although inexperienced observers often think that paddling a kayak involves pulling back with the hand on the side where the stroke is being made, the thrust is actually provided by pushing forward with the opposite hand and levering. When it is done correctly, paddling a Klepper feels something like shelving innumerable volumes of the *Encyclopaedia Britannica*, each of which is shoved home with an even and surprisingly easy shove with the ball of the hand.

The Humptulips, which drains the southwestern corner of the Olympic Peninsula, is a deceptive river to navigate. Because of the tidal effect on the lower river, the same bend can be either smooth and broad or a narrow, twisted jumble of debris. The gentlest of the major peninsula rivers from the standpoint of current, it nonetheless requires more attention from a kayaker or canoeist than many more exuberant streams. Tide tables must be consulted before embarking, and once underway great care must be taken to avoid submerged obstacles. Lane, who paddled in the bow, was responsible for early warnings. When the situation permitted, we would steer away by both stroking on one side, but when she shouted "left, left" with alarm and began to dig hard, I would backstroke on the other side. This had the disadvantage of slowing the boat down (steerage is directly related to speed), but allowed me to pry the bow of the kayak around rapidly in the direction Lane was paddling.

By ten o'clock the rising tide had not yet begun to swell the Humptulips through the full seven miles of its tidal reach, and so we had to do some digging as we floated down through the oxbow to a point within hailing distance of where we had spent the night, and just departed. There was a solitary fisherman casting from the next bar and a herd of hysterical cattle on the other side, several of which had just been dehorned, judging from the vivid blood streaming down the sides of their white faces. Out in the pasture with the bawling cows was a remnant of the forest that once stood here. Sixty feet tall where it had been snapped off, and a dozen feet through at the base, this old-growth Sitka spruce dominated the landscape like a broken-armed colossus from antiquity. It had been burned all over, and by the look of the scrap lumber piled a third of the way up the trunk, its final pyre was being prepared.

The burning of this tree—which has no doubt already taken place—marks the end of an age. When it stood 200 or more feet tall in the prime of its 1,000-year life, the Humptulips and nearby Chehalis valleys were covered with the heaviest stands of timber on the Olympic Peninsula. Several 640-acre sections contained more than one billion board feet of prime western red cedar, western hemlock, Douglas fir and Pacific silver fir apiece. At first awed by the majesty of the trees, white settlers soon began setting forest fires to clear land and highlight casual outings which "materially altered the face of the country," as James Swan recalled of one such incident in 1852. Many, like Swan's Shoalwater Bay blaze, burned out of control until doused by the fall rains.

Commercial logging of the forests around Grays Harbor began in 1882 with the construction of the Simpson Brothers' mill at Hoquiam, and spread to the Humptulips a decade later when a large log jam at the mouth of the river was dynamited. In order to get the logs out of the woods, the timber companies built a network of "splash" dams which were used to flush the logs down the sleepy Humptulips. Of the thirty or so logging dams built on the Humptulips (and the more than 100 in the entire Grays Harbor area), not a single dam was equipped with a fish ladder as required by Washington law since the first year of statehood. "Although a few dams were low enough to pass [salmon] during high flow periods, the majority were total blocks [to migration]," according to a 1955 report by the Washington Department of Fisheries. "The length of time that the dams remained in the streams ranged from less than one to more than 50 years, with an average of about 20 years. During this time when most were in existence, these barriers effectively blocked over 60 percent of the [salmon] spawning and rearing potential in Grays and Willapa harbors."

One early fish commissioner, activist Leslie Darwin, forced the Humptulips Driving Company to pay for the construction of four hatcheries in the Grays Harbor area to compensate for the damage done by its dams, but these hatcheries were soon abandoned, and it was not until thirty years later that any more attention was given to the salmon, or the law. In 1950 Fisheries Director Robert Schoettler ordered scores of splash dams torn out, and much lost habitat was restored to the salmon, who responded immediately. Referring to a splash dam that had blocked half the Hoquiam River for forty years, Henry Wendler of the department noted: "In the summer of 1952 many young silver [coho] salmon were noticed downstream from the dam but none were seen above . . . [O]ne month after the removal of the dam in the fall of 1952, 80 adult silver and chum salmon were observed moving upstream from the former dam site."

About a mile beyond the old Sitka spruce snag we met the tide coming the other way. Paddling harder now against the tide and the freshening salt breeze, we followed the right channel past a line of rotting pilings left over from the logging days toward the new steel highway bridge. The center portion of this bridge rests on an island that covers several acres in the middle of the river, and that—to our surprise—was still festooned with red, yellow, blue and white wild flowers. As we drifted through the big pool at the lower end of the island admiring the colors, a harbor seal poked its silver head out of the water not more than twenty feet from the kayak. His liquid eyes and tiny, pert ears focused on us immediately, and he was gone.

A yellow line of salt grass and beached snags in the distance marked the beginning of the actual harbor. Hundreds of delicate white feathers danced on the surface of the river all around us and an elegant common loon slowly submerged itself submarine fashion as we approached. Finding the opening to both

Gillis and Campbell sloughs choked with logs and running rapidly against us with the tide, we continued down the main channel of the Humptulips. A little further on we talked with two fishermen in a skiff who warned us in an offhand way, "You know there's nothing out there but the bay." Undaunted, we pressed on for North Bay, the large embayment that receives the Humptulips, and the wildest area remaining in Grays Harbor.

Directly ahead was Neds Rock, a seventy-six-foot-high slice of banded clay in the shape of a steamship stack standing three miles to the southwest off Point New. Five miles to the southwest was Point Brown, which (with its companion Point Chehalis) commands the two-mile-wide entrance into Grays Harbor and separates it from the Pacific Ocean. Due south across the widest part of the harbor, a wavering blue line along the horizon showed the hem of the Willapa Hills. Twelve miles of seemingly unbroken water lay between us and Bay City on the south shore, but as the U.S. Coast and Geodetic Survey map showed, there is no channel through. About three quarters of a mile out onto North Bay our kayak, which draws only a couple of inches, ran aground on a glistening sand bar.

Leaving the kayak pulled up on the sand, we walked to the far side where we could see some of the great number of birds for which Grays Harbor is noted. Nearly 90 percent of the birds found in Washington can be seen in Grays Harbor, especially during the fall and spring migrations when the area is a prime feeding and resting spot for birds on the Pacific flyway. Members of three endangered species (brown pelican, Aleutian Canadian goose, peregrine falcon) and five rare species (Caspian tern, American flamingo, emperor goose, snowy plover, bald eagle) have been observed in the harbor in recent years. For some, like the 1,200 Caspian terns that make Whitcomb Island the birds' largest colony in the state, Grays Harbor plays a vital role in their continued survival. Many more common birds also rely on the harbor for their principal winter or summer grounds, among them dunlin and western gulls, which are found in greater numbers in Grays Harbor than anywhere else on the West Coast.

North Bay itself boasts the harbor's largest concentrations of waterfowl, with as many as 50,000 ducks present at one time during the fall migrations. The importance of Grays Harbor to the birds on the Pacific flyway has increased in recent years as other West Coast estuaries, such as San Francisco Bay and San Diego Bay, have been degraded. The autumnal wanderings of waterfowl down that chain of bays and lakes from Alaska to Baja California had begun ten days before and were now gaining force. Nearly a mile away across the gray waters of the bay we could see ten thousand widgeons, pintails, mallards and scaups rafting together in loose flocks. While we stood gazing through the binoculars at one group to the southwest between us and the staccato light at Point Brown, a noise like the breaking of heavy surf startled us into a hasty examination of the incoming waves until we realized that the roar came from another group of several thousand widgeons rising at once in an explosion of white-epauletted wings.

The widgeon is one of the many creatures in Grays Harbor dependent on the extensive beds of eelgrass that carpet the shallow areas such as North Bay. While widgeons graze along on the living grass muttering companionably, a host of tiny, bottom-dwelling invertebrates devour the dead and dying remains of the plants. Because of this long, graceful grass, wetlands like those found in Grays Harbor are among the most biologically productive areas on the globe, outproducing even cultivated farmland in terms of biomass or gross amount of living matter. According to a report issued by the Corps of Engineers, the harbor's 5,420 acres of salt marsh produce 46,568,105 pounds of living matter per year, dry weight.

As the dominant seagrass of the North Pacific, eelgrass resembles the Pacific salmon in its ability to take advantage of a rich food source (in this case, river-borne nutrients) and convert it into a widely palatable form. Each is at the center of a great circle of life, but neither stands alone. Eelgrass benefits from the nutrients provided by salmon dying in the rivers that feed its estuaries, and young salmon utilize eelgrass for cover and the eelgrass-eating invertebrates for food. Numerous studies have shown that juvenile Chinook and chum salmon largely subsist on eelgrass-eaters like harpacticoid copepods, gammarid amphipods and mysids during the sometimes extended periods they spend in river estuaries.

Based on the productivity of North Bay, one would expect the Humptulips to have stronger salmon runs than less well-endowed Grays Harbor rivers of similar size, and despite the Humptulips' previous abuse, this is the case. In the mid-1960s the Department of Fisheries conducted a series of tests to compare the survival of salmon from the Humptulips and the Chehalis, which is the largest river flowing into the harbor. The tests, which involved the release of identical hatchery salmon the same distance from the Pacific, showed that the survival for coho released into the Humptulips was 250 percent higher than that of the same fish released in the Satsop, a major tributary of the Chehalis. Humptulips coho were also significantly larger than their counterparts from the Satsop.

The Department of Fisheries had designed the tests to measure one variable: the need for the Chehalis River fish to swim through inner Grays Harbor, an area of "notorious water quality problems due to pulp mill waste discharges," where dredging and filling has wiped out large areas of eelgrass and its allies. With a drainage of more than 2,000 square miles (three times the size of any other river on the Olympic Peninsula), the Chehalis and its tributaries were once famous for their large runs of Chinook, coho and chum salmon. The harbor's first industry was a salmon cannery built at the mouth of the Chehalis in the early 1870s, and before long Grays Harbor had become one of the premier pound net fisheries in the state. The industry reached its peak near the turn of the century, when 1.5 million pounds of salmon were packed in Grays Harbor, but after that the timber industry took over.

Milling the 31 billion board feet of timber taken out of Grays

Harbor in the early years produced an almost incomprehensible amount of sawdust, the bulk of which was dumped into the lower Chehalis. As it decomposed, this sawdust drew so much oxygen out of sections of the river and harbor that fish passing through them were suffocated. Because they were generally located at the mouth of the Chehalis and its lower tributaries, pollution from the sawmills owned by companies like Polson Brothers blocked the salmon's access to the entire Chehalis system at certain times, depending on the flow of the river and the strength of the tides. As early as 1893, E. A. Chase of the Puget Sound Fishing Company wrote in the Tacoma *Ledger* of similar sawdust dumping at the mouth of the Puyallup River on Puget Sound:

> . . . [T]he experience of all Eastern fishermen in the states of Maine and Massachusetts for 100 years back has shown conclusively that dumping sawdust and offal into the rivers and creeks has driven fish from their haunts and therefore has been prohibited by law.
>
> . . . Now it would seem to me that this country would profit by the experience that the older settled portions of the United States have paid so dearly for. Anyone should be very careful throwing anything in the water which is liable to decompose and make it unhealthy, and the wholesale dumping of garbage of this city [Tacoma] into Puget Sound ought to be stopped at once.

Washington's first legislature had, in fact, already passed a law prohibiting "throwing into the water any substance deleterious to fish," including waste from sawmills. Violations were so flagrant, however, that at least one early state fish commissioner felt compelled to comment in his annual reports on "Why the Law Has Not Been Enforced." (Answer: not enough money.) In 1899, the Federal Refuse Act established criminal penalties and fines for polluting to be administered by the Corps of Engineers. This law also was not enforced. When fishermen protested the increasing numbers of "dead and maimed" fish found in the harbor after the first pulp mill went into operation in 1928, they were told that nothing could be done. By 1937, the pulp mill was flushing 275 tons of sulphite waste a day into Grays Harbor.

That same year, however, the State of Washington began work on a landmark investigation entitled *The Occurrence and Cause of Pollution in Grays Harbor.* Prepared by the new state Pollution Commission, this study reported that "dead and distressed fish, shrimp, crabs and other aquatic animals were observed in large numbers in Grays Harbor in 1937, 1938 and 1939." Typical of these kills was the one witnessed by commission personnel on September 27, 1938 near the mouth of the Hoquiam River. "Several hundred adult silver [coho] salmon were distressed along a mile or more of channel," wrote authors Arne Eriksen and Lawrence Townsend. "Many of these fish were killed or drifted helplessly at the surface of the water, the [rising] tide carrying them into the Hoquiam River and up the channel past the pulp mill toward Aberdeen."

Despite the continued dumping of sawdust, raw sewage and caustic wastes into the lower Chehalis and inner Grays Harbor, *The Occurrence and Cause of Pollution in Grays Harbor* singled out the pulp mill owned by the Grays Harbor Pulp and Paper Company (which has since become a part of ITT-Rayonier) as the greatest single polluter. The oxygen demand of the mill's waste was calculated to be the equivalent of the sewage produced by a city of 1.4 million people, or roughly the total population of the state at the time. Sampling revealed oxygen concentrations as low as .4 parts per million in the vicinity of the mill. Such water was as lethal (salmon require at least 5 parts per million of oxygen to breathe) as it was common. Similar situations existed at the time in the water around pulp mills in Tacoma, Everett, Bellingham, Port Townsend, Port Angeles and other cities in Washington.

Ten years later, Fred Niendorff of the *Post-Intelligencer* reported a macabre scene near the Weyerhaeuser and Scott Paper Company mills in Everett: "As the tide slowly ebbed on the afternoon of July 31 residents and workers along 5½ miles of beach between Mukilteo and Everett gazed upon one of the most astonishing waterfront sights . . . in many a day. By mid-afternoon the receding waters had reached extreme low and there, in the blazing rays of the sun, lay a shimmering stripe of white along the water's edge as far as the eye could see. . . . Dead fish, running into the millions, solidly packed the 5½ mile strip of beach the width of a yard or more. . . . There were cutthroat trout, poggies, little rock fish—and countless baby salmon from fingerlings up to ten and 12 inches."

Stung by this account and the relevation the following day that the waters near Weyerhaeuser's Everett mill were so polluted that they could kill herring in three minutes, the timber company's president, Philip Weyerhaeuser, told the *Post-Intelligencer* that "it was never proved to our satisfaction that pulp mill waste was responsible" for the death of salmon and other aquatic life. At the same time, Weyerhaeuser maintained that his company was working on a new pulp mill process that would substantially reduce the amount of pollution the mills released. The Weyerhaeuser pulp mill at Longview on the Columbia River had recently been equipped with experimental equipment designed to reduce emissions by 75 percent, and Weyerhaeuser strongly implied that the pulp mill pollution problem "appears on the verge of being solved," as Niendorff put it in the story's lead.

Two years later the state Pollution Control Commission reported that toxic wastes from the Grays Harbor pulp mill were still blocking the entire lower Chehalis for considerable periods of time, especially during the migrations of the fall Chinook. The waste storage lagoon built at Rennie Island after the commission's first report had proved useless, and one third of the harbor's tidelands were by then closed to the gathering of shellfish because of contamination from human sewage. Water quality continued to deteriorate when Weyerhaeuser built the harbor's second pulp mill at Cosmopolis in 1957. Although it used the same magnesium-based process as the touted Longview plant, the new Weyerhaeuser mill still dumped millions of gallons of "sour sewer" waste into the harbor a day.

To feed the mill, Weyerhaeuser began liquidating its extensive holdings of old-growth timber in the Grays Harbor area, one tract of which is said to cover 250,000 contiguous acres. As the clearcuts spread over the mountainsides, tremendous amounts of silt slurried into rivers and streams as a result of typically poor logging practices. On land owned by Weyerhaeuser, the ratio of miles of unpaved logging roads to square miles of river basin ran as high as nine to one, according to Jeff Cederholm. This is nearly 400 percent more than the lethal threshold for salmon observed by Cederholm and his associates on the Clearwater River. The Chehalis does not have exactly the same drainage characteristics as the Clearwater fifty miles to the north, but there is no doubt that logging has created a massive erosion problem in the valley. "You should take a look at the mouth of the Wishkah or Hoquiam rivers after a heavy rain," said Dan Kruger of the Washington Department of Ecology. "It's dark brown." According to a Department of Ecology report: "About 85 percent of the suspended sediments [in the Chehalis] are due to erosion of deforested watershed areas."

As on the Quinault, Elwha and Dungeness rivers, this basic change in the river has apparently been reflected in a basic change in the system itself. The estimated 500,000 tons of silt and sediment that washes off logged land in the Grays Harbor area has combined with more sediment traveling north along the Pacific Coast to speed the filling of the harbor. Dredging commenced in 1905, and after the failure of the Corps of Engineers' rock jetties at Point Chehalis and Point Brown, it grew substantially in area and volume. Between 1916 and 1942, the Corps of Engineers dredged an average of more than three quarters of a million cubic yards of sediment annually from the harbor and the lower Chehalis. By the 1950s, the desire of the forest products industry to bring larger vessels into the shoaling harbor increased the dredging to nearly two million cubic yards annually.

All of this dredged material was dumped inside the harbor, where it became another major source of water pollution. Speaking of its plans to fill more Grays Harbor wetlands with dredge spoils after the National Environmental Policy Act required a public assessment of the impacts of the action, the Corps described the process by which it had been killing salmon for half a century: "Shallow water areas which provide salmonids with protection from predators will be eliminated, subjecting them [juvenile salmon] to greater predation." The supply of food for young Chehalis River salmon also probably declined as a result of the Corps's work, for as H. B. N. Hynes noted in *The Ecology of Running Waters*, "dredging greatly reduces the variety of the flora and invertebrate fauna." This destruction was especially acute around the mouth of the Chehalis and Hoquiam rivers, where dredge material was used to eliminate almost entirely areas that had formerly produced lush stands of eelgrass.

It is interesting to note that the government agency that performed the destructive dredging in Grays Harbor was the same one charged with enforcing federal water pollution law. When pressed on the issue, spokesmen for the Corps of Engineers publicly blamed lack of money and manpower for their failure to enforce the Refuse Act of 1899, but a more fundamental problem was actually at the heart of the Corps's inaction. Through the Rivers and Harbors Congress (a lobby which includes members of Congress, many polluting industries and the Corps), the Corps developed a deep political alliance with the very groups it was supposed to police. Although no money could be found to enforce the Refuse Act, the Corps became famous for its ability to win congressional approval for environmentally destructive projects, such as the diversion of water from Lake Okeechobee which killed much of Florida's famed Everglades.

In 1977, for instance, the Corps fired Steven W. Simpson when he attempted to cite violations in the dumping of slag from the Tacoma smelter into Puget Sound. No one denied that ASARCO had been dumping 700 tons of slag a day without a permit—and hence illegally—since 1962, but District Engineer John Poteat saw this as slight cause for concern, let alone alarm. He granted the company an emergency permit to continue dumping under the guise of repairing what was described as storm-caused erosion, and fired the enforcement officer who issued the original citation, reportedly, because his manner was abrasive and he would not follow orders. Simpson, a twenty-eight-year-old Vietnam veteran, claimed that the Corps had knuckled under to industry pressure, and added that he had observed many uncited Refuse Act violations during his travels up and down Puget Sound. Poteat responded that the Refuse Act was now the responsibility of the Environmental Protection Agency. The Corps, he said, "must be tactful in dealing with industry, just like anyone else. . . ."

At the time that Poteat spoke, Corps of Engineers activities in the Northwest included a half dozen major dams, along with projects for navigation, coastline stabilization and irrigation. There is no doubt that some Corps projects, such as Chittenden Locks joining Lake Washington and Puget Sound, have been a great public benefit, but others have been dubious at best. "[W]aterways development is a pork barrel operation," acknowledged a Corps officer responsible for reviewing the agency's work for the Bureau of the Budget. Regarding the Corps's all too frequent practice of greatly exaggerating the benefits of projects while downplaying negative impacts, Charles Curran told former Tennessee Valley Authority Director Arthur E. Morgan: "There are no degrees of integrity; either you have integrity or you have not. And I must say that I am not impressed with a number of my colleagues [in the Corps] in that they consider themselves honest if they don't accept any personal gain. The fact that they come up with an unsound report that will help someone politically means that they do not recognize intellectual dishonesty."

A good example of the situation described by Curran is the $22 million dam the Corps built on the Wynoochee River, another major tributary of the Chehalis. This dam was originally proposed by the Port of Grays Harbor, the City of Aberdeen and others as a means of supplying water to new industries they hoped to attract to Grays Harbor. The Corps prepared a report that justified the dam in terms of "multipurpose" benefits to the area's community, and it was authorized by Congress in 1958. No additional demand for industrial water developed, however, and when the dam was finally completed in the early 1970s, the City of Aberdeen had to obtain a congressional moratorium on its share of the cost of the dam to avoid bankruptcy.

The other major justification for the dam used by the Corps was that it would "improve river conditions" for salmon and trout. The Corps maintained that the wild salmon of the Wynoochee would benefit from water released from behind the dam during periods when the river was low, but experience has proven otherwise. The wild salmon of the Wynoochee have actually declined significantly since the completion of the dam, primarily because of the failure of fish passage facilities designed and installed by the Corps. The Department of Fisheries estimates that the Wynoochee River has lost an annual run of 3,460 wild coho along with significant numbers of fall Chinook and chum as a result of the dam. No compensation for this loss has been made by the Corps or any other group involved with the dam. (Unless you count the "Coho Campground" the Corps installed above the dam, which it advertises as "designed to meet the needs of the mobile traveller, with ample space for trailers and campers.")

While the Corps was busy building the dam on the Wynoochee, some major changes were taking place in water pollution law, and its enforcement. In 1966, Congress passed amendments to the Water Pollution Control Act, which led to joint federal and state standards requiring Washington's thirteen pulp mills to substantially reduce pollution by 1972. These goals were not met owing to the intransigence of several pulp mill owners, but the newly created U.S. Environmental Protection Agency stepped up the pressure. The EPA's plan was to approach the pulp mill pollution problem in a step-by-step fashion, requiring the installation of a series of filtering and recovery systems as technology made further pollution reduction possible. On Grays Harbor, where Weyerhaeuser and ITT-Rayonier were forced to install the first phase of pollution control equipment, tests conducted by the Washington Department of Ecology during the 1970s showed that "primary treatment" was having a measurable, if mixed, effect.

On the minus side, waste processing increased the presence of lethal bacteria in the water of Grays Harbor. According to a Department of Ecology study, the primary treatment equipment at the two Grays Harbor mills serve as breeding grounds for *Klebsiella pneumoniae*, the bacteria which causes pneumonia in human beings. It remains to be seen whether the increased presence of pneumonia in Grays Harbor will be linked to disease in humans or other creatures, but as V. T. Vlassoff noted in a paper published by the American Society for Testing and Materials, "their presence denotes deteriorating water quality." At the same time, another ecology study found that primary treatment had reduced the death rate among young salmon in the vicinity of the mills from 97 to 67 percent. The water was still toxic at times, but during the early 1970s certain aspects of Grays Harbor's water quality appeared to be improving for the first time in a century.

Then the Corps of Engineers announced plans for the biggest dredging project in the history of the harbor. The Corps and the Port of Grays Harbor wanted to deepen the existing twenty-mile-long channel from thirty to forty-eight feet so that larger vessels could call at Grays Harbor and leave more heavily laden. The project also included the construction of a new highway bridge over the Chehalis River at Aberdeen, which would allow the larger vessels to go as far upriver as Cosmopolis. Upon completion, Grays Harbor would be able to compete with Portland, Oregon, Vancouver, British Columbia and Seattle. The Corps estimated that the deep dredge would cost $66 million initially, plus operational costs along the line.

Studies at the University of Washington concluded that the project could cause large-scale damage to bottom life, perhaps killing as many as half the crabs in the estuary. At the same time, the dredging would activate pesticides and other poisons buried in the mud of the harbor. Acting as a natural trap for pollutants, the harbor had, after a century of industrial development, reached the point where its "capacity to assimilate wastes is being exhausted," as a Corps report noted. By 1974 DDT, Lindane, mercury, cadmium, copper and some sulphides already exceeded concentrations reported hazardous to marine life by EPA. The deep-dredge project would inevitably increase the presence of these substances and further their penetration up the food chain, where they might pass from eelgrass to harpacticoid copepod to salmon to man.

The Corps proposed to dump most of the project's 20 million cubic yards of dredge spoils at sea off the mouth of the harbor, so as to avoid filling in more salt marsh, but it was opposed in this by its alter ego, the Port of Grays Harbor. "It's a waste of a natural resource to dump spoils in the open ocean," said Port Manager Hank Soike, who advocated using the material to fill Bowerman Basin, the largest shorebird feeding area remaining in the inner harbor. Since 1940 the Port and the Corps have cooperated in the filling of approximately 700 acres of salt marsh, or 20 percent of the total, for the benefit of various large industrialists.

The ones who stood to take immediate advantage of the deep dredge project were the timber exporters. Weyerhaeuser was particularly blessed in that a quarter of the project's cost was specifically required to pass larger vessels to the company's docks at Cosmopolis. In addition, dredge spoils from the Cosmopolis reach were slated to be deposited as fill on land owned by Weyerhaeuser and others. "We can only conclude that this entire project is a [$66 million] gift from the public to Weyerhaeuser," said David Ortman of Friends of the Earth. "Not only is the public forced year after year to pay to dredge out the results of poor forest practices upstream, now the public is asked to pay for a deeper channel to Weyerhaeuser's docks, . . . all for the purpose of increasing shipments of log, lumber and pulp exports to the Orient."

Much of the timber shipped out of Grays Harbor was old-growth from valleys like the Clearwater, and much of it was shipped unprocessed as raw logs. During the early 1970s, Boise-Cascade, Georgia-Pacific, International Paper and others began to sell large amounts of unprocessed logs to the wood-starved Japanese, who were willing to pay two to three times as much as independent Olympic Peninsula mills could afford. By 1978, export log sales accounted for one-third of the industry's business, and on Grays Harbor, which was the leading export terminal in the state, nearly 90 percent of the logs were being loaded raw and shipped to the Orient. Industry spokesmen like George Weyerhaeuser justified the export of the Olympic Peninsula's last old-growth timber in terms of economic stability and self-sufficiency.

"No family, corporation or *country* can afford over the long term to spend beyond its income," Weyerhaeuser wrote in a guest column for Nick Thimmesch in January 1981. "But the United States has placed itself in position of dangerous international vulnerability by doing exactly that. In every year since 1970, with the exception of . . . 1973 and 1975 . . . our country has imported more than it has exported. In each of the past three years, our international trade deficit has stood at about $30 billion. Were it not for sales abroad of renewable agriculture and forest products, which together pay for about two thirds of America's imported oil, we would be even more deeply in the red." Weyerhaeuser called on America to "develop an export mentality" and make increased government assistance to export firms "a national goal."

The Weyerhaeuser Company and the other timber exporters already enjoyed a number of special economic privileges. Foremost among these is the Domestic International Sales Program, known as DISC. Part of Richard Nixon's new economic policy of 1971, DISC essentially established a tax shelter for firms involved in the business of exporting timber. Under the program, the big timber companies were allowed to charter special corporations to engage exclusively in the export business.

These enterprises are allowed to defer payments (sometimes permanently) on half the profits they show. According to the Pacific Northwest Research Center in Eugene, Oregon, the DISC tax break for Weyerhaeuser amounted to $7.5 million in 1972 alone. Export sales also enable timber firms to maximize the amount of their income taxed at capital gains rates, rather than the significantly higher standard rate for corporate income.

Other attractions for the timber companies in the export business have been the reduction in payroll resulting from the fact that the timber is not processed in the United States, and the elimination of their weaker and smaller competitors. Congressman Don Bonker, whose Southwest Washington district boasts Weyerhaeuser as its largest landowner, observed: "The fact is that small mills are shutting down in the Northwest, and part of the reason is log exports. When we export logs we also export jobs." The predictions of the Pacific Northwest Forest and Range Experimental Station regarding declining timber harvests and forests products employment are being borne out. More than a dozen Oregon sawmills closed in 1978 and 1979, bringing unemployment to thousands and economic hardship to communities like Mill City, Philomath and Willamina.

The timber multinationals meanwhile were being lavished with more privileges from foreign countries. Consider the offer of the Philippines as described in a full-page advertisement in the *New York Times*. Under a photo captioned "Filipino children wave flags for the New Society," the ad proclaimed: "We like multinationals." To prove it, the government of this timber-rich Southeast Asian country ("Our country is lovely . . . And loaded") was offering "tax exemptions and credits. Tax deductions for reinvestment and labor-training expenses. Accelerated depreciation. Carry over of net operating loss incurred during the first ten years of operation." In addition, the regime of Ferdinand Marcos promised to spend nearly 75 percent of the national budget on "economic and social development" projects like ports and dams.

Such blandishments have become increasingly persuasive to the big timber companies as the Northwest's tremendous old-growth forests have dwindled toward the vanishing point. To continue to expand production and profitability, the timber companies needed to secure control of another source of prime timber. Investment in the Far East and the Southern United States began during the 1950s, and by 1973 Weyerhaeuser Vice President C. W. Bingham could declare that the forests of the South "provide the next major region for forest development, both in hardwood and softwood plantations."

It is worth noting that much of timber giants' expansion outside the Northwest and the United States has been financed with the profits from export sales, which Merrill Lynch reported earned some companies more than 60 percent profit in 1979, compared to a relatively sedate 11 percent for domestic sales. In this way, export timber sales have not promoted self-sufficiency, as George Weyerhaeuser suggested, but actually fostered the process of resource depletion, which was the root cause of the country's trade deficit in the first place.

The shifting of the timber industry away from the Northwest that is now underway marks the third time in less than a century that American lumbermen have exhausted an area and moved on. First came the pine forests of upper New England, and then the Great North Woods of the upper Midwest. Now, three-quarters of a century after Frederick Weyerhaeuser began buying land in Washington, Oregon and Idaho, history seemed to be doubling back on itself like the big oxbow on the lower Humptulips.

Neither Weyerhaeuser nor any other of the timber giants were abandoning the Northwest entirely, of course. They had invested millions in pollution control and mechanization, and they intended to be around to take advantage of the next harvest cycle, which current state and federal policies seemed to insure would give them a monopoly on the supply of timber.

There was, however, a certain similarity between the "cut and run" policies of Frederick Weyerhaeuser and George Weyerhaeuser's modern gambit. Once again the company had overlogged an area in a manner destructive to the environment. And once again, the profits from the venture were great enough to allow it to continue the process in another part of the world.

ELEVEN

THE FIRST REPORTS WERE EXCITED and vague. Something about the top of a mountain giving way in the rain. No one was hurt, but the scene obviously made an impression on those who saw it. "It's like a moonscape made of mud up there," one person said.

Within a matter of hours it was official. Several thousand cubic yards of earth at the site of the Satsop nuclear power plants had sloughed off into three creeks that join the Chehalis River about twenty miles upstream from Grays Harbor. Hurried calls shot back and forth between the utility consortium that was building the reactors and various state and federal authorities, while in the towns of Elma, Satsop and Montesano, people began to talk about the brown stain in the Chehalis.

The rain that triggered the first slides continued through the next day, August, 23, 1977, dropping a total of two inches in twenty-four hours. Such storms are relatively common in the

Chehalis Valley, which annually receives nearly 100 inches of precipitation. Residents have adjusted to this fact of life by making the rain porch an almost universal feature of home architecture, and the Atomic Energy Commission recognized it as well by making a substantial erosion control system a prerequisite for sanctioning the reactors' construction. In order to get the necessary federal permit for its plants, the Washington Public Power Supply System had to pledge to install a $1 million drainage system capable of handling 5.5 inches of rain in twenty-four hours, more than twice the amount that actually fell.

The immediate cause of the mudflows in Workman, Fuller and Purgatory creeks was the failure of the public utility to keep its word. "They had all this money allocated for erosion control," Tom Cropp of the Washington Department of Game recalled of the first phase of construction at Satsop, "but they were speeding along and didn't want to divert the people to do the work." The utility, which is commonly known by its acronym WPPSS (pronounced "Whoops"), later admitted that the bulk of the promised system had never been installed, and that most of what had been completed was subsequently covered over in the process of construction. In early September, an investigation by the state determined that WPPSS had violated the terms of its license. Shortly thereafter the utility suspended all other work to fight the growing erosion problem full-time.

"Something broke down someplace," WPPSS Managing Director Neil Strand said of his agency's efforts to build some of the largest nuclear power plants in the United States, "[but] we're going to be able to handle whatever rain we get here. I'm telling you we'll be doing everything to make sure nothing like this ever happens again." But it did happen again. During October and November, the seasonal rains overwhelmed the check dams and pumping stations WPPSS had hastily installed over the preceding weeks, and a large amount of mud was again washed down the creeks into the Chehalis. In desperation, WPPSS finally decided to cover sixteen acres of the excavation in plastic, which was done at a cost of $1 million. Before spring, WPPSS had spent a total of $18 million on erosion control at Satsop.

"The horse was already out of the barn by that time, of course," observed Department of Game biologist Bob Watson. Watson made a survey of the damage to the three creeks early that winter. He found that one—Fuller Creek—had been completely devastated, and that the two others were seriously clogged with silt and debris. It was clear that the wild salmon and trout in these streams were lost. The exact extent of the damage was not known, however, because WPPSS had failed to conduct an adequate survey of fish life prior to construction as promised, according to Game spokesmen. Watson estimated the annual loss of trout alone at $28,120 and termed the incident a "biological catastrophe." WPPSS estimated the annual loss of trout at $14.75.

Amid howls of outrage from people like Jake Metcalf of the Northwest Steelheaders, the issue went before the Energy Facility Site Evaluation Council (EFSEC) for a determination of the utility's responsibility. At the time, the council was already considering the case of a much larger fish kill caused by the construction of two other WPPSS reactors near Hanford on the Columbia. An estimated 3.6 million fall Chinook fry from the last free-flowing section of the Columbia were killed in April 1976 when WPPSS ignored the warnings of Department of Fisheries biologists during an experimental drawdown of the river. The State of Washington was asking $1.6 million in damages in this case, while WPPSS countered with an offer of $180,000.

WPPSS had killed significant numbers of wild salmon in both instances, but in keeping with the longstanding bias of all parties concerned, the only remedy under serious consideration was the increased propagation of hatchery salmon. On the Columbia, the state energy council ordered WPPSS to pay for a $500,000 expansion of the state's Priest Rapids hatchery, along with the cost of producing 834,000 Chinook smolts for four years. Assuming that the Priest Rapids hatchery would be able to create a self-sustaining hatchery run of comparable size, newspapers and television stations in Washington hailed the energy council's ruling as environmental justice: "A Fish for a Fish" the headlines read. Unfortunately, the Department of Fisheries' own hatchery records for the mid-Columbia showed little rational basis for the belief.

Returns to all five state facilities had been erratic for a decade, and in 1977 four (including Priest Rapids hatchery) were unable to return their seed. As a result, stations like the large Klickitat hatchery had to import eggs every year. Some of these eggs came from hatchery surpluses elsewhere, but others came from native fish that otherwise would have spawned in the wild, where their chance of successfully propagating was better than at "zero escapement" state operations. By 1979, Klickitat, Ringold and Rocky Reach alone represented a drain of nearly ten million eggs annually. To increase artificial propagation of salmon meant stealing more eggs from wild runs that were already under consideration for the threatened or endangered species list. At best, the WPPSS-supported hatchery work at Priest Rapids could offset this additional loss of wild fish with the creation of a hatchery run under the control of the Washington Department of Fisheries. At worst, it could repeat WPPSS's kill of 3.6 million Chinook fry and double the impact of the original accident.

On the Chehalis, the Washington Department of Game used the money it received from WPPSS to expand another troubled hatchery system at the expense of the wild fish. In 1973, the year that WPPSS announced plans for the Satsop nukes, a revealing report on Game's efforts to artificially propagate steelhead was prepared for the department by noted fisheries biologist Loyd Royal. He observed that the wild steelhead population in Washington had dropped sharply over the previous twenty years, and singled out the state's own hatchery program as a part of the reason. "One can only conclude," Royal wrote, "that the wild winter and probably summer steelhead populations have declined with the development of the hatchery program. . . ." Competition for food and space, genetic pollution and egg robbing were the principal means by which hatchery steelhead were killing their wild counterparts, according to Royal's *An Examination of the Anadromous Trout Program of the Washington Department of Game.*

Regarding the ability of the state's steelhead hatcheries to show a return of fish, Royal found "striking evidence that planting increased numbers of [hatchery] steelhead smolts in recent years has not increased the number of returning adults." Between 1960 and 1970, the number of steelhead released by the Department of Game had grown 43 percent, while the number of fish caught had increased by only 3 percent, and the actual number of returning spawners appeared to show "a modest decline." Royal noted that poor record keeping by Game's hatchery division made it impossible to precisely assess hatchery performance, but from the evidence that existed the picture was clear: "Most [hatchery] operations have been an economic failure and have failed to substantially increase the runs." Modification of existing Department of Game policies might increase the survival of hatchery or wild steelhead to a degree, but Royal made no secret of his view that "artificial propagation of salmon will kill the wild runs."

Royal, who was sixty-seven at the time, spoke with some authority on the subject of wild salmon. For the previous twenty-four years he had been chairman of the International Pacific Salmon Fisheries Commission, a compact that exercises joint Canadian-American authority over the sockeye runs in the Fraser River. During Royal's association with the commission, the famous Fraser sockeye were one of the few major runs on the West Coast to actually increase in number. It was also during this period that the Fraser supplanted the Columbia as the dominant salmon river south of the Yukon. More impressive still, the Fraser sockeye were entirely wild. "They had a hatchery when I went there," Royal recalled after his retirement to Centralia, Washington, "but I closed it down." Instead of artificial propagation, Royal attempted to offset environmental degradation on the Fraser by making more good habitat available to the wild fish. Beginning in the early 1950s on British Columbia's Horsefly Lake, the commission built six spawning channels for sockeye and pink salmon on the Fraser. Although differing somewhat in design, these facilities were essentially man-made replicas of pristine rivers packed as tightly as intestines into a limited space.

The Department of Game chose to ignore the larger implications of Royal's report, but on smaller technical matters it paid respectful attention. "I believe every recommendation [of Royal's] has been implemented," Jack Ayerst, the head of Game's hatchery program, told me in 1978. Among these was no longer starving young hatchery fish to artificially induce the smolting transformation, and no longer planting the culls from the hatchery process. Of particular importance to the Satsop was an accompanying change in Game's policy concerning the kind of eggs they used in their hatcheries. For years Game had relied heavily on one race of fish, an early winter run from Chambers Creek on Puget Sound. Plants of Chambers Creek fish worked well at times (a 20 percent return is the record), but at others their survival was considerably less than the wild steelhead. This was the case on the Satsop, where hatchery plants had returned hardly any fish at all. Hoping to take advantage of the superior survival of the wild Satsop steelhead noted by Royal and others, the Department of Game decided to use them as the stock for future hatchery operations.

Like Quinault, the word Satsop originally referred to a river, a tribe of Indians, and a prized run of salmon. Known as *tsá tsap*, these steelhead and spring Chinook (the term appears to have referred to both) were famous on nearby Puget Sound, where pioneering icthyologist George Suckley observed in 1848: "The Puget Sound Indians take a salmon in summer which is known to the . . . bands speaking the Nisqually dialect as *sat-sup*. This they consider to be the best of all the kinds of salmon they catch." The *tsá tsap* had suffered horribly at the hands of dam builders, loggers, industrialists and fishermen since Suckley's time, but a few wild steelhead persisted in returning to the river every year. The Department of Game's plan was to take as many eggs as possible from these fish, incubate and raise them in its hatcheries, and then plant them back in the Satsop. And so when EFSEC awarded Game $13,000 in 1979 for damage done to wild trout by construction of the Satsop nuclear power plants, the state used the bulk of the money not on habitat improvement for wild fish, but on collecting the eggs of wild Satsop steelhead for hatchery propagation.

By then, some curious discoveries were being made about the site where the two Satsop nuclear power plants were under construction. Fuller Hill south of the Chehalis River had supposedly been chosen as the best place in the state to build a reactor by a WPPSS study, but the actual choice of the area had more to do with Wynoochee Dam than anything else. Faced with the politically nightmarish prospect of trying to pay for the dam out of local property taxes, the political leaders of Grays Harbor were extremely anxious to find a buyer for the water before their congressional debt moratorium expired. Working in concert with representatives of the groups who stood to lose the most in a property tax spiral (Weyerhaeuser, ITT-Rayonier, numerous savings and loans and mortgage-holding banks, real estate speculators, and so on), the City of Aberdeen, Port of Grays Harbor, Grays Harbor County and Grays Harbor Public Utility District mounted a campaign to have a nuclear power plant built in the area. Port Manager Hank Soike was the driving force and "inspiration" behind the effort (as with the Grays Harbor Deep dredge project and so many other industrial development schemes), but the man who made it possible was WPPSS Managing Director Jack Stein, a friend of Soike's who had recently resigned as manager of the Grays Harbor Public Utility District to become head of WPPSS.

Stein and WPPSS selected the Grays Harbor area as the site for two nuclear power plants in 1973. Strong opposition to the plants was expressed by local residents, but the pronuclear interests were able to obtain state approval for the project without the popular referendum it would clearly have lost. The City of Aberdeen and the rest eventually got their $13 million contract with WPPSS for water from Wynoochee Dam, but before the first year of construction was completed at Satsop, a much less glowing picture of the site began to emerge. First it was learned that a small earthquake fault ran through it, and then Frank McElwee, assistant director of projects at WPPSS, compared the soil to "the flour your mother used to sift." McElwee noted flatly that such "a soil with 40 percent moisture and 40 percent fines [sand] is very difficult to work with . . . when you're trying to build an embankment." WPPSS had previously indicated that on-site sandstone would provide all fill needed for the construction of the plants. But after the slides and discoveries like McElwee's, it became necessary to truck in 2.5 million cubic yards of gravel, enough to cover sixty football fields to a depth of 10 yards. Most of this came from the strip mines that proliferated on what had been rich agricultural land in the nearby Chehalis Valley.

During the fall of 1978, problems began to develop over substandard workmanship in the twin 1,100-megawatt plants themselves. In October, eleven concrete inspectors were fired for falsifying their work qualifications; none had passed the written exam required for such work. Several months later it was discovered that two sixteen-foot vibrators and some hose had been imbedded in the foundation of one of the reactors when the concrete was poured. Unable to locate their exact whereabouts, WPPSS decided to leave the vibrators and hoses where they were. Two months after this, a former quality control inspector at the plant charged that X-rays revealing defective welds had been falsified to obtain their approval. While WPPSS and an independent inspection firm were denying these charges, workmen failed to install 200 steel bars designed to give earthquake protection.

Many of these incidents were the fault of subcontractors hired by WPPSS, but through the whole saga ran the thread of bad management by WPPSS itself. The erosion control fiasco (which cost the public an eventual $138 million when the job could have been done right in the first place for $1 million) was one of many examples of how decisions by Jack Stein, Neil Strand and others drove the cost of the projects higher and higher. Another example was the $2 million WPPSS paid to a Denver prospecting firm for fraudulent uranium claims in the Red Desert area of Wyoming. According to a story by Dan Seligman in the *Post-Intelligencer*, WPPSS ended up paying millions for claims it could have secured (had they been properly staked) for $500,000. A congressional committee termed WPPSS's behavior in the affair "questionable management by a municipally owned corporation which is utilizing public bond money." During December 1978, another report commissioned by the Bonneville Power Administration concluded that WPPSS management had lost control over "future schedule and costs" at the five nuclear power plants it was building in Washington. The report by Theodore Barry and Associates of Los Angeles detailed fifteen areas of management weakness and charged that the true condition of the projects was being hidden from the twenty-two public utility districts for which WPPSS serves as the construction arm.

The cost of the two Satsop plants was estimated at $400 million in 1973. Six years later, the cost had risen to $4.4 billion, and the project was a total of sixty months behind schedule. During the same period, the cost of building all five WPPSS plants had climbed from $4 billion to $10.5 billion. By late 1978, the cost of WPPSS's nukes was climbing at a rate of $1 *billion* a month. Unalarmed, most of the WPPSS board felt, like Benton County Public Utility Commissioner John Goldsworthy, that the Bonneville report complaining about costs was a "hatchet job." Only one member of the public board that nominally controls WPPSS had any misgivings about what was going on. This was William Hulbert, manager of the Snohomish County Public Utility District. At a meeting on January 13, 1979, Hulbert rebuked the board for its lack of supervision over WPPSS staff and projects, specifically objecting to the routine approval by the board of a $43 million item. He told his fellow board members, "for months we've been automatically approving change orders [amendments to existing contracts] worth millions of dollars and [there hasn't been] a goddam explanation."

Echoing the Barry report, Hulbert went on to read a memorandum between Bonneville Power officials in which they discussed construction problems at WPPSS plants in detail. "You're not getting that kind of information from your staff," he told the board. "You'd never know how bad things are over there [Hanford and Satsop]. It's enough to curl your hair." Bonneville's interest in WPPSS's affairs stemmed from the fact that it was Bonneville, and not WPPSS, that ultimately had to worry about what happened to the reactors. For just as the City of Aberdeen was able to pass its debt for Wynoochee Dam on to the larger public body of WPPSS, WPPSS had succeeded in passing its debt for the reactors on to the larger public body of Bonneville Power. Between 1971 and 1973, Bonneville agreed to purchase the output from two plants at Hanford and one at Satsop, no matter what the electricity finally cost. By 1980, WPPSS cost overruns had helped raise the electrical bills of people in Washington, Oregon, Idaho and California as Bonneville was forced to raise its wholesale rates between 88 and 112 percent.

Curiously, one thing that WPPSS did not want to pay for was the pollution control equipment required to meet the terms of its original federal and state licenses. Three months after Hulbert's outburst, EFSEC began considering WPPSS's request for relaxation of thirteen water pollution standards set for the Satsop plants. WPPSS was asking to increase the discharge of copper, zinc, nickel, some other heavy metals and hot water. Spokesmen for the utility claimed that the release of additional pollution would not have an adverse affect on the salmon of the Chehalis River, but the Departments of Fisheries and Game disagreed. At the heart of the issue was copper, which is known to inhibit the production of an enzyme needed by salmon to make the transition from fresh to salt water. Copper, particularly in its ionized form, is also recognized as directly toxic to salmon in sufficient doses.

Both sides mustered considerable scientific evidence to support their cases, but with the experts for WPPSS (Roy Nakatani of the University of Washington) and the state (Patrick Davies of the Colorado Division of Wildlife) waiting in the wings, the proceedings took an unexpected turn. On the first day of testimony in Olympia, Ken Wise, environmental engineer for WPPSS, told EFSEC Chairman Nicholas Lewis that WPPSS had never expected to have to comply with the original pollution standards, and therefore had not designed the plants to meet them. Wise said that if the state actually required WPPSS to meet the terms of its original licenses for Satsop, it would cost the public an additional $60 million and cause additional delays. "The council has an opportunity to save rate payers a substantial amount of money," he said. Under questioning from Lewis, Wise added that the decision to design the plants to standards then illegal was made at the assistant director level, and he did not know if the WPPSS board had been informed.

Testimony introduced by Assistant Attorney General James Johnson cast an even more bizarre light on WPPSS's behavior. Under subpoena, Boeing Environmental Products President John Andrew told the energy council that his company had sold "zero discharge" pollution control equipment since 1973 that would eliminate the need to dump any heavy metals into the Chehalis River. The Boeing system, which had already been purchased by a number of public utilities in the South and Southwest, could have been installed at Satsop for less than the polluting system that WPPSS had chosen, according to Andrew. "We talked to them," Andrew said of WPPSS, "but they didn't seem to be excited about the idea of zero discharge." Asked if the Boeing system could still be installed for less, Andrew said no. WPPSS had already cast the wrong kind of piping into the concrete foundation of the plants.

As this new controversy flared, WPPSS attempted to disassociate itself from Wise's testimony, even though he remained in his position and did not personally retract any of his previous statements. Managing Director Strand denied that the utility intended to ignore pollution standards, and denied that it was trying to use the additional cost of compliance as a club to get its way. Plans had been prepared to both meet and not meet pollution standards, explained WPPSS counsel John Granger. "We are looking for a determination on which way to proceed," he said. "What's important now is to make certain the council understands we're not trying to pressure them," Strand said, adding with a rhetorical wink: "If saving the rate payer's money is putting pressure on the council—well, boy that's pretty bad."

Strand's solicitous tone did not mollify the local rate payers of the Chehalis Valley. At the council's first public meeting in the small town of Elma, an angry crowd of more than 100 shouted down an administrative law judge and proceeded to verbally attack almost every aspect of the twin nuclear power plants under construction on the hill to the south. Led by local state representatives John Erak and Carol Monohon, speaker after speaker accused WPPSS of "economic blackmail" in its efforts to obtain relaxation of the pollution standards, and they urged the council to enforce the original conditions under which the plants were approved. When hearing examiner Patrick Biggs attempted to limit the comments of Jim Todd of the Northwest Steelheaders, he was shouted down with cries of "WPPSS gets unlimited time to tell you what they think," and "Sit down and let the man talk." Biggs did sit down, and for the next hour and a half he and a dozen other sweat-drenched council representatives were treated to a vivid picture of local sentiment.

One eighty-four-year-old woman, Mrs. Dale Willis, hobbled up to the microphone and described the large salmon runs she and her husband saw in the Chehalis when they moved to the area in 1925. "No one in this country will see that again if this pollution is allowed," she said. "One gallon is one gallon too much." In a cracking voice, the white-haired dairy wife spoke bitterly of the farm land that was being destroyed by WPPSS gravel mining operations. "We have to think of the generations to follow us. . . . These nuclear power plants should be discontinued, and no more work should be done on them at all." Lanny Carpenter, a much younger resident of Pe Ell in the upper Chehalis Valley, brought the evening to its dramatic climax when he told the Energy Facility Site Evaluation Council, "If you are so remiss as to allow WPPSS to increase discharges of chemical and thermal waste into the river, the death of those fish will be on your hands, and every one of my children will know your names." Carpenter scanned the faces of the panelists before him while the room fell silent. Not one local resident testified in favor of WPPSS's request that night.

As it turned out, neither the feelings of local residents nor the testimony of the experts had much effect on the outcome. In August, 1979, Administrative Law Judge Biggs allowed all of the modifications sought by WPPSS. Biggs told the council (which later approved his ruling) that the increased pollution from the nuclear power plants would not harm salmon or the "pristine Chehalis" in any way. According to the Associated Press, Biggs said the critical evidence favoring WPPSS was the fact that salmon do not spawn or rear in the vicinity of the plant. In making this determination, Biggs apparently did not realize that all parties (WPPSS included) agreed that large numbers of adult and juvenile salmon were found in exactly the section of the Chehalis where the waste was to be discharged. These fish represented runs of all species to the entire upper river.

The Department of Fisheries had presented evidence that the amount of heavy metal pollution sought by WPPSS would impede the salmon's ability to migrate, and possibly kill the juveniles when they tried to go to sea. WPPSS countered with tests showing that the pollution would not kill the salmon outright. WPPSS testimony never addressed the meat of the state's case, and apparently neither did Biggs. The original energy council license for Satsop allowed WPPSS to divert 17 percent of the Chehalis to cool its plants, thereby eliminating Elizabeth Creek during the summer, and drying up the salmon holding area on the Chehalis known as the Green Banks. The new action allowed WPPSS to increase the pollution discharged into the other major salmon holding area just below the mouth of the Satsop.

There was little doubt that the council's ruling would affect life throughout the Grays Harbor area since it would increase the presence of heavy metal pollution that was already sufficiently severe around harbor dredging operations to be hazardous to marine life. On the Chehalis itself, the increased pollution at Satsop would draw the noose a little tighter around the upriver runs of wild salmon. For the past half century or more, the Chehalis had been losing its salmon and trout like a tree dying back from the top. While many runs disappeared altogether (the famous *satsup* spring Chinook were killed off, as were the sockeye that used to run into Nahwatzel Lake), the remaining runs abandoned the upper reaches of their range. The Department of Fisheries estimated in 1978 that the upper Chehalis supported roughly one-fiftieth the number of wild coho it should. Chum salmon were found "in great quantities" by a Hudson's Bay Company agent in 1824, but a century later this species no longer ventured beyond Cloquallum Creek, forty miles downstream. Now migration-retarding pollutants from the Satsop plants would be released five miles downriver from this.

The more cynical observers of the situation on the Satsop had predicted this outcome all along on the basis of the governor's power over EFSEC, and the prejudices of the person who then held that office. Washington's governor at the time WPPSS sought to increase its pollution of the Chehalis was Dixy Lee Ray. A squat, forceful woman of sixty-two, Ray was one of the most outspoken advocates of nuclear power in the country. She was also a marine biologist with a Ph.D. from Stanford. Christened Margaret, Dixy Lee chose a new name for herself as a child growing up in Tacoma, and a new life as well when she later joined the faculty of the University of Washington Department of Zoology. Boring marine animals were her specialty, but her narration of a science series for the university's television station soon showed something of the broader power and appeal of her personality. Bright, eccentric and blunt, she gave the impression of being a person whose judgment was based on logic, rather than the silly conventions of the everyday world.

Passed over for promotion at the University of Washington, Ray resigned in 1962 to become director of the Pacific Science Center, a low-budget "house of science" left over from the Seattle World's Fair. Here she functioned as a public relations agent for the general causes of science and development. Speaking of her subsequent appointment to the Atomic Energy Commission, she recalled: "The [Nixon] administration and Jim Schlesinger obviously could see what was coming—a growing opposition to nuclear energy, thanks to Ralph Nader and his pals. Schlesinger wanted to be able to say to the Naderites, 'You see, we are deeply concerned about the impact of nuclear power production on the environment. That's why we've invited one of the nation's leading environmentalists, and a reputable scientist, at that, to sit on the [Atomic Energy] Commission.' What a masterpiece of irony lay ahead!"

Appointed by Nixon to the Atomic Energy Commission in 1972, Ray quickly established herself as a proponent of things nuclear. She compared the blast of an atomic bomb to "sculpture," and gleefully mocked those who questioned the safety of nuclear power. Eating was more hazardous to human health than nuclear power, Ray declared, because "in 20 years, only seven people lost their lives in atomic accidents, while . . . 300 people choke to death every year while eating." Her quick tongue and unusual style (she lived in a trailer on a Maryland dairy farm and squealed around Seattle in a Jaguar with a bulb horn) made her one of the few Washington characters of the gray Nixon years. She fully enjoyed the attention her style brought, but when a duel with Henry Kissinger went against her, she quit with a vocal public attack on the Secretary of State, and returned to her Fox Island home on Puget Sound.

Eighteen months later, she and her constant companion, a white poodle named Jacques, moved again—this time to the governor's mansion in Olympia. Elected as a Democrat, Ray's political framework remained decidedly Nixonian. While cutting social services, she expanded state aid to the largest economic interests in the region. On the Columbia River in 1977 Ray's Department of Ecology allocated a substantial amount of water that had already been requested for salmon to a Mormon-controlled agribusiness venture that wanted to irrigate the Horse Heaven Hills. On the Skagit River in 1978, she personally ordered the Department of Ecology to oppose the departments of Fisheries and Game when they sought to prevent practices at Seattle City Light's Ross Dam that had killed as many as 239,000 Chinook fry in one night. Where the Department of Ecology had functioned as a quiet force for the degradation of the state's wild salmon under Governor Evans, Ray made the department an active agent against its namesake.

Considering energy essential to industrial expansion, Ray pursued its development with special enthusiasm. She advocated relaxing licensing procedures for nuclear power plants so they could be built more quickly, and volunteered Washington as a storage site for nuclear wastes from other areas. When the Barry report found WPPSS virtually out of control in 1978, Ray jumped to the utility's defense by attacking the paper that broke the news. She called the story in the *Post-Intelligencer* by Bill Prochnau and Larry McCarten "a classic example of bad journalism" that only "picked out what was negative and adverse. . . ." (Questioned later, Ray admitted that she herself had not read the report.) The twin Satsop nukes had first been proposed when Ray was at the Atomic Energy Commission, and there was simply no way she was going to let a technicality like pollution control stand in the way of their expeditious completion.

The summer that WPPSS got its pollution waiver, it was already apparent that a number of the Chehalis runs were *in extremis*. "Call it horrendous, terrible, disastrous, groty, awful or whatever," said Department of Fisheries biologist Rick Brix of the Chehalis chum. "There hasn't been a strong enough adjective invented to cover what we're looking at here." On a typical spawner survey of the Maple Glen area on the Middle Fork Satsop the year before, the department found 179 chum salmon, of which 89 were alive and 90 dead. At the same time and place in 1979, there were two chum, one dead and one alive. The great danger for the salmon in this is that one of their generational links may be broken, and the whole run weakened, like an engine missing on one cylinder. Given time and protection, wild salmon runs can often rebuild a lost year class (through the combined efforts of jacks, older fish and strays from other rivers), but on the Satsop that fall I found the wild chum had neither.

The rain on the windshield turned to a very wet snow as I drove west from Olympia on the last day of November 1979. There were mallards wading in the puddles along the road and seagulls were strolling in the vivid green fields of new-sown grass outside Oakville. At Elma, where the Chehalis Valley broadens dramatically, the nuclear power plants appeared on a distant, cloud-racked ridge. Speeding closer, I studied the growth of the dark cooling towers, which seemed to be erecting themselves around their red-lit gantries like the martian machines in H. G. Wells's *War of the Worlds*. Farther west, I found the Satsop River brown and swollen, while the small stream just beyond it was dry and filled with rusty machinery. Officially known as Chehalis system stream 0361, this creek was once a chum producer, but water diversions and other human activities have since eliminated nearly all of its former three-and-one-half-mile length.

At Brady, I left Highway 12 and headed up the Satsop into a bosky country studded with lichen-hung white oaks. Throughout this lower section, the Satsop flows through a land of giants.

Geologists believe that the Chehalis Valley was formed during the last glaciation when a mile-high tongue of ice cut off the opening of the Strait of Juan de Fuca, blocking the escape of the Fraser River as well as all the rivers of Puget Sound and the eastern Olympics. The result, according to Bates McKee's *Cascadia*, was the formation of a several-hundred-square-mile lake covering "the entire lowland between the ice wall, the mountains, and [southern] Puget Sound. . . ." The only way out was around the Olympics, and so one day, 15,000 years ago, a huge torrent cut a new channel to the sea at Grays Harbor. This unnamed giant, which was several times larger than the modern Columbia, reshaped much of the southern Olympic Peninsula, and then, with the subsequent retreat of the glacier, vanished.

Ever since, the three forks of the Satsop have been reworking the lower valley into the kind of world most preferred by chum salmon. Chum, *Oncorhynchus keta*, are the largest Pacific salmon after Chinook, but their nature is entirely different. Instead of strong rivers, chum seek springs, sloughs and braided side channels as spawning grounds. They will even run "in rivulets by the roadside, where the water is not over two or three inches deep," as one nineteenth-century observer noted. Known as dog salmon because of the pronounced canine teeth of the mature males, chum were not fished heavily by whites until choicer runs like the *satsup* spring Chinook had been exterminated. The now extinct Satsop Indians, however, considered them to be the chief of all the salmon. According to Katherine Van Winkle Palmer's *Honné: The Spirit of the Chehalis*, the transformer Honné created live salmon from the dead, saying: " 'Your name is *Klahwhi*, dog salmon. This is as far as you will go up the river. You will come up the river quickly and . . . your life will be short.' And Honné gave the fish a striped blanket made of cedar bark dyed with alder. That is the coat of colors which the fish still wears."

It had stopped snowing by the time I splashed through the deserted parking lot at Shafer State Park, about a half mile down the Middle Fork Satsop from one of the best springs on the river. Between slugs of cookies and apple cider, I began laying on layers: two pairs of wool socks, long underwear, wool pants, wool shirt, felt insoles, rubber hip boots, wool coat, red, white and blue wool gloves, scarf, foam-insulated baseball cap, Polaroid glasses and finally my walking stick. Stepping into the river right in front of my car, I startled three big, gray Chinook that had been holding in the deeper water along the bank. Pleased to find fish so quickly, I paused to survey the situation. There were six redds visible on the tail of the riffle in front of me, and at least that many more in close to the shore under a canopy of salmonberry. Here two female Chinook erupted into combat, thrashing the water with a sharp report like shaking out a sheet in a stiff souwester. In the confusion, I edged close enough to touch a thirty-pound Chinook male with the end of my stave, which ignited another rocketing display.

Once across the dozen-yard-wide riffle, I headed up the south shore toward a large green pool that was almost entirely overhung by a mossy old maple. There were two dozen apple-colored coho swaying like sea grass in the middle of the pool, and on the other side of the river at the mouth of the spring, a dead chum. Stepping across this unnamed spring in one stride, I found the remains of some long-dead ten-pound chum laid out on the grass. I had examined them more closely a couple of weeks before, and been struck by the puncture marks on their backs. At the time, I guessed the fish had been gaffed and then abandoned. Ahead, the clear, grassy-bottomed spring led back along the edge of a cliff into twenty acres of alder thicket laced with rivulets of running water. I followed a heavily used animal path bearing the prints of deer, raccoon, lynx and dog along the side of the spring until I came into a clearing where I saw a small chum female holding tensely in a pool at the base of a thirty-foot wall of rock and clay.

It was just beyond in the alder maze that I began to realize what was happening. A freshly killed chum male lay on a bed of buttercups by the spring. There were two parallel gashes in his back, but no other marks. He appeared to be in his prime and still contained milt, or sperm. Rolling him over, I found matching slashes on the other side and blood oozing from the gills. I stood up and looked around me in the drear light. Whatever had killed this fish (and the others too, I began to suspect) was not killing for food. Farther in, where the spring braided and braided again to the point where it was often less than three inches deep, I found several more freshly killed chum thrown on the bank amid a mosaic of what was now exclusively dog tracks. The air had the gagging stink of rotting flesh, and on a small island in the midst of the many channels, I discovered why.

Eight chum carcasses lay on the muddy remnant of a grassy flat. There had obviously been quite a struggle here. Bending down to examine a gaping female with one bite taken out of her back, I saw her eggs showing through the stumps of bloody, exposed bones. A dozen more chum in similar condition were strewn around. None had been eaten, or even lost their eyes. Only in a few cases had a fish been torn up in the frenzy of the kill, as in the case of a beautiful rust and green male that had his gills ripped off, and a female who had her back cruelly broken and her orange eggs spread in the mud around her. From the heavy tracks around the dead fish and the well-established network of trails along the sides of the twisting springs, it appeared that these wild Satsop chum were being killed by two dogs, one with a print the size of my palm, the other half that size.

In this setting it wasn't hard to imagine them at work. The big dog could easily dash through the deepest water, and the little dog could follow the fish under the overhanging bushes. In their desperate desire to procreate, the chum would have streaked about, sending up great wakes that would have further reduced their running room. There was no place to hide, and with dogs killing for fun, no way to satiate the predator. Altogether that day, I counted twenty-six chum killed by dogs, and another sixteen either dead in the water or too deteriorated to determine the cause of death. Only one fish was alive. Since the Department of Fisheries' most recent survey had found many fewer fish and made no mention of killing by dogs, I decided to call the department's regional office in Montesano.

Hurrying back to the ranger station at Shafer State Park, I found Ranger Al Sinclair working on his truck. His big collie barked menacingly at first, but let me pass to use the phone in the house. While Sinclair leaned on the kitchen counter and listened, I told a Fisheries biologist what I had just seen. The longer I talked, the weirder I felt. "Some of those fish were killed last night," I said finally, "which means it's still going on." The man from Fisheries replied that he "might come up and take a look," but his voice did not sound convincing. "I'm not exactly sure what I could do," he continued. "We just don't have the manpower to do a decent job of enforcement—you know that." The Department of Fisheries had, of course, received approximately $10,000 from WPPSS for the death of wild Chehalis chum and coho, but like the other money, this went to the hatchery division. "Well, sorry to bother you," I heard myself saying. "I just thought you'd like to know."

Meanwhile, the nuclear power plants named for the salmon were experiencing difficulties of their own. Despite Governor Ray's assistance, WPPSS proved unable to deliver workable plans on schedule during 1979 and 1980, resulting in extensive and costly delays. At Satsop, WPPSS was forced to renegotiate its contracts for piping, heating and electrical work (which had already doubled once) from $740 million up to more than $1 billion in 1981. Joel Connelly reported in the *Post-Intelligencer* that despite the expenditure of hundreds of millions of dollars, the last two contracts were still less than 5 percent complete at the time of the financial "realignment." By the early 1980s, the cost of WPPSS Satsop reactors had increased 1,750 percent to more than $7 billion, and the plants were still years from completion. The cost of all five of WPPSS's nuclear power plants had meanwhile risen to $24 billion.

This made WPPSS the single most expensive nonfederal

project ever undertaken in the United States, but it was in fact only the tip of the iceberg. According to a Washington State Senate report prepared by Jim Lazar, the actual cost of the five reactors—that is to say, purchase price plus debt service, depreciation and so forth—would total more than $200 billion over the thirty-five-year span of the bonds WPPSS issued to finance the reactors. (By comparison, NASA spent $36.5 billion during its first eleven years work, which included putting man on the moon.) Figured on the basis of population, WPPSS public debt had reached the equivalent of a $31,000 mortgage on every household in the state, with an obligation to pay $100,000 per household over the next thirty-five years to retire the bonds. To meet these expenses, utilities predicted that electrical rates would jump 400 to 500 percent by the end of the decade.

Soon a U.S. Nuclear Regulatory Commission investigation revealed that one of WPPSS's Hanford plants was so poorly built that it might never be able to operate, and the U.S. Internal Revenue Service began investigating WPPSS in connection with tax fraud, according to a story by Joel Connelly in the *Post-Intelligencer.* The pressure on WPPSS grew still greater in the spring of 1981, when the utility consortium's bankers quietly cut off the credit. By August 1981, it was clear that WPPSS was in the terrifying position of not being able to continue construction on all of its nuclear power plants and not being able to stop either. WPPSS had neither the money to pay its crews beyond October, nor the money to pay for the decommissioning of any of its partially completed projects.

Weeks of desperate negotiations between WPPSS, Bonneville Power, the governors of Washington and Oregon, the aluminum industry and others produced a plan to mothball two plants (one at Satsop and one at Hanford), but the agreement fell through in January 1982 when Tacoma City Light refused to pay its share. This meant that WPPSS had to come up with $335 million to terminate the partially built reactors, as well as the debt service on the $2.5 billion in bonds already sold for plants three and five—sums it could afford even less than mothballing. A note of real fear swept over the proceedings that spring. Edward Carlson, chairman of United Airlines and a former member of the WPPSS board, warned that all five of WPPSS's nuclear power plants were in financial jeopardy, and the possibility of receivership was raised by Seattle City Attorney Doug Jewett.

For the first time, people began to realize how much hung on the fate of the tottering public-utility consortium. If WPPSS went under, it could bankrupt its member utilities, since their obligations to WPPSS must be paid before their own bonded debt. Other governments such as the City of Aberdeen (which badly needs its WPPSS contract for water from Wynoochee Dam) and the State of Washington (which has already had its credit rating lowered, partially as a result of WPPSS) were also threatened.

Equally vulnerable were the large national insurance companies and banks that had purchased large numbers of WPPSS bonds, and were then using them to back their own obligations. It was in this way that the *tsá tsap* touched the life of virtually every American who owns an insurance policy or has a bank account.

TWELVE

I HUNG SUSPENDED in a circle of light. The earth doubled over to envelop the sky. Iridescent rings blazed like a corona around the rim and hid the apparitions hovering outside.

A duck could be seen swimming in two places at once, while my car, which was parked forty feet away on the other side of the stream, had disappeared. I myself was transformed into a creature with the immense head and compressed body often found in Pacific Northwest Indian totem poles.

It took me several seconds to realize that this probably made my red hat the single most obvious element in the entire scene. I reached to remove it, but as I did, the three chum salmon who had been observing me shot away up the glide with a sound like a high diver hitting the water in a tuck. By their alarm, I knew they had recognized me as a man.

Stuffing the hat into my pocket, I continued up Richert Springs in a misty rain. To get beyond the fish who had spotted me, I bushwhacked through the salmonberry until I was wet from head to toe. Such precautions are normally not necessary to view chum, but the salmon native to this tributary of the Skokomish River are exceptional fish.

While chum can become wasted and lethargic before they reach their spawning grounds, Richert Springs chum arrive silvery and electric. As quick as any coho, they tend to have the red flesh characteristic of Alaska's great chum runs. They are also quite large, averaging thirteen pounds in weight, or one-third more than chum in the rest of Washington.

Easing my way back to the edge of the stream, I found six of the wild chum orbiting around a redd that had been dug in the lee of an undercut alder. From my position above and behind them, I was now able to turn the tables and observe the fish at will. Because salmon have a field of vision of approximately 300 degrees, I was in the blind spot of all the fish except those that were chasing downstream.

Much of the fundamental research on what fish can—and can't—see was carried out as a hobby by a turn-of-the-century Englishman named Francis Ward. A physician by profession, Ward described the classic "fish eye" distortion that results when the outside world is viewed from under water, and made the first photographs of the phenomenon. He also documented the existence of the surrounding iridescent ring and area of "total reflection," where the dark bottom of the stream is reflected back down from the surface of the water.

Of Pacific salmon, chum are considered among the most visual at the time of spawning. Biologists base this judgment on the importance appearance plays in finding and keeping a mate. Chum males develop grotesquely pronounced canines, a hump and a ragged series of burgundy slashes resembling claw marks on their green and black sides. The hump is often dusted with a powdery blue, and the wicked teeth accentuated by a gaping white mouth. Females, by comparison, appear to be black, disembodied streaks. Slender and sleek, they are the warm golden gray of the stream bed except for a black lateral line.

Five of the chum on the glide before me were males, and one was a female. The largest of the males, a bruiser weighing close to twenty pounds, was wallowing in the pea gravel at the bottom of the redd and quivering violently. His smaller mate passed back and forth over him with a continuous caressing motion, but never actually lowered herself into the pocket of the nest. The rest of the bucks (or "satellite males" as they are often called) darted around downstream where their V-shaped wakes made the only waves on the clear water.

Although they repeatedly approached the redd and attempted to take the dominant male's place, the satellites were much different in appearance. Where the big male was boldly marked with the burgundy slash pattern, the other males had only a black stripe like a female. So close was the resemblance, in fact, that I at first mistook them for members of the opposite sex. Cornelius Groot of the Pacific Biological Station at Nanaimo, British Columbia, has shown that chum males can change from one of these color patterns to the other as quickly as a chameleon.

When Groot, in experiments, drove the dominant male from the redd with a broomstick, he found that the fish lost the slash pattern. Only when it had regained its confidence enough to reclaim the redd did the pattern reappear. Groot also noted that the red marks were an indicator of which male would prevail in combat between suitors, for the weaker fish usually telegraphed its condition with the fading of the slash pattern during the final phase of the fight. "The color is contained in the layers of the skin," Groot said. "They can open one, close another, and let it shine through. . . . This is a characteristic of all [salmon], but it's more apparent in chum than Chinook or sockeye, for instance."

On Weaver Creek a tributary of the Fraser, chum males sometimes put on yet another set of clothes. Mimicking the brilliant red body and green head of sockeye males, they attempt to spawn with sockeye females. The product of such unions is viable, but generally less so than purebred fish of either species. Other Pacific salmon also hybridize to one degree or another. The Washington Department of Fisheries briefly bred a cross between chum and humpy salmon (called "chumpies") at its Hoodsport hatchery during the 1960s, and I myself have observed a lecherous six-pound pink male attempting to spawn with a twenty-five pound Chinook female in the Graywolf River.

Deciding to let the chum copulate in privacy, I headed upstream toward where the blue flanks of the Olympics loomed through the leafless branches of the trees. Around the next bend I found four more chum indulging the penchant for shallow water that has brought their kind such grief since the coming of the white man. The fish were lazing in a four- or five-inch-deep side channel when I appeared on the bank above. Instantly, three of the fish took off, their tails churning up clouds of silt. The fourth started just a moment later, but the silt stirred up by the others prevented him from seeing the way over the bar into the main stream. After dashing about in a panic for a few seconds, he settled slowly to the bottom where he lay gasping as the silt cloud closed in around him.

It was not yet midafternoon, but dusk was already well advanced. Fingers of low fog were stretching through the valley, and the cars on Highway 101 had begun to turn on their tiny headlights. As I started back the way I'd come, it seemed to me that the tempo of spawning picked up. Chum are active at all times of the day, but like pinks they seem to prefer the cover of darkness, especially for migration. "You can hear them [Richert Springs chum] going over the bar at the Skokomish all night," said Skokomish Tribal Fisheries Manager Dave Herrera. "If you were out there during the daytime, you wouldn't see a thing."

Hererra and I had joked earlier about whether discarded beer cans were taking the place of salmon carcasses in Pacific Northwest streams, but on Richert Springs that day the salmon still held the upper hand. The final count for the lower half-mile of the stream was twenty-two beer cans and fifty-one spawned-out chum. These springs are the favorite spawning grounds for wild

Skokomish chum, which annually number around 15,000 fish. The return to Richert Springs was roughly half the normal number in 1979, but still there were many more fish than on Grays Harbor rivers like the Satsop.

The reason for the greater abundance of Richert Springs chum is the fishes' environment. Although the springs on the Skokomish and Satsop are both fed by a steady welling of cool, clean water, those on the Skokomish are considerably larger. This, and the fact that the low wooded land along Richert Springs has been left almost entirely free of agricultural and residential development, gives the fish that spawn there better protection against predators. Best of all though, the mouth of the spring is only seven miles up the Skokomish from the long, hook-shaped fjord known as Hood Canal.

Named by Captain George Vancouver for the English admiral, Lord Samuel Hood (as was Mount Hood in Oregon), Hood Canal forms the eastern boundary of the Olympic Peninsula. Here the Olympic Mountains rise abruptly from sea level to a mile-high escarpment that has been cut with deep, hatchetlike strokes by five rivers: the Skokomish, Hamma Hamma, Duckabush, Dosewallips and Quilcene. Few places in North America are as visually stunning, but the importance of the canal goes beyond its scenic qualities. With no polluting industries or large population centers anywhere along its sixty-mile length, Hood Canal is the healthiest large estuary remaining in Washington State.

Eelgrass beds abound, and with them the tiny bottom-dwelling invertebrates that live on decaying plants in shallow delta areas. Young chum salmon feed heavily on two of these, harpacticoid copepods and gammarid amphipods, during their stay in the canal. These species comprise a small portion of the total invertebrate population, but wild chum make the most of them by spawning from mid-September through late January. This causes the fry to emerge from the gravel over an equally long period the following spring and helps prevent the fish from overwhelming their food supply.

The amount of food consumed by young chum salmon during this period is crucial to their later survival, according to Charles Simenstad of the University of Washington's Fisheries Research Institute. "The more growth chum put on during their first few weeks in the near-shore environment," he said, "the better chance they have of surviving in the ocean." During the late 1970s and early 1980s, Simenstad studied the invertebrate populations of Hood Canal, Grays Harbor and other Washington waterways. He found many more of the tiny creatures in Hood Canal than Grays Harbor, but also noted that the species that chum eat diminished each year during the course of the fishes' migration through the canal.

By pairing the declines in the harpacticoid copepod population that he was observing in Hood Canal with the times when hatchery chum were released into the area, Simenstad concluded that the hatchery fish were severely depressing the source of both their own sustenance and that of the wild fish. "I have data for 1977, 1978 and 1979," he said, "and it shows that these declines are very clearly correlated to the release of hatchery chum into the canal. During the months of April and May you'd expect to see a rising curve of copepod abundance. . . . Instead, their numbers actually fall." Simenstad urged that hatchery programs be evaluated in light of the finite carrying capacity of the canal, but found little interest in the idea at the Department of Fisheries, which was in the process of dramatically increasing its egg collection and hatchery release program on Hood Canal.

The department was particularly keen on hatchery expansion on the canal because of the notable success of its existing facilities in the area. Hoodsport hatchery, located on Finch Creek five miles up the canal from the mouth of the Skokomish, was one of the best producers in the entire state. Between 1966 and 1971, returns of Chinook, coho and chum to this one hatchery averaged more than 20,000 fish, or more than twice the combined return to the two state salmon hatcheries in the Grays Harbor area. Since the completion of the Hoodsport and nearby George Adams hatcheries, Chinook and coho catches had rebounded from a combined average of 2,500 to a modern high of 44,000 fish a year. Reasoning that the success experienced with relatively small plants of hatchery chum into Hood Canal would hold true for plants forty or more times larger, the Department of Fisheries included a new hatchery program for Skokomish chum in the $33 million Salmon Enhancement Program approved by the state legislature in 1977.

The Department of Fisheries told the legislature that the new hatchery would add 250,000 chum to the Washington catch, a substantial contribution to the Salmon Enhancement Program's overall goal of doubling the state's catch. The planned facility was to be built on Weaver Springs, a tributary of the lower Skokomish, but apparently owing to sloppy drafting of the bill, the location was incorrectly identified as nearby Hunter Springs. In order to obtain the $1.4 million appropriated for the project, the department was forced from this point on to refer to Weaver Springs as "Hunter Springs." Shortly after passage of the enhancement program, the department gave the "Hunter Springs" hatchery a "Declaration of Nonsignificance," meaning that it would have no effect on the environment of the area, and therefore would require no environmental impact statement.

When the Skokomish Tribe protested that the new hatchery could kill the still sizable wild Skokomish chum runs through genetic pollution, competition for food and the overharvest inherent in a mixed stock fishery, Fisheries backed down and agreed to assess the hatchery's impact. The resulting document, which was released in May 1978, contained little mention of the wild fish or discussion of how the state would harvest the hatchery chum without overharvesting the wild chum of areas like Richert Springs. Discussion of Simenstad's research was similarly omitted. Director of Fisheries Gordon Sandison met with representatives of the Skokomish Tribe several times during the winter of 1978, but the tribe continued to oppose the planned release of large numbers of hatchery chum into "Hunter Springs."

The Department of Fisheries, for its part, remained committed to the hatchery, despite diminishing estimates of its contribution to the Washington catch. In January 1979, the department quietly acknowledged to the legislature that its original estimate of the hatchery's production was inflated and unrealistic. Instead of a quarter million fish for the million-plus dollar investment of public funds, the fishermen of the state should expect to catch 150,000 chum a year from the "Hunter Springs" hatchery, according to Fisheries spokesmen. Fisheries also acknowledged around this time that the new hatchery operations in the Hood Canal area would kill approximately 50,000 wild chum. This meant that the net production of the "Hunter Springs" facility was likely to be 100,000 or less. It also dramatically altered the project's cost/benefit ratio, but Fisheries did not advertise this fact to either the legislature or the Indians.

The stage was set for the showdown between the Skokomish Tribe and the Department of Fisheries on March 29, 1979, when the tribe sent Director of Fisheries Sandison a letter declaring that it could not accept the state's planned release of 13 million hatchery chum into "Hunter Springs." Since the Boldt decision required the State of Washington to obtain approval from affected treaty Indian tribes before undertaking enhancement activities, the tribe's letter seemed to place an insurmountable obstacle in the state's path. The tribe indicated that it would expect to hear from the state before any action was taken, but this was not to be. In late April the Department of Fisheries triumphed over the Skokomish the same way it had over the Olympic National Park the year before on the Soleduck: it released the fish into "Hunter Springs" without permission. Later, the department renamed the hatchery after the late Donald Mekernan, avoiding the Hunter/Weaver issue altogether.

When the tribe found out, they were enraged. Their fury was due to the fact that at the same time the state was killing large numbers of wild salmon with its growing hatchery program, it was arguing before U.S. District Judge William Orrick that the Indians had no right to *any* fish produced by the state hatchery system. These fish were the sole property of non-Indian fishermen, the state maintained, since they did not exist at the time that the treaties were signed, and the Indians did not contribute to their support. The Indians were meanwhile asking Judge Orrick in phase II of *U.S. v Washington* to recognize their right to a say in resource development decisions affecting rivers and salmon in Washington. The Indians' case, which was based on the claim that Fisheries had flagrantly failed to protect the resource entrusted to it, was a direct attack on the authority of the State of Washington, and the practices of virtually every resource-dependent industry within its boundaries.

Not surprisingly, the state vehemently opposed Indian participation in resource management decisions on the grounds that even if the treaties gave them the right to half the fish, they certainly did not give them the right to see that the runs were maintained. At the same time, the Department of Fisheries began a publicity campaign designed to blunt criticism of its own management of the salmon resource. To hear the state tell it, there was no current shortage of salmon, and no prospect of shortage in the immediate future. A 1979 report entitled *The Record of Puget Sound Salmon Harvest Management in the 1970s* stated:

> Contrary to popular opinion, Washington State salmon runs have not declined drastically in recent years and are not threatened with extinction. A few individual cases can be cited, but these are definitely exceptions, not the rule. On a statewide basis, a convincing case for optimism can be put forward with respect to the three species predominating in Pacific salmon production from Washington watersheds. The long-term trends for the abundance of Chinook and coho salmon are definitely upward even though we project temporary declines for these species in 1979. The highest number of coho salmon landed in the state (since the inception of a reliable statistical system in 1935) occurred in 1976 —a total of nearly 3.4 million fish. The greatest number of Chi-

> nook salmon landed statewide in a single year also occurred in 1976—1.3 million fish. The third major species produced in Washington streams, chum salmon, has not enjoyed this pronounced long-term upward trend in abundance. Large-scale artificial production efforts are well underway, however, and the preliminary statewide landing estimates for 1978 are the second best on record since 1935. We expect record landings to be the rule in the early 1980s.

Because statements like this constitute the basis upon which the State of Washington has recently spent millions on more hatcheries, it is worth exploring its full ramifications. It is true, for instance, that Washington's 1976 coho catch was the largest since 1935, but it is also true that this catch was achieved by overfishing the wild (and some hatchery) runs to a serious degree. In 1976 the spawning escapement of wild coho in Puget Sound was 110,000, or 40,000 less than the state's own rather modest goal. The same was true for the record catch of Chinook that same year: only 30,000 of the needed 50,000 Puget Sound Chinook survived to spawn in 1976. Seen in a fuller light, these 1976 catches were not so much a tribute to the success of the state's hatcheries as they were a sign of the continuing failure of state management, especially with respect to the wild runs.

Further, the total number of hatchery and wild salmon had not really enjoyed a "pronounced long-term upward trend in abundance." In order to construe a basis for this contention, the state had to restrict its discussion to one part of the state, Puget Sound, during the "long-term" period of six years, 1970–77. During this time the combined state salmon catch did climb slightly, but the spawning escapements of wild and hatchery fish both dropped steadily as a result of overfishing and other elements under state and federal control. Viewed over any significant period of time, the graph of Puget Sound (the best producing area remaining in the state) salmon catches heaves like the chest of a drowning man.

Beginning with the earliest available records, the cyclic peaks and troughs of the Puget Sound salmon catch have been 39 million fish in 1913 and 3.9 million in 1918; 11 million in 1929 and 2.5 million in 1938; 8 million in 1949 and 1.4 million in 1956; 7 million in 1963 and 1.9 million in 1968; 5.5 million in 1977 and . . . ? Clearly, a decline in the peak harvest of 86 percent (since 1913), 31 percent (since 1949), and 22 percent (since 1963) do not support the state's claims that its management has been successful in maintaining the resource. And given the decreased number of spawners that would be returning from the years when insufficient wild spawning escapements were achieved, there was realistically little reason to expect "record landings to be the rule by the early 1980s," unless one intended to continue the plunder of the runs.

During the first years of the enhancement program, this is in fact what happened. While catches increased, escapements of hatchery and wild fish continued to decline, often by design. In June 1979, for instance, the Department of Fisheries announced a new management plan for Puget Sound salmon that would kill one-third of the wild fish remaining in the sound. Except for three rivers (Skagit, Snohomish, Stillaguamish) and a few individual runs elsewhere, the state planned to manage exclusively for hatchery salmon, which meant overfishing the wild stocks. Maintaining that its aim was "to provide protection for a major portion of natural stocks," the department proposed eliminating an estimated minimum of 38 percent of the wild fish, and quite likely more, since Director of Fisheries Sandison admitted that the department's planned mitigation "will require additional refinements derived from applied research." Although not accepted by many of the treaty tribes, the state's plan was instituted de facto in a number of areas.

The wild salmon runs designated by the state for preservation were generally able to meet escapement goals in the years that followed, but the state's hatchery runs were not. Only nine of the state's forty-three hatcheries were able to meet production goals in 1979, according to a story by Robert Mottram in the Tacoma *News-Tribune*. Among those with shortfalls were the

Skagit (48 percent below its goal), Priest Rapids (61 percent below its goal), George Adams (53 percent below its goal) and Humptulips (45 percent below its goal) facilities. The greatest shortfall of all occurred on the Olympic Peninsula at the Satsop Springs Enhancement Program, where the state got only 16 percent of the eggs it needed. Mottram also reported that salmon production in the state's hatchery system had decreased every year since the passage of the enhancement program. Fisheries discounted the report (the original goals were inflated, said enhancement chief Frank Haw), but a similar trend had been observed for some time in Oregon. According to an Oregon Department of Fish and Wildlife study by Alan McGie, returns of Oregon hatchery coho dropped by at least 9 percent a year between 1965 and 1980, while hatchery releases more than doubled from 21 million to 47 million coho annually.

In Washington, during the first few years of the enhancement program, the total poundage of salmon produced by the state's hatcheries dropped 4 percent, but the cost of operating them increased by 15 percent, to $6.2 million a year. During the next biennium, 1979–80, the operational cost of Fisheries' hatcheries jumped to $17 million, and capital expenses for the construction of new hatcheries totaled $42 million. (By comparison, the state spent $403,000 in operational costs and $2.8 million in capital costs for projects to benefit the production of wild fish.) By 1980 the cost of producing salmon in the state's new hatcheries was averaging between $6 and $10 per fish caught, according to a Department of Fisheries report. At some facilities like the enhancement program hatchery on the South Fork of the Willapa River, the projected per-fish cost of production ran as high as $24. Figured on this basis, the full cost to the public of that four-pound, $18 coho in the Port Angeles supermarket would actually be between $28 and $42.

To its credit, the Department of Fisheries' own research and development branch attempted to prevent construction of the Willapa hatchery on the grounds that the cost was "definitely out of line." Tony Rasch of the department advised his superiors in late 1980: "My inclination would be to figure out some way not to build it despite the political pressure to the contrary." The political pressure to which Rasch referred came from the state House and Senate Natural Resources Committees, which were responsible for legislative oversight of the Department of Fisheries. Joining with legislators from the area, the chairmen of these two committees told Director of Fisheries Sandison they wanted the project to proceed. "While the number of fish returning to Washington fishermen per dollar of state expenditure is our most important concern," they wrote, "we also believe very strongly that a project should be built on the South Fork of the Willapa River."

Although the legislature did not get its way on the South Fork Willapu, it played a similar role following the release of the report by the Presidential Task Force appointed by Jimmy Carter to "solve" the Northwest's chronic salmon wars. Like the Royal report four years before, the task force found that many of the state's hatcheries were not producing significant numbers of fish. "A variety of enhancement programs have been undertaken," it noted, "frequently with little control or effort to determine the value of the activity. They have often been continued without any real concern for their value and contribution to the resource." Asked by the press if the state was operating useless hatcheries, the Department of Fisheries' hatchery director, Harry Senn, replied, "I think that's true. I'd rather not name them though, because I'd have a pack of legislators down my neck."

State Representative John Martinis, chairman of the House Natural Resources Committee, ordered an inquiry into the effectiveness of the state's hatcheries a short time later, but he obviously found the prospect disconcerting. "I'm a part of this," he told me of the enhancement program. "I voted for it and my name is associated with it." After the first flush of publicity, Martinis and the Natural Resources Committee's interest in the hatchery study waned until the project was quietly dropped in the summer of 1979. As a result, Senn was never required to identify the hatcheries that represented a chronic drain on the state's general fund, and the promised independent examination of the hatchery program was never conducted. During this period, the Department of Fisheries built eight new hatcheries, including the problematic facilities at Bear Springs on the Soleduck, Satsop Springs on the Satsop, and "Hunter Springs" on the Skokomish.

On September 29, 1980, U.S. District Court Judge William Orrick (who had replaced the ailing Judge Boldt) delivered his verdict in phase II of *U.S. v Washington.* Orrick found for the Indians on both counts, recognizing their right to protect the environment on which the runs depend for their survival, and their right to half the hatchery salmon harvested in Washington. Although Director of Fisheries Gordon Sandison said the decision "won't change the way we do business," it soon became apparent that many non-Indian fishermen, who were the main supporters of the state's century-long war with the Indians over salmon, were finally willing to make peace. "If the goal now is to protect all salmon and we get half of those fish," said Paul Anderson, executive director of the Purse Seiners Association, "I see nothing wrong with the Indians having the rights to environmental protection." Others continued the fight. In late 1981 several Indian fishing boats were destroyed by arson, as was the Squaxin Tribal Center. At the same time, yet another effort was made to extinguish Indian treaty rights, this time through initiative vote.

A somewhat nervous-sounding Assistant Attorney General Ed Mackie added that "the potential for impact on the economy and development and use of resources would be substantially greater under this decision than we've seen under [Judge Boldt's] 1974 decision. This may address how we continue our forest practices, the use of pesticides, what water may be withdrawn from rivers and the priorities, where you can build highways and docks, real estate and shopping centers—the whole bit." Almost immediately the treaty Indian tribes of Washington began to press the cause of the salmon and to bring about what

Mackie had described. Although Orrick had not established a mechanism for the Indians to exercise their environmental protection right (and was clearly not pushing the case with one-tenth the verve of his embattled predecessor), the Indians took legal action against a number of major developments proposed for the state.

On Puget Sound, they sued to prevent Seattle City Light from building Copper Creek Dam on the Skagit; and on the Strait of Juan de Fuca, they sued to prevent Northern Tier from building an oil port and transcontinental pipeline. The Indians also attacked existing developments to obtain relief and redress for the wild salmon. The Skokomish Tribe, for instance, brought suit against both Tacoma City Light and Simpson Timber for their respective practices on the upper Skokomish. On the North Fork, where the wild spring Chinook have been exterminated by two Tacoma City Light dams, the Indians were asking the utility to pass enough water to allow fish to spawn (for much of the year, the North Fork is dry for four miles below Cushman Dam). On the South Fork, where clearcut logging by Simpson Timber has increased river siltation and contributed to the virtual disappearance of the wild spring Chinook, the Indians were asking for an end to damaging logging practices.

At the same time, the Indians' position on hatcheries was changing. Guaranteed half the production of the state's hatchery system by Orrick's ruling, the treaty tribes of Washington began to view artificial propagation a little more benignly. Many of them were attracted to the higher rate of harvest allowed with hatchery fish, and the fact that it is possible to determine through the run-timing of a hatchery run who will have a chance to intercept the fish. "Through stock manipulation you can control the fishery," said Dave Hererra. "We're very aware of this because it's been used against us for so many years." With the help of federal funding, the Quinault, Quileute, Makah, Klallam and Skokomish tribes were all operating hatcheries of some sort by the early 1980s. Sometimes these projects were clearly beneficial, as with the Stillaguamish Tribe's cooperative program with the Department of Fisheries. In this instance, the tribe took summer Chinook reared at a tribal facility and released them above Granite Falls, an impassable barrier on the south fork of the Stillaguamish. Before the fish return, the Department of Fisheries will build a ladder on the falls so the fish can ascend to the upper river.

Inevitably, however, the tribes' increased reliance on hatcheries has involved them in some of the practices they have protested for years. As an example, the same tribe—the Stillaguamish of Puget Sound—also undertook a cooperative program with the Department of Game to release 200,000 steelhead fry into the Stillaguamish River. Explaining why the fish were released at a stage that maximizes residualization and conflict with wild salmon, the tribe echoed the rationale used by Washington Fish Commissioner A. C. Little in 1899. "Rearing and releasing steelhead is an expensive venture," said Terry Martin, tribal fisheries biologist. "Ideally, the steelhead are reared for two years until they become smolts and then released, but costs [approximately $20,000] are prohibitive at this time for the tribe to hold them for that period."

Another reflection of changing Indian attitudes was the cooperative management plan signed by the Skokomish Tribe and the State of Washington in January 1981. The agreement, which was the first in history between a tribe and the state, stipulated that plants of hatchery Chinook and coho would be increased, in the case of Chinook to the highest level on record. Regarding chum salmon, the two parties agreed that hatchery plants should not exceed 50 million annually, or almost fifty times more than a decade before. Tribal hatchery releases were to make up part of this number, and the Skokomish Tribe chose the wild Richert Springs chum as the stock they would use. When the administration of President Ronald Reagan killed the effort to place the wild salmon of the Columbia River on the threatened or endangered species list because "enough conservation programs already exist," it appeared that no one remained to speak for the wild salmon in their hour of greatest need.

Salmon hatcheries, meanwhile, were the subject of ever-increasing interest. During the 1980s, yet another group made a bid to enter the salmon hatchery business in Washington. These were private hatchery owners, or ocean ranchers, who had recently begun operating in Oregon. Although the Oregon Department of Fish and Wildlife had halted expansion of public hatcheries in the late 1970s because of poor returns, private hatcheries owned by Weyerhaeuser, Crown Zellerbach and Charter Oil had been allowed free rein. The companies' plan was simple: raise and release salmon to the ocean, then harvest and sell the fish that returned as adults; for the majority of their lives, the fish would feed on the public resource, rather than company expense, and when the time came to catch them, the fish would present themselves at the slaughterhouse door.

Acknowledging the plight of the salmon (if not the degree to which it has been caused by timber companies), Weyerhaeuser aquaculture manager Harlan Freeman said, ". . . we have seen, of course, a continuing decline of salmon on a nationwide basis, coupled with population growth and an increased demand for the product. Prices for salmon are at a record high with prospects of going higher and higher. So in our viewpoint, the business prospects for salmon never looked better economically." Due largely to Weyerhaeuser's $14 million investment in its Newport, Oregon, facility, private hatchery coho releases in Oregon increased from 87,000 to 14 million annually during the late 1970s. To date, Weyerhaeuser has not had great success at Newport, where returns have averaged around .5 percent instead of the 5 percent predicted by corporate planners. Oregon fishermen have also complained that the fish are small, some of them so small that they are under the sixteen-inch limit for coho.

In general, hatcheries have worked best on smaller rivers with a clean, hospitable environment. The Department of Game has had quite good returns on the Olympic Peninsula with steelhead plants in the Lyre River, and the same has been true of the somewhat similar Samish River on Puget Sound. In both these instances the release of hatchery winter-run steelhead has produced a 300 to 500 percent increase in the number of fish returning to the river. The Department of Fisheries has had similar luck at hatcheries like Hoodsport and Minter Creek, where hatchery returns have tended in recent years to be substantially larger than the wild returns before. At stations like the Soleduck, hatcheries have also been able to introduce a species of salmon that did not exist there historically to any significant degree.

Despite such successes, however, hatcheries have demonstrated certain real limitations. Not once has the Department of Fisheries been able to replicate the number, variety, or quality of the wild salmon runs killed by major developments such as dams. Despite three-quarters of a century's labor on rivers like the Elwha, Skokomish, Cowlitz and the once-mighty Columbia itself, not a single Washington dam is in compliance with the letter of the state's hatchery lieu law, which requires "compensation" (or full replacement) for the fish lost. Hatchery salmon do well where wild salmon do well, and they do badly where the wild fish also suffer. State and federal hatcheries have yet to demonstrate that they can succeed on rivers where the environment has been seriously degraded, and judging by the experience of the *tsá tsap* steelhead of the Chehalis, they may actually have a lower tolerance for pollution than the wild fish with which they compete.

The wild salmon are a different fish with a different ecological function. They are Quartz Nose, Two Gills on Back, Three Jumps, Lightning Following One After Another; *tsá tsap*, *tyee* and the finest of them all, the blueback "Quinnat"; the salmon of "100 pounds or more in weight" that the Spanish explorer Manuel Quimper found at Neah Bay in 1792 and the 102-pound salmon that Ernie Brannon caught on the Elwha 140 years later. They are the early Chinook that people remember used to "knock the boat up out of the water" when they floated over them on the glides of the upper Calawa, and the near-record 31-pound steelhead that was caught on the Bogachiel within the last ten years; the sound of violent splashing off a lonely bridge at night, and the bleached carcass lying on the edge of a gravel bar where a seagull pecks the eye out.

Gifted with the ability to move from one medium to another and then return again to exactly the place where their lives began, the wild fish of the genera *Oncorhynchus* and *Salmo* have played a crucial role in the development of the general ecology of the Pacific Coast of North America. In a region that has been reworked by waves of glaciers for the last million years and which otherwise counts leaching rains as its predominant meteorological phenomenon, the wild salmon serve as nature's principal means of returning nutrients from the sea to the land. Through their passionate, seemingly perverse death, they give life not only to their own progeny, but also to a host of predators and other dependent species. They are, in short, an engine of general enrichment, and an important element in the long-range stability of the Pacific Coast ecosystem.

Even at their most successful, hatcheries cannot fulfill the broader purpose of the wild salmon runs. Their effect is to increase the salmon harvest of one predator (man) at the expense of other species (among them the next generation of salmon, which as fry consume creatures which themselves consume the remains of the preceding salmon generation) and the system as a whole. They are, as Larry Lestelle once observed, the biological equivalent of living on the principal of a bank account, rather than the interest. The long-term effect of Washington's traditional policy of relying on hatcheries while not enforcing environmental laws has been the reduction of nutrient cycling from the sea, and a rearrangement of those who benefit from the process.

At one level, the ongoing story of the wild salmon's destruction can be seen as a simple, if persistent, case of short-sighted self-aggrandizement. For government agencies with resource responsibility, allowing the degradation of the wild salmon has been a self-fulfilling prophecy of greater hatchery production, expanding budgetary allocations and increased agency power. For the legislators who have approved (and often demanded) the course followed by the state and federal governments, these policies have offered a highly visible way of demonstrating their sympathy for the salmon without curtailing the activities of the elements of society on whose support they depend. (From a political standpoint in Washington, the brown and white "State Salmon Hatchery" signs posted on all nearby highways have been more valuable than a wild salmon run hidden somewhere back in the woods.) And finally for the various private development interests, "business as usual" has meant they could proceed with illegal projects and often actually be subsidized by the public to do so, since the public paid in both the loss of wild salmon and the cost of running the hatcheries that partially took their place.

Almost every aspect of modern human society in the Northwest has played some part in the liquidation of the wild salmon, but the most prominent players are relatively few. An approximate roster of the groups that have most heavily profited from, and served to bring about, the ongoing salmon crisis in Washington can be obtained from the campaign contributors to almost any state legislator active in the natural resources arena. Running for reelection as the chairman of the House Natural Resources Committee in 1976, for instance, Representative John Martinis received the bulk of his money from utilities (Puget Power, Washington Water Power, Washington Natural Gas); timber companies (Boise Cascade, Georgia-Pacific, Simpson, Weyerhaeuser); oil companies (Arco, Shell, Standard of California); banks (Seafirst, Rainier, Pacificbank); non-Indian fishermen (Puget Sound Gillnetters, Association of Pacific Fisheries); and labor organizations (Washington State Labor Council, Washington Education Association).

It is tempting to see these and other allied groups as the root of the salmon's problems, but there is a darker reflection in the story of the salmon that suggests that they may only be the agents of a more basic impulse. The current plight of the wild salmon on rivers like the Queets, Elwha and Satsop marks the third time during the last three centuries that wild salmon have been threatened with extinction by modern industrial society. To understand the larger implications of the salmon's decline, one must look back to the destruction of the Atlantic salmon in the United States during the nineteenth century, or even better, the similar fate that met the wild salmon of England during the course of the Enclosure Movement and the dawn of the Industrial Revolution.

Prior to the sixteenth century, the largest class in England was comprised of yeomen who subsisted on a combination of resources that had traditionally been held in common, such as fields and hunting and fishing rights. Although never as numerous as their Pacific cousins, the Atlantic salmon, *Salmo salar*, provided a significant part of the yeoman's yearly food supply. James Bertram has written of the period: ". . . the people resident on a river were allowed to capture as many fish as they pleased, or . . . purchase all they required at a nominal price. . . . Farm-servants on the Tay and Tweed [rivers] had usually a few poached fish, in the shape of a barrel of pickled salmon, for winter use. At that time, . . . men went out on a winter night to 'burn the water,' but then it was simply by way of having a frolic. In those halcyon days country . . . farmers kept their smoked or pickled salmon as they did pickled pork or smoked bacon. The fish, comparably speaking, were allowed to fulfill the instincts of their nature and breed in peace. . . ."

This modest economy was destroyed over four centuries by monied interests who were able to enclose what had been common land, and convert it from the field system to pasture, primarily for sheep. Hunting and fishing were similarly curtailed through private closures and the decline in the salmon runs because of pollution from the early mills that processed the sheep's wool. By the beginning of the Tudor period many rural English freemen were being forced to leave their longtime homes for the cities where they became factory workers in the service of the same interests who had evicted them. Wages fell steadily in relation to prices from the middle of the eighteenth century onward, and so did the fortunes of those who found that wages were all they could hope to get. For the rising manufacturing class, however, the process was exceedingly attractive, since it provided them with both labor and markets. While the wild salmon of the Thames were being rendered extinct by industrial abuse, and more than four million acres of English common land were appropriated by large private interests, the English bowed to new lords.

There is a suggestion in the English experience, and the subsequent imperialism of newly industrialized Europe, of a basic mechanism of modern hegemony. It is that the destruction of common food resources is not a sad byproduct of modern industrialism, but rather a necessary prerequisite for its success: that industrial society extends and consolidates its control by creating scarcities that can only be met by entering the money economy. It was, for instance, the nascent English capitalist's destruction or theft of common public food resources, such as common land and wild salmon, that gave them control over the laboring weight of the nation for so low a price. In more recent times, Frances Moore Lappé, Joseph Collins and Richard Barnet have noted how multinational corporations control Third World economies through a similar pattern of induced dependencies.

The future of the wild Pacific salmon may possibly be glimpsed in the English extinction of their Atlantic counterparts in the Thames, or the more recent experience of another insular people, the Japanese. During the headlong drive for modernization that began with the Meiji Restoration, the Japanese built unladdered dams, dumped industrial pollution into rivers, and transformed many of the Hiroshige's famous *Fifty-three Stations of the Tokaido* into scenes of urban squalor. The Japanese also became heavily involved with the artificial propagation of salmon. The hope was that the hatchery fish might be able to offset some of the environmental damage, but instead they drove out the wild fish so completely that there are no salmon in Japan today that are not hatchery salmon. The Japanese have had considerable success with some of their hatchery efforts, especially with chum salmon, but as Richard Van Cleve, dean of the University of Washington College of Fisheries, and others have noted, the total production of the Japanese hatcheries is a fraction of the wild fish that used to run.

Ninety years after Private Harry Fisher feasted on Queets Chinook, the process is well advanced on the Olympic Peninsula. Where once there were free salmon in abundance, there are now expensive salmon for the affluent. Where people once built their homes out of the abundant local lumber, they now buy "mobile homes" made of aluminum that cost thirty times as much and probably won't last half as long. Where peninsula homesteaders once lived independently and self-sufficiently, most people must now work for the same development interests that are impoverishing the public's natural wealth. There is no saying where the Northwest salmon story will eventually conclude, but it is certain that man and salmon will be linked, for as the Indians said from the start: the fate of one mirrors the fate of the other.

During the course of my three years' wandering around the Olympic Peninsula, I saw wild salmon of every Pacific species, as well as the two anadromous trout, the steelhead and sea-run cutthroat. Many were beautiful fish, and occasionally the massed display was stunning (as on the humpy glide of the Graywolf River), but nowhere did I find the old glory, or the life it supported. To see relatively unsullied salmon runs and a yeomanry of subsistence salmon fishermen today, one must travel to Alaska, the Northwest Territories and British Columbia. I remember sitting deep in Alaska with a bowl of chum salmon and turnip stew in my lap listening to subsistence fishermen tell about the rise of commercial salmon fishing in the Yukon system. It was a little after 11 P.M. on the first evening of the season that a star pierced the midnight sun sky.

There were nine of us gathered around a bonfire on the cliffs above the muddy, mile-wide Tanana River. A young man named Curt, whose beard glowed ruby-red in the firelight, talked between bites. He observed that the commercial salmon fishery begun only a few years before had already grown roughly a hundredfold to more than one million summer chum annually.

Out on the river, three Indians on a beer run to Manley Hot Springs waved as they passed at high speed. A moustachioed man in the rear, who was known to some of the people in our camp, let out a whoop and threw an empty beer can far out across the water. Opening beers of their own, the fishermen around the fire agreed that some subsistence salmon fishermen were illegally selling roe, or eggs, to commercial buyers. It is against Alaska law for subsistence fishermen to sell any part of their catch, but the Japanese are willing to pay so much for roe that the problem has been spreading. "They take maybe a dozen ounces of eggs, and then dump forty pounds of fish," one person said. "It's a kind of a shame." A bush pilot named Steve, who had flown surveys for the Alaska Department of Fish and Game, said the situation was further complicated by the lack of any real sound, long-term information on the size of the salmon runs in Interior Alaska and the fishery they can presently support.

"There's talk of a dam on the Yukon."

"U.S. Borax wants to put a molybdenum mine down in the Misty Fjords."

"And oil, don't forget oil."

"Yeah, but you have to admit the runs have been good over the last few years, really the best I can remember seeing."

"They're talking a lot about hatcheries in Southeast Alaska. That's bound to help."

I looked out across the Tanana into an immense and typically austere Alaskan landscape. Unbroken spruce forest ran away across a country of rolling mountains resembling a stationary sea viewed from the trough of a swell. Caught by the evening sun, the grove of white-barked birch on the opposite shore lit up like a thousand incandescent filaments, while the forest behind settled into the long, hazy shadows. On the horizon, doughy clouds rose to a mauve veil that was softened with distant rain falling somewhere to the west. The azure of the clear northern night was visible overhead, but to the south the sun, which had been setting for about four hours, continued its roseate display.

Curt, Yvonne, and the two Steves are subsistence salmon fishermen. They depend on the salmon they catch to provide the staple of their own diet, and the diet of their dogs, through the winter. Every summer they leave their cabins in small villages like Manley Hot Springs or Tanana, and move to fish camps strung along the river. Over the course of two or three weeks time, they try to catch, filet and preserve at least 100 pounds of salmon per person, plus 500 pounds for each dog. The Tanana has strong runs of Chinook, but chum are the mainstay of the subsistence fishery, which captured an estimated 303,000 of the fish in 1978, according to the Alaska Department of Fish and Game.

This was the last evening that the group would be spending in camp that summer, and although it might not have looked different from any other campfire scene, a party was in progress. More stew, more beer, another bowl of soup made from wild mushrooms gathered in the woods along the river, followed by handfuls of raw, sweet blueberries picked on an old burn. Yvonne recalled how the river rose so high in July that they had to wade in up to their waists to work at the fileting tables. Steve told of a number of near-crashes in his plane, and the other Steve pondered the possibility of selling Tanana River mud in California as "genuine Pleistocene silt."

After midnight, the lapses in the conversation became longer as we repeatedly fell silent to watch the sky. Steve saw a shooting star fall across the newly risen, butter-yellow moon, then disappear behind a low group of clouds only to reappear one more time before vanishing into the mountains. It was deep twilight when the aurora borealis appeared high in the sky to the south. A white glow that shifted in vertical columns like shimmering draperies, the northern lights grew more intense with each pulse. Curt mentioned that the University of Alaska had been doing barium release missile experiments to accentuate the lights for the purpose of studying the Van Allen belt. "It's the way I imagine nuclear war would be," he said. "Fireworks make a lot of light, but you can see that what's involved here is much, much more powerful. You get a lot of magentas and deep reds all over the sky."

The next morning we ate another meal of chum (fried this time, with potatoes and onions), and broke camp. Curt and the two Steves each had outboard-powered skiffs of the flat-bottomed design so common in the Yukon system. Loaded heavily with the last gear from camp, including a cast-iron cook stove, we made slow but steady progress upriver against a current Curt estimated at eight miles per hour. Although not well known, the Tanana is one of the largest rivers in North America, with twice the length and discharge of the Hudson. Forests of whole trees drifted past, and periodically a great roar would signal the sucking funnel of the whirlpools that appear and disappear without apparent cause. Dragging my hand in the water, I found it was so muddy that I could not see the first joint of my finger.

We passed three of the fish wheels used by some subsistence fishermen as we wound our way between a series of large forested islands. These traps, which belonged to an Indian family in Manley Hot Springs, were tied to the shore in the main current, which provided the force to keep the dippers spinning. Salmon thus caught were thrown into a hopper by the continuous motion of the wheel as it went around. All were empty. Our next stop was an abandoned fish camp on the shady side of the river. Here we picked lustrous high-bush cranberries and explored about the ruins of several cabins back in the forest. One had been dropped to its knees by a spruce that had fallen directly across the crown, and in another the floor dropped away like a psychology experiment in spatial disorientation.

Cans of Gargoil by Mobil Oil were almost as common as Hills Brothers Coffee cans and bottles of Philadelphia Whiskey ("famous since 1894") in the garbage middens among the ruins. On a table in the main cabin we found a two-color flier for Liberty Blue Ribbon Motor Oil and a calendar page from January 1941 with each day carefully crossed off. The winter of '41: plutonium had just been discovered, and Hitler would shortly invade Greece. As we headed back to the skiff I couldn't help wondering if Alaska was an appreciably wilder place then.

We met the proprietors of the next fish camp upriver as they completed the last 100 yards of a canoe crossing from the other side of the Tanana, three-quarters of a mile distant. Nate and Joe told us they were going to can the twenty or so chum buzzing with flies in the bottom of the canoe, but they seemed more intent on the coming run of fall chum and coho than on the fish then in the river. Both said they would be there for the wintry end of fishing, and then return to Fairbanks to get a marten trapping grubstake.

As Nate showed his watercolors of the river and the mountains to the east, he became reflective about the virtues of their camp: a rich eddy to fish, a cold water stream for drinking, southern-exposure bluffs to catch the sunlight and moderate the temperature, and an easily climbed spruce on the ridge above to view Mount McKinley, 140 miles away.

They are virtues worthy of some reflection.